THE
BEER
COMPANION

A Connoisseur's Guide to the World's Finest Craft Beers

Stephen Snyder

SIMON & SCHUSTER

To my agent, Susan P. Urstadt

SIMON & SCHUSTER
Rockefeller Center
1230 Avenue of the Americas
New York, NY 10020

Copyright © 1996 Quintet Publishing Limited.

All rights reserved, including the right of
reproduction in whole or in part in any form.

SIMON & SCHUSTER and colophon are
registered trademarks of Simon & Schuster, Inc.

Creative Director: Richard Dewing
Designer: Simon Balley
Senior Editor: Laura Sandelson
Editorial Assistant: Clare Hubbard
Photographers: Ian Howes, David Armstrong

Designed and produced by
Quintet Publishing Limited,
The Old Brewery, 6 Blundell Street,
London N7 9BH

Typeset in Great Britain by
Central Southern Typesetters, Eastbourne
Manufactured in Malaysia by
C. H. Colour Scan SDN BHD
Printed in China by
Leefung-Asco Printers Ltd.

1 3 5 7 9 10 8 6 4 2

Library of Congress Cataloging-in-Publication Data

Snyder, Stephen, 1961–
     The beer companion: a connoisseur's guide to
the world's finest craft beers / [Stephen Snyder].
          p.   cm.
     Includes index.
     1. Beer.   I. Title
TP577.S62   1996
641.2'3—dc20   96–16848
     ISBN 0-684-83125-2   CIP

AUTHOR ACKNOWLEDGEMENTS
Although this book could not have been created without
the work of dozens of people, I must acknowledge the
extraordinary efforts of those who made my job so much
easier. They are: Clare Hubbard for her herculean efforts
on all fronts; Stephen Paul for his expert guidance and
support; Laura Sandelson for her deft leadership; and the
intrepid Ian Howes. Thanks to Greg Noonan and Paul
White of The Seven Barrel Brewery, Jeff Close of
Catamount, and Dave Ebner of Otter Creek for letting me
invade their breweries at short notice. Thanks to my wife
Melissa for her patient support, and especially to Michael
Jackson, Roger Protz, Tim Webb, and Graham Lees, to
whom I could always turn in times of doubt. Finally, I
must thank the breweries who gave their knowledge and
time, and the generosity of the following importers:
Wendy Littlefield of Vanburg & DeWulf, Matthias
Neidhart of B. United International, Monroe B. England
& Ian McAllister of Merchant Du Vin, Hank Hague of St.
Killian Importing, Alan Kaplan of Westwood Importing,
Jeff Dafoe of Dafoe International, Martin Wetten of
Wetten Importers, Lanny Hoff of All Saint's Brands,
George Saxon of Phoenix Importers, and Brian Harris
and Jeffrey House at Thames America.

C O N T E N T S

INTRODUCTION

Why is a book like this necessary? Beer, after all, is commonplace in our society and most people, whether or not they drink beer, feel fairly confident that they know all there is to know about it. Furthermore, to most Americans, "beer" is equated with a pale, inexpensive beverage of ignoble reputation. Quite simply, all of that has changed. The newfound appreciation for quality beer is part of the movement away from the mass production and artificial ingredients of our modern world. Beer has been rediscovered and now enjoys status as a relaxing and restoring libation and an accompaniment to fine dining.

The "Craft Beer Renaissance" as it is often called, is in its third decade, with the rate of change within the industry moving at an astounding pace. The connoisseur or would-be connoisseur of beer is faced with a dizzying array of choices of handcrafted beers from around the world.

Today, the terms microbrewery, brewpub, regional brewery, and contract brewery have come into wide usage and tend to cause confusion among those learning about craft beer. A microbrewery is technically defined as a small independent brewery producing no more than 20,645 hectoliters annually. However, the success and subsequent growth of many such breweries has rendered the term "microbrewery" increasingly obsolete. In this book, we often use the term "craft brewery" as it refers to a brewer of high quality beers without regard to the annual output or age. These make up the majority of the entries in the Beer Directory. A brewpub is an establishment that brews its own beers for consumption on its premises. Contract breweries are breweries that do not actually brew, but hire another brewery to brew their beer "under contract" for them; in most cases, a well-established regional brewery. We have included contract breweries only if their award-winning beers have made a notable contribution to the craft brewing world.

In our efforts to educate and entertain, the purpose of this book is not to list every good beer in the world. Indeed, there are number of fine breweries not listed, and we regret that not everyone could be included. To offer the connoisseur a deeper knowledge, we have included a representative sampling of the world's best breweries and profiles of a few less well-known ones.

A solid, working knowledge of the world's artisanal beers is the best tool to avoid disappointment and to assure the lifelong enjoyment of quality beer. If champagne is to be served in commemoration of life's great moments—births, graduations, weddings, and successes—then let beer's place be to celebrate the day-to-day joy of living.

Stephen Snyder
Perkinsville, Vermont, 1996

PART ONE

The Story
of Beer

BREWING BEER

*O*n the surface, beer is one of the simplest and most natural products that people consume. Four basic ingredients—malted barley, hops, water, and yeast—are all that are needed to create a world-class brew. That simple formula, as perfected over the centuries in Belgium, Britain, Germany, and France, is just as reliable today. Strange techniques, preservatives, and additives used to make a beer drinkable are only necessary when a brewer diverges from the tried and true recipe in order to produce beer faster and cheaper.

Beer is infinitely complex because of the variations that can be achieved with its four simple ingredients and because of the problems that can be encountered in the brewing process. That is where the skill of the brewer comes into play. With a thorough knowledge of all the separate elements and how they interact, the brewer carefully plans the recipe and selects the proper grains, hops, and yeast for the style to be brewed and makes sure all the mineral elements in the water are properly adjusted. It is the knowledge and experience of the brewmaster, or "head brewer," that will determine the final outcome of the beer. This skill is vital in a craft-brewing environment, where there is less reliance on computers and sophisticated machinery to oversee the brewing process. The grain must first be crushed enough to allow thorough extraction of sugars, but not so much as to create flour and an inefficient mash. The proper varieties of hops must be chosen, and they must be fresh and well cared for if the beer is to have the correct bitterness, flavor, and aroma. The yeast must be viable, uncontaminated, and the appropriate strain for the style being brewed in order to achieve the proper flavor and character in the beer. The water must be correct in pH and purity, and must have a precise balance of mineral ions if proper mashing, hop bitterness, and fermentation are to be achieved.

HOPS

YEAST

MALTED BARLEY

WATER

Ingredients of beer

MALT

Perhaps the making of beer has such a long tradition in human history because its foundations,

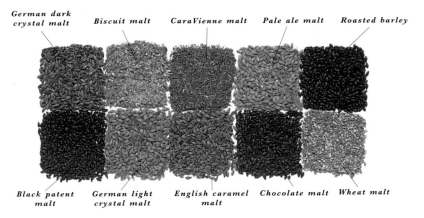

German dark crystal malt   Biscuit malt   CaraVienne malt   Pale ale malt   Roasted barley

Black patent malt   German light crystal malt   English caramel malt   Chocolate malt   Wheat malt

particularly the malting of cereal grains and the act of fermentation, are so closely mirrored by naturally occuring processes. Despite the technical advances made in modern brewing, malting of barley is merely a replication of the transformation that a grain of barley experiences when it falls to the ground and is soaked with rainwater. When it begins to sprout, it draws on its starch reserves to send a shoot up into the sunlight and a root down into the earth as it creates new plant. By carefully imitating and controlling this process, the maltster encourages the germination, then halts it when sufficient enzymes have been produced and some of the complex starches have been transformed into simple sugars. After the tiny sprouts are gently removed, the green malt is kiln dried and cured before it is sent to the brewery. At the brewery the malt is gently cracked and immediately mixed with hot water or what brewers call "brewing liquor." This process, called "mashing," activates the enzymes in the malt, which break down complex starches into simpler sugars that will be more readily consumed by yeast during fermentation.

HOPS

The earliest record of the cultivation of hops in Europe dates to 768 and was made by Christian monks. The documents are kept in what is now the famous Bavarian state brewing college at Weihenstephan. Whether the hops were used in brewing or not is not recorded, but it is almost certain the monks experimented, for nearly every other bitter herb was at some point used in the brewing of beer. Flemish brewers initiated the widespread use of hops on the Continent around the year 1500. For many years, the English considered the use of this foreign herb to be an adulteration of good ale although immigrants from the Netherlands employed hops in brewing. King Henry VIII prohibited the use of hops in any ale not specifically designated "beer" by publicans, so that consumers would know exactly what they were getting. At the time, the producers of English ales employed such herbs as horehound, bog myrtle, alehoof, buckbean, and the bark of various trees to balance the overwhelming sweetness, characteristic of malted barley.

Hops' flowers grow into cone-shaped structures ("strobiles") on the female plant. These cones bear the lupulin glands which provide the aroma, flavor, and astringent bitterness that balances the sweetness of the malt and acts as a preservative and natural clarifier. The word "hop" comes from the Anglo-Saxon "hoppan," which means "to climb."

While the flavor and aroma come from essential oils in the plant, the bitterness of hops comes primarily from the alpha acids contained in the resins of the lupulin glands. These alpha acids also provide the preservatives that retard spoilage. Alpha acid percent is a measure of the percentage of the flower's weight that is composed of the alpha acid resin, and is used as a measure of bittering potential and preservative power. Hops for brewing are used in different forms: loose whole flowers, plugs of compressed whole flowers, pelletized powder, and extracts. For brewing purposes, hops are classified primarily as bittering or finishing hops. Hops with high alpha acid percentages are generally used for bittering, and hops with lower alpha acid percentages are usually considered the best for aroma and flavor (collectively referred to as finishing). This is a greatly over simplified categorization, as most hops can serve both purposes if the correct quantities are used, or if they are properly blended with other varieties.

YEAST

Beer yeasts are single-celled microscopic fungi which transform malt sugar into alcohol, carbon dioxide, and other by-products that give beers their unique flavors. For centuries, the importance of yeast in brewing was not fully understood. Monks euphemistically referred to it as "God is good," because they considered the work of yeast something of a miracle. Because of the work of Louis Pasteur in analyzing yeast activity and that of Emil Hansen at the Carlsberg brewery in isolating single strains, yeast management is now more high-tech microbiology than faith.

There are two main species of beer yeast. That used in ale brewing, *Saccharomyces Cerevisiae*, sometimes called top-fermenting yeast, prefers warmer temperatures and tends to settle on top of the beer at the end of fermentation. The so-called bottom-fermenting *Saccharomyces Uvarum* lager yeast prefers cooler temperatures and sinks to the

Louis Pasteur

bottom of the vessel during fermentation. Neither yeast ferments only at the top or bottom, but throughout the beer. Both ale and lager yeast species have a wide variety of strains that give each beer style its unique character in flavor, body, and aroma.

WATER

Brewing water, referred to as "liquor" by professional brewers, constitutes ninety-five percent of the final product and has great influence on both the taste of the beer and the brewing process. The brewer is most concerned with six main component salts of water, bicarbonate, sodium, chloride, sulfate, calcium, and magnesium, which are carefully balanced to achieve the desired flavor and quality in the finished product.

Bicarbonate is considered the most crucial factor in brewing liquor. Low levels result in high mash acidity, especially when using dark malts. High levels result in poor yields from the malt. The concordant high pH compromises the effectiveness of the enzymes in the grain to convert starch to sugar. Sodium contributes body, full mouthfeel, and character to the beer. Chloride brings out malt sweetness and, like sodium, contributes to the overall mouthfeel and complexity of the beer. Sulfate is the main water element influencing hopping rates, as it brings out a sharp, dry bitterness if the bittering units (BU) are too high. Calcium

encourages the precipitation of proteins ("the break") during the boiling stage. Magnesium is valued primarily as a yeast nutrient.

THE BREWING PROCESS

Malted barley is crushed in the roller mill, mixed with hot water, and augered into the mash tun, a large copper, wood, or stainless steel vessel in the brewhouse. In an infusion mash method, the oatmeal-like mixture, or mash, yields a sweet golden liquid called wort (pronounced "wert"). In the decoction mash method, developed by German brewers to accommodate their types of malt, portions of the mash are pumped into a kettle and boiled to facilitate protein breakdown. It is then pumped back to the mash tun, where the temperature is raised slowly over several hours. This method is used primarily in weissbiers and bocks and creates a deeper maltiness of flavor. In a compromise between the two traditional methods mentioned previously, many breweries now use a temperature controlled mash where the temperature of the mash is raised in precise steps over several hours in a single vessel. After the mashing is complete, the sweet wort is drawn off from the mash tun into the brew kettle or the mash is pumped to a lauter tun, where the grain bed is sprayed with hot water— or "sparged"— to draw off the wort and remove residual sweet liquid trapped in the malt.

The spent grains are then discarded or

used as livestock feed. Next, in the brew kettle, the wort is brought to a boil, hops are added, and the mixture is usually boiled for one-and-a-half to three hours. When the boil is completed, the wort is strained of hop particles, whirlpooled to remove coagulated protein, chilled to fermentation temperature, and then sent to the primary fermentation vessel, where a fresh dosage of yeast is "pitched." In most cases, fermentation lasts for five to ten days in the primary fermenter, after which the young or "green" beer is pumped to the conditioning tank, where it clarifies and ages for one to two weeks. Lagers usually undergo a much longer fermentation, with two weeks in the primary fermenter, two weeks in a secondary one, and one to six months in the conditioning tank.

Before mature beer leaves the brewery, it is sometimes filtered and variously packaged. There are several methods to produce carbonation in the finished beer. Many modern breweries inject carbon dioxide into the flat beer that emerges from the conditioning tank. German breweries sometimes "krausen" their beer by adding a dose of actively fermenting beer. Another method is to package the beer before fermentation has ceased, thereby trapping the required amount of carbon dioxide in the beer. In bottle-conditioned beers, a fresh dose of yeast and priming sugars are added to produce natural carbonation or refermentation in the bottle.

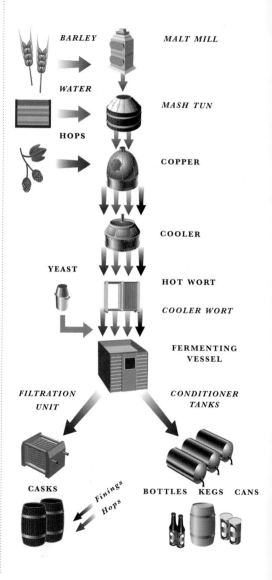

THE BREWING PROCESS

BARLEY — MALT MILL

WATER

HOPS — MASH TUN

— COPPER

COOLER

YEAST

HOT WORT

COOLER WORT

FERMENTING VESSEL

FILTRATION UNIT — CONDITIONER TANKS

CASKS — *Finings Hops* — BOTTLES KEGS CANS

BEER STYLES

An understanding and appreciation of the classic beer styles of the world greatly increases the enjoyment of craft beer. Below is a brief summary of the major beer styles, including their history, taste and color profiles, and some traditional ingredients that produce their unique qualities.

ALTBIER: Also known as Düsseldorfer alt. "Altbier" means "old" or "traditional" beer in German, referring to the way beer was brewed prior to the nineteenth century. Alts were originally lagered for long periods in ice-cold caves after a warm fermentation, which mellowed the fruitiness of a top-fermented ale. These beers have pronounced bitterness, with subdued hop flavor and aroma compared to a pils. The term "alt" can also be applied to beers outside of the Düsseldorfer style. A prime commercial example is Diebels Alt.

BARLEY WINE: British strong ale with high, winelike alcohol content (6–12% alcohol by volume (ABV)) and usually reddish amber or copper in color. High final gravities give this beer a sweetness that is balanced by high hopping rates. Barley wines are excellent beers for laying down and improve dramatically with age if bottle con-

Barley wine

ditioned. A prime commercial example is Sierra Nevada's Bigfoot Barleywine Style Ale.

BELGIAN RED ALE: A tart West Flanders style of ale deriving its reddish color from Vienna malt and its trademark acidity from bulk aging for one to two years in oak tuns. Aged Belgian red is sometimes blended with new beer to reduce the high acidity level. An exceptionally refreshing beer. A prime commercial example is Rodenbach Grand Cru.

BELGIAN STRONG ALE: A strongly alcoholic Belgian ale similar to English strong ale or barley wine, that varies in color from pale amber to deep brown. The use of various refined sugars gives these vinous beers strength without the heaviness found in all-malt beers. A prime commercial example is Brasserie Dubuisson's Scaldis.

BIÈRE DE GARDE and **BIÈRE DE PARIS:** (French country and

Parisian beer). Characterized by a smooth, sweet, fruity, and earthy taste, these beers can be lagers or ales; color ranges from deep blond to reddish brown. Traditionally, bières de garde are brewed in the northern area of France near the Belgian border, corked in wine bottles, and then aged for months or even years to mellow out the estery/phenolic overtones. Bière de Paris is often fermented with lager yeast, giving it a more rounded and less fruity character than its country cousin. A prime commercial example of bière de garde is Castelain Blonde. A prime commercial example of Bière de Paris is Lutèce.

BIÈRE DE MARS: Light-colored, seasonal French ales brewed from the best of the summer barley and fall hops. These beers are subjected to a long, slow fermentation over the winter and have been drunk in celebration of the arrival of spring since the late fourteenth century. They are usually strong and robust, but also rounded and sophisticated. A prime commercial example is Brasserie Castelain's Bière de Mars.

BITTER: A well-hopped, cask-conditioned English ale. Bottled versions can be found quite readily, but purists define these as draft beers. Lightly carbonated, and not as bitter as the name would suggest, the beer is more often floral/spicy from English hops and only slightly drier than standard pale ales. Varying in color from bronze to deep reddish copper, this very popular pub style encompasses three sub-styles classified according to original gravity: ordinary, best bitter, and strong bitter (or ESB). A prime commercial example is Fuller's ESB.

BOCK: Bocks were originally consumed by fasting monks because they provided a good source of nutrition when no solid food was allowed to be eaten at all. The standard bock styles include bock, doppelbock, helles bock, and maibock (see also eisbock and weizenbock). Bock is a rich, malty, brown German lager that is brewed in fall or winter for consumption in spring. The less common helles bock and maibock, however, are more honey colored and appear in mid to late spring. Contemporary American bocks are usually lighter in body and color than the original German bocks. Prime commercial examples of bock, doppelbock, and helles bock are Einbecker Ur-Bock

Bitter

Dunkel, Paulaner Salvator, and Sierra Nevada's Pale Bock, respectively.

BROWN ALE: Southern English brown ales are generally dark, sweet, and low in alcohol. The northern English version is often drier and more potent. Both are made with softer water than pale ales. The commercial popularity of this ancient brew style had waned over the past few centuries, but brown ales are currently enjoying a revival among craft brewers. American brown ale typically has more pronounced hop bitterness, flavor, and aroma, reflecting our love of that herb. A prime commercial example is Brooklyn Brown Ale.

CREAM ALE: An American mild, golden, full-bodied pale ale generally brewed with North American–grown barley and hops, cream ale is typically top fermented and then cold aged like a lager or even blended with lager. It is one of North America's few indigenous beer styles. A prime commercial example is Riverside Brewing's Raincross Cream Ale.

DORTMUNDER EXPORT: This popular style of beer was originally brewed in the area around the city of Dortmund in western Germany and is typically a full-bodied, premium lager somewhere

between the dryness of German pils and the sweeter maltiness of Munich helles. Referred to simply as "export" in Germany, this is not to be confused with other beers in Germany that carry the adjective export, which merely indicates a premium lager. A prime commercial example is Stoudt's Export Gold.

DUBBEL: A malty Belgian ale that may have taken its name from being approximately double the original gravity of the "simple" beers of medieval Belgium. These fairly sweet, nutty, reddish-brown beers are considered a subcategory of the Abbey style and are generally bottle-conditioned. A prime commercial example is Affligem Dobbel.

EISBOCK: This is a lager beer created by freezing doppelbock after fermentation is complete. The resulting ice is removed— and, therefore, much of the water—resulting in a much sweeter, heavier, and alcoholically strong beer. A prime commercial example is Kulmbacher Reichelbräu's Eisbock.

FARO: A pale to brown Belgian lambic originally served on draft in and around Brussels. Faro is fermented with wild yeast and bacteria, and refermented with candy sugar, the result is a lively, faintly sweet but

Maibock

acidic ale, with a soft, winelike palate. A prime commercial example is Frank Boon Pertotale.

FEST BIER: A term commonly used to describe German "holiday" beers such as märzen, but it also refers to German Christmas (*Weinachten*) or Easter (*Ostern*) beer and a variety of beers commemorating lesser feast days. Typically, fest biers are ruddy, malty, rich lagers. A prime commercial example is Würzburger Hofbräu Bavarian Holiday.

FRAMBOISE: Belgian fruit lambic flavored with raspberries. Like other styles of lambic, this is effervescent, tart, turbid, and very lightly hopped. A prime commercial example is Lindemans Framboise.

GRAND CRU: A term for Belgian special occasion beer that is often arbitrarily bestowed on a brewery's strongest beer. Originally brewed for weddings, village celebrations, and other important events, it is typically high in alcohol. A prime commercial example is Celis Grand Cru.

GUEUZE: Old lambics and young lambics that are blended then refermented in the bottle for at least one year. A prime commercial example is Cantillon Gueuze.

INDIA PALE ALE (IPA): A style of English pale ale that has traditionally been a premium, extremely well hopped ale. IPA

Framboise

gained its name because of its popularity with the British troops in colonial India—its alcoholic strength and high hopping rates helped it withstand the long ocean voyage from England. This is a beer now found mostly in bottled form, although it was originally cask conditioned. A prime commercial example is Brooklyn Brewery's East India Pale Ale.

IRISH RED ALE: A slightly sweet Irish cousin of English bitter, this brew is red-hued from the use of roasted barley. Greatly influenced by the Scottish ales, Irish reds are malty, lightly hopped, light to medium bodied, and have a slight diacetyl quality. Top- and bottom-fermented versions are brewed commercially. A prime commercial example is Kilkenny Irish Beer.

KELLERBIER: A fruity, dry lager brewed primarily in Bavaria in the Franconia region. Kellerbier is highly hopped and lightly carbonated. Bottled versions do exist, but this unfiltered or minimally filtered beer is usually served on draft in local village "bräustüberls." A prime commercial example is Modschiedler's St. Georgen Bräu.

KLOSTERBIER: Literally, "cloister beer," denoting a beer in any particular style that is now, or was sometime in the past, brewed in a monastery or convent. A prime commercial example is Klosterbräu Ettal's Dunkel Export from the Bavarian monastery of Ettal in the Alps. **KÖLSCH:** The appellation of a pale, often cloudy, and blond "old style" German ale originally brewed in the Köln area before the lagering revolution. Moderately or lightly hopped in the boil, kölsch is dry with a slight lactic taste, and moderately high in alcohol. A prime commercial example is Long Trail Kölsch.

KRIEK: Belgian, cherry-flavored lambic made by adding macerated cherries to the secondary fermenter—usually after an extended primary fermentation. A prime commercial example is Cantillon's Kriek Lambik.

KULMBACHER: Dark German lager from the town of Kulmbach in northern Bavaria that is both heavier and darker than Erlanger or the more popular Münchner Dunkel. A prime commercial example is Dixie Blackened Voodoo.

LAMBIC: Belgian wheat beer spontaneously fermented with wild airborne yeast and bacteria. The style originated in the town of Lembeek in the Pajottenland and by law must contain a minimum of 30 percent wheat, usually un-malted. It is cloudy yellow, very lightly hopped, frothy, and slightly sour or citric in taste. Lambic is often flavored with fruits such as

peaches (pêche), cherries (kriek), or raspberries (framboise). It is cooled in large, open vats, then fermented in large, oak wine casks. A prime commercial example is Boon's Kriek Boon.

LIGHT BEER: Typically low in flavor, light beer is intended to be low in alcohol and/or low in calories. The low flavor profile often requires that these beers be served well chilled. A prime commercial example is Upper Canada's Light Lager.

MALT LIQUOR: An American legal definition which varies from state to state, but typically refers to lagers with a minimum of 4 percent and a maximum of 6 percent ABV. In some states, imports with these alcohol levels must contain the words "malt liquor" on the label. As a style definition, "malt liquor" is generally considered to be a strong American lager meant to be served ice cold. A prime commercial example is Schlitz Malt Liquor.

MARS: A rare "march" beer from the region around the famous Belgian brewing town of Louvain (Leuven). Traditionally, a "small beer"—brewed from the low-gravity runoff of the mash—that is then aged several months before summer consumption. The French march beer is completely different, being high in alcohol. Mars is currently commercially extinct in Belgium.

India Pale Ale

MÄRZEN/OCTOBERFEST: Bavarian lager fest bier that is amber, smooth, and malty, but well balanced by German or Czech hops. True Märzen, by the German definition, is brewed in March and aged until late September or early October. Octoberfest is the American term for the Märzen style. A prime commercial example is Hübsch Märzen.

MILD ALE: Mild ales are low-alcohol English beers (roughly 3–3.5% ABV) that have a medium to light body and a slightly sweet finish. Some are copper colored and are sometimes referred to as nut brown, but most are lower-gravity, dark brown ales and are called dark mild. A prime commercial example is Adnams Southwold Mild.

MÜNCHNER DUNKEL: The Bavarian version of dark lager also referred to simply as "dunkel" (German for "dark"). Mastery of this beer style is credited to Spaten Brewery's Gabriel Sedlmayr II in the mid-nineteenth century. Malty in aroma and taste, but well balanced by German hops, a good dunkel should not be at all bitter or heavy. A prime commercial example is Frankenmuth Dark.

MUNICH HELLES: Munich-style pale lager developed in the 1920s as an answer to the overwhelming demand for Pilsen-style light lagers. These gold- to straw-colored lagers are noted for their smooth, well-balanced maltiness and unassertive hop bitterness. A prime commercial example is Heckler's Hell Lager.

OLD ALE: This is a medium-strong British dark ale also known as "stock ale." This beer was named "old" because, centuries ago, it was mild ale aged a year or more before drinking. A mixture of expensive old ale and inexpensive mild became the basis for the porter style. A prime commercial example is Gale's Prize Old Ale.

OUD BRUIN: The dark reddish brown to black East Flanders ale—also known as "old brown" or "Flanders brown" that is subjected to a long primary ferment and an even longer secondary ferment, often in wooden casks where it is exposed to beer-souring bacteria. The result is a well-aged, slightly sour, acidic beer with a vinous nature. Some oud bruins are also flavored with raspberry or cherry. A prime commercial example is Liefmans Goudenband.

Pale ale

PALE ALE: First brewed at Burton-on-Trent, England, this beer became a wildly popular style that supplanted the porters, browns, and milds. By modern standards, these ales are far from pale, but the name was first used in comparison to the dark brown or black stouts and porters. This classic British ale that developed in the eighteenth century is well hopped, full bodied, and bronze, golden, or copper in color. Originally, pale ales were cask conditioned and many in the UK still are. In the U.S., they are primarily kegged or bottled, although there is a growing interest in cask conditioning. A prime commercial example is Eldridge Pope's Royal Oak Pale Ale.

PALE ALE, BELGIAN: This is a maltier and more carbonated counterpart to English pale ale. Belgian pale ales are often stronger than the English versions, emphasizing fruity yeast and malt character over hops. A prime commercial example is De Smedt Op-Ale.

PILS, GERMAN: A lighter, drier, hoppier, more effervescent, and less smooth version of the malty Czech pilsner. A prime commercial example is Warsteiner Premium Verum.

PILSNER, AMERICAN: Also referred to as "American premium lager." Lightly colored and hopped, these often include adjuncts such as corn and rice for their character, and bear little resemblance to authentic Czech Pilsner. They are usually highly carbonated and served ice cold. A prime commercial example is Anheuser-Busch's Budweiser.

PILSNER, CZECH: The world's most famous and popular beer style, originally brewed in the Bohemian city of Pilsen in 1842. This is the classic European lager that others raced to imitate in the nineteenth century lagering revolution. Straw to deep gold in color, Czech pilsner has a flowery Saaz hop aroma, a dry finish, and extremely well balanced maltiness. European and American imitations lack its complexity and full body. A prime commercial example is Pilsner Urquell.

PORTER: A dark, moderately strong ale that was born as a mixture of inexpensive "green" beer such as mild or brown ale with expensive aged beer. Porter has a spicy, chocolatey character and is hopped with English varieties such as Fuggles and Challenger. Gypsum, chocolate malt, black malt, unrefined sugar, licorice root, wormwood, and roasted

German pils

barley have all contributed to the recipes of this stout predecessor. Dark malt flavors dominate, yet porter is lighter in body and malt character than stout. American porter is sometimes bottom fermented. A prime commercial example is Samuel Smith's Taddy Porter.

RAUCHBIER: These German "smoke beer" lagers were made famous in the city of Bamberg in northern Bavaria. Seasonal märzen as well as bock-strength versions are brewed in the region. The smoke character originally was a by-product of the ancient practice of drying malt over oak or beechwood fires. A prime commercial example is Aecht Schlenkerla Rauchbier.

SAISON: A smooth, mellow, liberally hopped, slightly estery, and acidic summer ale from the French-speaking region of Belgium, particularly the town of Liège. These complex, thirst-quenching ales are brewed by farmhouse breweries in winter and aged several months before serving. They are top fermented, dry hopped, and bottle conditioned. A prime commercial example is Saison Dupont.

SCHWARZBIER: Literally "black beer," Schwarzbier is a dark German lager that often has bittersweet, dark chocolate notes in addition to roasted malt flavors. These are generally darker, more robust, and less delicate than Munich dunkel. The modern benchmarks of the style are now brewed in Japan as well as in eastern Germany. Prime commercial examples are Köstritzer Schwarzbier and Sapporo Black Beer.

SCOTTISH AND SCOTCH ALE: The standard gravity Scottish ales include the sub-categories light, heavy, and export. These beers are also known by their archaic designations of 60 shilling, 70 shilling, and 80 shilling, respectively, and are roughly the counterparts of English bitter. A fourth category, strong (90 shilling) is a rich, creamy ale of varying strengths that is often called "Scotch ale" or "wee heavy" because it is traditionally served in small, aperitif-sized portions. Strong Scotch ale is typically black or deep, walnut brown from the use of roasted barley or dark malts in addition to pale ale malt. It is low in hop bitterness, flavor, and aroma, reflecting that Scotland's climate is unsuitable for hop

Porter

cultivation. The taste is complex, with hints of raisin, plum, and currant. A prime commercial examples is Traquair House ale.

STEAM BEER: Technically, the name "steam" now belongs to Anchor Brewing Company of San Francisco, but it is used colloquially to refer to what is more accurately called the California common beer style. Theories abound concerning the reason for the moniker "steam" being attached to this style of lager, ranging from the nineteenth century use of steam for industrial brewery power, to the high temperature of the primary fermentation, and even the sound created when casks of the lively beer were broached. Several Bavarian brewers have produced a style called dampfbier (German for "steam beer") in the past two decades. Produced mainly around the Bavarian towns of Bayreuth and Zweisel, these are fruity, top-fermented, but cold-lagered beers. The commercial example is Anchor Steam Beer.

STEINBIER: "Steinbier," literally "stone beer" in German, is a top-fermented specialty beer from Altenmünster. In an ancient brewing technique, wort is poured in a sluice over porous stones that have been heated to 2192°. This causes the sugars in the wort to scorch and crystallize. After the stones cool, they are returned to the young beer so the caramelized sugars can be fermented out, giving the beer a sweet, smoky flavor. A prime commercial example is Rauchenfels Steinbier.

STOUT: This derivative of porter is a dark, heavy, opaque ale with a high percentage of roasted grains. Stouts may be "sweet" (also called "European"—the old description "milk stout" was banned by British food trade law), "dry" (Irish), or "imperial." Dry stout is often dispensed with a high pressure nitrogen carbon dioxide mixture to give it the traditional intense, creamy head without overcarbonating the beer. The sweet stout category includes oatmeal stout. Prime commercial examples are Young's Oatmeal Stout in the sweet stout category, Guinness Extra Stout in the dry stout category, and Courage Imperial Russian Stout in the imperial stout category.

TRAPPIST ALE: An "appellation" or protected class of top-fermented, bottle-conditioned, and usually lightly hopped Belgian ale. By law, only

Stout

beers produced by Trappist monasteries have the right to be called "Trappist." Although widely varying in character, these world-renowned ales are generally regarded as strong, estery, phenolic, and malty. A prime example is Chimay Première (red label).

TRIPEL: A subcategory of the Abbey style with Trappist origins. These beers are made from very pale malt and a generous quantity of refined sugar. Tripel is more alcoholic than dubbel, but drier and much lighter in color than British ales of similar strength, such as barley wine. A prime commercial example is La Trappe Tripel.

VIENNA: Vienna is a style of lager beer developed by brewing pioneer Anton Dreher in Vienna, Austria, during the mid-nineteenth century lagering revolution. Pale red to deep amber color, they are moderately strong, light to moderately hopped, and malty. The darker, stronger Märzen lagers are based on the Vienna style, as are the traditional, dark Mexican lagers. It is one of the world's best food accompaniments. A prime commercial example is Abita Amber Lager.

WEISSE: Often a designation referring specifically to the Berliner Weisse style of wheat beer, it is just as often a term used for the Bavarian style of wheat beer. A prime commercial example of Berliner Weisse is Berliner Kindl Weisse.

WEIZEN: A term primarily used to designate the Bavarian or south German wheat beers that include hefe-weizen, dunkel, weizen, kristall weizen, and weizenbock. Except perhaps for Vienna lager, there is no other beer that pairs so perfectly and diversely with food. Prime commercial examples of hefe, dunkel, and kristall are Spaten Franziskaner Weissbier, Tucher Dunkles Hefe Weizen, and Maisel's Kristallklar.

WEIZENBOCK: Weizenbock is a German wheat beer that ranges from a deep, reddish amber to black, but these are usually much lighter in body and intensity than the standard all-barley malt bock. A prime commercial example is G. Schnieder's Aventinus.

WHEAT BEER: American wheat beer is much milder in flavor and usually lacks the distinctive clove and banana notes of the Bavarian-style varieties, but it has the same refreshing taste and generous carbonation. A prime commercial example is Catamount Wheat Beer.

WITBIER: A Belgian-style wheat beer also known as "biere blanche" or "white beer" that originated around Louvain and Hoegaarden, witbier is cloudy, frothy, and pale, with a low flavor and aroma profile. Special ale yeast strains, unmalted wheat, and spices such as coriander, cumin, and bitter orange peel are often used in addition to malted barley. A prime example is Celis White.

ZOIGL: A beer primarily "homebrewed" in small towns in the Oberfalz region of northern Bavaria. Zoigl may be top or bottom fermented, but is is usually amber to dark brown, full bodied, unfiltered, dry, and served on draft.

TECHNICAL PARAMETERS OF THE MAJOR BEER STYLES

STYLE	O.G.	IBU	Color (SRM)	ABV
Altbier	1.043–48	28–60	10–16	4.5–5
Barley Wine	1.065–1.120+	50–100	8–22	7–12
Belgian Strong Ale	1.063–95	20–30	3.5–20	7–12
Bière de Garde	1.060–80	25–30	8–12	4.5–8
Bitter, Best	1.038–42	25–30	12–14	3.5–4.5
Bitter, Ordinary	1.035–38	20–25	8–12	3–3.5
Bitter, Strong	1.042–55	30–35	12–15	4.5–6
Bock	1.065–74	20–35	9.5–22	6.6–7.5
Bock, Doppel	1.074–80	17–27	12–30	6.5–8
Bock, Eis	1.092–1.116	28–40	18–50	8.6–14.4
Bock, Mai	1.066–68	20–35	4.5–6	6–7.5
Brown Ale, American	1.038–55	25–55	15–25	3.5–5.5
Brown Ale, English	1.038–50	14–38	18–34	3.5–4.5
California Common	1.040–55	35–45	8–17	3.6–5
Cream Ale	1.044–55	10–22	2–4	4.5–7
Dortmunder-Export	1.050–60	24–37	3–5	5–6
Dubbel	1.050–70	18–25	10–14	6–7.5
Faro	1.044–56	11–23	6–13	5–6
Gueuze	1.044–56	11–23	6–13	5–6
India Pale Ale	1.050–65	40–60	8–14	5–6.5
Irish Red Ale	1.035–65	20–35	10–12	3.5–7
Kellerbier	1.048–50	30–40	8–12	4.5–5
Kölsch	1.042–47	16–34	3.5–5.5	4.5–5
Kulmbacher	1.043–48	28–60	10–16	4.5–5
Lambic	1.040–72	15–21	5–10	5–7
Light Beer	1.024–40	8–15	2–4	2.9–4.2
Malt Liquor	1.045–70	7–22	2.5–3.5	5.3–6
Märzen/Oktoberfest	1.050–60	20–25	8–12	5–6
Mild Ale	1.030–37	10–30	10–26	3–3.5
Münchner Dunkel	1.049–60	23–30	14–20	5–6
Münchner Helles	1.045–52	25–30	3–4.5	4.5–5.5

TECHNICAL PARAMETERS OF THE MAJOR BEER STYLES

	O.G.	IBUs	SRM	ABV
Old Ale	1.055–75	30–40	10–16	6–8
Oud Bruin	1.044–56	15–25	12–18	4.8–5.2
Pale Ale, American	1.044–56	20–40	4–11	4.5–5.5
Pale Ale, English	1.045–55	25–45	6–12	4.5–5.5
Pale Ale, Belgian	1.044–54	20–30	3.5–12	4–6.2
Pils, German	1.044–50	30–40	2.5–4	4–5
Pilsner, American (Megabrewery)	1.044–48	11–16	2–2.5	4–5
Pilsner, Czech	1.043–49	30–43	4–4.5	4–4.5
Porter	1.048–60	35–40	20–40	5–6
Rauchbier	1.048–55	20–35	15–20	4.5–5
Saison	1.044–54	20–30	3.5–12	4–6
Schwarzbier	1.044–52	22–30	25–30	3.8–5
Scotch Ale	1.072–85	25–40	15–50	6–8
Scottish Export	1.040–50	15–20	10–20	4–4.5
Scottish Heavy	1.035–40	10–15	10–20	3.5–4
Scottish Light	1.030–35	8–18	7–18	3–4
Stout, Dry	1.040–50	30–50	35–70	4–5.5
Stout, Imperial	1.072–80	50–80	20–50	7–9
Stout, Sweet	1.045–56	15–25	40+	3–6
Tripel	1.070–95	20–25	3.5–5.5	7–10
Vienna	1.048–55	22–28	8–12	4.4–6
Weisse, Berliner	1.028–32	3–6	2–4	2.8–3.4
Weizen, Dunkel	1.048–56	10–15	17–22	4.8–5.4
Weizen, Helles Hefe-Weissbier	1.048–55	10–18	3–10	4.5–5.5
Weizen, Kristall	1.045–55	10–19	3.5–5	5–5.5
Weizenbock	1.066–80	10–20	7–30	6.5–7.5
Witbier	1.044–50	15–25	2–4	4.5–5.2

KEY:

O.G. — Original Gravity. A measure of the fermentables in the beer wort prior to fermentation.

IBUs — International Bitterness Units. A measure of hop bitterness.

SRM — Standard Reference Method. A measurement of beer color.

ABV — Alcohol by Volume. Expressed as a percentage, this figure is 25 percent greater than the Alcohol by Weight figure used by many U.S. breweries.

ENJOYING BEER

he styles and appropriateness of a particular beer for a given occasion are nearly limitless. Using the Directory and the Beer Styles sections of this book, choose a beer that suits the mood, the season, and, most importantly, your personal preference. Although there is a great deal of fun to be had in "beer hunting," for your regular purchases of beer try to find a store with a strong selection of both imports and microbrews. A good beer seller will have a solid working knowledge of a wide range of beers and can make recommendations to meet your needs. The best beer sellers are enthusiastic about the subject and eager to discuss it with you.

Listed below are some terms that will help your understanding of terminology and words that may be used on beer labels from different countries.

GERMAN

Alt—Old

Bayerische/Bairische/Bayrisch—Bavarian

Doppel—Double

Dunkel/Dunkle/Dunkles—Dark

Feines/Fein—Fine

Fest—Stronger than normal and usually malty and reddish in color

Flaschengärung—Refermented in the bottle for natural carbonation

Hefe—Yeast

Herb—Dry

Klassiche—Classic

Kristall—Filtered

Nach dem Reinheitsgebot gebraut—Brewed

according to the Bavarian purity law with only malt, hops, yeast, and water

Obergärig—Top fermented

Schankbier—A low gravity beer between 7 and 8°P and usually about 3% ABV

Stark—Strong

Trüb—Naturally cloudy from yeast sediment

Rauch—Smoked

Stammwurze—Specific gravity. Germans use the percent sign (e.g., Stammwurze 24%) to indicate degrees Plato (24°P)

Vollbier—A standard gravity beer between 11 and 14°P and usually about 5% ABV

FRENCH

Aucun Additif Ni Agent de Conservation—

No additives/no preservatives

Bière artisinal à triple fermentation—Triple fermented craft brew

Bière Forte—Strong Beer

Bières Spéciales Du Nord—Special beer of the north of France near the Belgian border

Bouteille Consignée—Returnable bottle

Brassée en—Brewed in

Brasserie—Brewery

Conservation: tenir au frais et à l'abri de la lumière—Storage: keep cool and away from light

Fermentation Haute—Top-fermented (an ale)

Houblon—Hops

La Levure—Yeast

Malt D'Orge—Barley malt

Non-filtrée/Non-pasteurisée—Unfiltered and unpasteurized

Refermentée en Bouteille—Bottle conditioned

Servir Frais—Serve cool

ENGLISH/AMERICAN

Malt Liquor—Usually, beer containing more than 5 to 5.5% ABV

Fire brewed—the brew kettle is heated directly by open gas flames as opposed to being heated by steam in a steel jacket that surrounds the copper. Although there is no hard scientific evidence to support this, many brewers feel that direct-fired kettles provide a harder boil, better carmelization of the wort, and a maltier-tasting beer. It is certainly more traditional.

Cold Filtered—There is little significance in this; all filtered beers are cold filtered.

Unfiltered/Unpasteurized—The beer will have at least a light sediment and requires careful pouring. A lager should have been refrigerated in the store where you purchased it, and should be kept chilled when you get it home. Ales should be kept in a cool, dark place, preferably at cellar temperatures.

STORING BEER

Once you have chosen your beer, it needs to be stored correctly in your home. Bottom-fermented lager beers should be kept cold (40°F) and dark, especially if they are unpasteurized. Ales should be kept cool and dark, and, in the case of some sedimented Belgian ales, at the upper end of cellar temperatures, or approaching room temperature at 55–60°F. If possible, dedicate a spare refrigerator to beer storage. The standard refrigerator setting of 35°F is much too cold and a lager stored at this temperature should be allowed to warm for at least 15 minutes before opening. It is possible in some refrigerators to set the thermostat so that you can keep lagers close to their 45°F serving temperature in one section and ales close to their 50–55°F ideal when placed near the motor compartment.

GLASSWARE

The proper drinking vessel is essential to obtaining maximum sensory pleasure from a craft beer. Although bland, nondescript, mass-market lagers may all taste the same regardless of the manner in which they are served, brews of more distinct character require fairly specific glassware, developed to allow them to express their true individuality. Reflecting the growth and range of beers, the glassware for which they are suited has evolved from the simplest tankards and steins of medieval times to, in the case of Belgian ales, an individualistic design for nearly every beer. The primary glassware for beer consumption falls generally into the following categories: fluted, goblet, tulip, flared tulip, cordial, tankard, weissbier tumbler, snifter, straight-sided tumbler, pilsner glass, dimpled pub mug, shaker pub pint, stoneware stein, and the noninck bulge pint.

FLUTED GLASS

Fluted glasses are best suited to fruit-flavored beers such as raspberry and those beers with a winelike bouquet. The tall design helps reserve the delicate bubbles of an effervescent lambic and concentrates the bouquet of aromatic beers, channeling it directly to the nose.

CORDIAL

Cordials are perfect for a small serving of a particularly strong or intensely flavored beer that is served as a nightcap or *digestif*. These glasses encourage the drinker to sip slowly and savor such complex beers as Eldridge Pope's Thomas Hardy's Ale, or Hürlimann's Samichlaus.

DIMPLED PUB MUG

The dimpled sides makes this large mug easier to handle, especially if hands become slippery during a meal. Its large, open mouth releases the floral, herbal bouquet of English hops as well as the fruity, malty aroma of a classic draft bitter. The design of the dimpled pint also encourages the drinker to enjoy the large gulps necessary to capture the big malt flavor of lightly-carbonated pale ales.

FLARED TULIP

Similar to the brandy snifter, except that it also has a flared lip allowing the beer to pass effortlessly under the foamy head and into the mouth while allowing the drinker to deeply inhale the aroma. This style of glassware is best demonstrated by Duvel's custom glassware and is perfect for Belgian tripels and other complex, generously carbonated dubbels, oud bruins, and Belgian red ales.

GOBLET

The goblet allows deep inhalation of the

bouquet of beers that have a more subtle aroma. Its shape also encourages a well-carbonated ale such as Belgian abbey ale to develop and maintain its full head without denying the drinker access to the beer. The goblet shape lets the beer warm quickly if cupped in the hands or more slowly if held by the stem.

NONICK BULGE PINT

Full, masculine, and substantial, these are intended to hold the ample serving that is an imperial pint. The vessel is gently bulged near the rim for easier handling, as well as to capture the fresh, earthy bouquet of English hops and fruity fermentation esters.

PILSNER GLASS

Whether in a stemmed, conical, or slightly bulging design, these are tall and graceful to channel the hop aromas to the fore. The clear glass showcases the brilliant golden color and lively stream of bubbles.

SHAKER PUB PINT

Originally designed as a bartender's mixing tool, these have come into wide use, particularly in brewpubs, as a sturdy, smart-looking vessel for holding pints of microbrewed pale ales, stouts, porters, and amber lagers.

SNIFTER

The snifter is considered by many to be the perfect vessel in which to "nose" an especially aromatic beer, particularly Belgian ales as diverse as lambic and abbey dubbel, because the design traps the aroma near the rim. The beer can be warmed in the palm for greater flavor detection or held by the stem to keep the beer cool.

STONEWARE STEIN

Once the standard vessel for beer drinking in Germany, the stein—in both decorative and utilitarian forms—is considered by many to be optimal for the consumption of bock beer in all its incarnations. The dense, heavy nature of

Fluted   *Tankard*   *Snifter*   *Tumbler*   *Stoneware stein*

these vessels provides efficient, consistent temperature control. The flip-top lid was originally designed to keep flying insects out of the beer. In a Bavarian *biergarten*, an open lid translates into a polite request for a refill. Open, conical versions have also been employed for weissbiers.

TANKARD

Although tankards crafted from pewter or another opaque material conceal the color and clarity of a beer, they often maintain the serving temperature and seem to accentuate the senses of taste and smell once sight is taken out of the equation. Clear tankards are often used for draft quaffing beers such as Bavarian helles or American lager.

TUMBLERS

The short, straight-sided versions are the traditional vessel for the service of Düsseldorfer altbiers. Taller, more delicate versions are used for Cologne's kölsch. Modest, fluted tumblers

are the traditional serving vessels for Belgian gueuze, allowing the drinker to deeply inhale the lactic aromas of this classic beer. It also facilitates a firm grip while negotiating the traditional Belgian accompaniment—a large pot of steamed mussels.

WEISSBIER TUMBLER

The weissbier tumbler is perhaps the trickiest beer glass to master. Without careful attention to your technique, you are likely to end up with a face full of wheat beer. Designed for easy grasping, these long, upwardly flaring glasses accentuate generous head formation and direct the cornucopia of aromas inherent to Bavarian weissbiers toward the nose. These are equally well suited to hefe, kristall, dunkel, and bock weissbiers. To pour properly, the glass should be turned nearly horizontal as the beer is poured gently down the side, then turned upright when one quarter remains to produce three inches of foam.

Goblet   *Flared tulip*   *Noninck bulge pint*   *Pilsner*   *Tulip*

Care of Glassware

Whenever possible, beer glassware should be hand washed, thoroughly rinsed of any soap, detergent, or rinsing agent, and air-dried until it is crystal clear. Just prior to serving, the glass should be rinsed with cold water. This will ensure proper development of a head on the beer by removing any dust or lint, and will prevent bubbles from clinging to the side of the glass. Glassware can be chilled in the refrigerator, but should never be frozen, as this will only introduce ice into the beer, giving it a watered-down taste. The low temperature will also completely mask most flavors and any sensations other than coldness and fizz.

Serving Temperature

Thankfully, much of the guesswork regarding proper serving temperature has been eliminated by considerate brewers, who now offer suggestions about temperature as well as proper glassware. Where possible, we have tried to include these in the Directory. However there are generally accepted guidelines for the major styles that will put you in the general vicinity. As in all other areas of beer enjoyment, there is a great deal of latitude for personal preference. Start with the basic parameters and move the temperatures up or down depending on the instincts of your palate. In the broadest possible terms, serve ale at 50–55°F and lager at 45–50°F.

Below are a few specific recommendations for serving temperatures. Store corked beers on their sides, just as you would wine. Store crown-capped beers upright.

Bavarian Wheat Beer: 45–50°F

Belgian Abbey Styles: 55–60°F

Belgian Witbier: 40–45°F

Bock: 45–55°F

British-style Pale Ales: 50–60°F

Czech Pilsner: 45–50°F

Dry Irish Stout: 55–65°F

Belgian Red: 45–55°F

Framboise: 45–50°F

Helles: 45–50°F

Kriek: 50–55°F

Lambic and Gueuze: 50–60°F

Low-Calorie and Low-Alcohol Beer: 35–40°F

Münchner Dunkel: 45–50°F

Oud Bruin: 55–60°F

Porter: 50–55°F

Scottish Ale: 50–55°F

Strong Ales and Barley Wine: 50–60°F

Undoubtedly, as your palate for fuller-bodied, richer brews develops, you will more than likely enjoy your beers at increasingly warm temperatures. If a style of beer is too intensely flavored on your first try, try serving it cooler the next time, and gradually develop your taste for it.

Proper Head Level

Many people wonder whether a beer should have a head of foam. In the U.S., many of us acquired great skill in our youth for ensuring that there wasn't the slightest trace of bubbles atop our beer. In keeping with the complexity of beer, the answer to the question of the proper amount of head on a brew depends on the style being served and the tradition of the area.

The appropriate head is linked to the carbonation of the brew. In southern England, the traditional pint of ordinary bitter in the pub is served with only a thin cap of foam. These ales are low in alcohol and lightly carbonated in order for them to be better session beers; in other words, beers that can be enjoyed in fairly large quantities over several hours without inflicting drunkenness or bloating upon its imbiber. In the north of England, around Yorkshire, the same session bitter is often dispensed with a thick, creamy head. As many Belgian ales are quite strong and are often consumed in limited quantities over a lengthy period, their generous carbonation facilitates a slow, steady release of aroma. These ales are often served with a large airy head of foam. Lagers fall somewhere in between, with many finding one to three inches of foam visually appealing, as well as a good way of releasing a dose of hop aroma in a pilsner or a warming whiff of malt esters in a doppelbock.

In summary, the amount of head on a beer is style specific, but generally a decent collar of foam will reward the drinker with more than just flavor as you drink; it will issue forth the wonderful aromas of hops, malt, and yeast.

North of England head

South of England head

German pils head

HOSTING A BEER-TASTING DINNER

I f you have ever held a dinner party at which wine was served, you are already reasonably well equipped to do the same with beer as the principal libation. Serve each selection in a separate glass, with between four to six ounces for each person. Less than that amount will prevent them from properly appreciating the beers' aroma, flavor, and development, and will not allow their palates to become accustomed to a new taste. Too much will fill your guests too soon and destroy their appetites.

Beers usually should be served from light to dark throughout the evening, with the richest, sweetest, and strongest beers reserved for the nightcap. Greet your guests with a dry, spritzy, and refreshing fruit lambic, gueuze, or Belgian pale ale aperitif. Pair appetizers with a light but flavorful pilsner. Light, and vegetable-based soups can generally be matched with dry, pale beers; serve dark, vinous brews if the soups are rich and meat-based. A salad course can be matched with the light, but more complexly flavored wheat beer. Depending on the main course, the next beer should be more robust and hearty. Two of the most versatile beers for accompanying entrées are

the reddish-hued English pale ale and the Bavarian märzen styles. Their rich, slightly sweet maltiness balanced by a firm hop bitterness makes them equally satisfying and cleansing to the palate. For light seafood dishes, a paler French biere de garde, a Belgian wit, or an American golden ale is more appropriate.

The cheese course is the time to serve beers with sherry or port like qualities, such as an English old ale, a Belgian dubbel, or an American barley wine.

The dessert course can be one of the most exciting and limitless arenas for beer service. The naturally sweet, chocolatey, and fruity qualities of many of the world's classic beers form a perfect partnership with rich desserts. Porters, stouts, and Belgian strong ales go wonderfully well with chocolate. Serve spiced beers with Christmas fruitcakes, creamy puddings, and pumpkin pie. Fruit-flavored ales are unequalled with berry pies, fruit tortes, and seasonal fruit pies. Some of the world's classic brews can even be served instead of dessert: try Kulmbacher Reichelbräu's Eisbock, Hürlimann's Samichlaus, or Schneider's Aventinus. A good after-dinner beer will often resemble other, more familiar digestifs, such as cognac, port, or whisky. Choose a beer that is rich, complex, and deep, with a sweetness that encourages slow sipping, such as a barley wine, Scotch wee heavy, or doppelbock.

BEER EVALUATION

Appearance assessment starts before the bottle is opened. To judge appearance, examine the unopened bottle against the light for signs of large bubbles at the top: this may be an indication that the bottle has recently been shaken and may gush when open. Ideally, the beer should rest one or two days before opening if this is the case, particularly in the case of highly carbonated or bottled-conditioned beers. Also, examine the sediment at the bottom of bottle-conditioned beers. It should be in a thin, densely packed layer. A cloudy, loose appearance may indicate recent rough handling and requires a day or two of upright settling. After carefully pouring the beer to produce an appropriate head of foam for that particular style, let the beer sit for a moment. A good all-malt beer will generally retain at least half of its head for one minute. This quality is referred to as "head retention." As the head falls, and as you drink, it should leave traces of foam on the sides of the glass, often referred to as "Irish" or "Brussels" lace. Judgment of appearance also includes the beer's color. Beer color is practically infinite in its subtleties and variations, but there are guidelines for each category of beer.

Aroma generally refers to the smell of the beer's basic malted and specialty grain ingredients—its base or underpinning. These aromas are often described as nutty, sweet, grainy, and malty. The aromas that result from the fermentation of cereal grains are called esters and are typically of a fruity nature. They exhibit themselves as the aromas of ripened fruit such as bananas, pears, apples, currants, and raisins. The terms "aroma" and "nose" are also sometimes used to describe the entire smell of a beer, including hops, malt, and esters.

Bouquet is more specific, referring to the aroma that hops alone bring to a beer. Hop bouquet or "hop nose" is best appreciated just after the beer is poured, as it dissipates quickly. Hop aroma is not always appropriate in every style of beer, and the variety of hops used for bouquet is also style specific. Terms used to describe hop aroma include herbal, pine, floral, resin, and spice.

HOW TO POUR A WHEAT BEER

Turn the glass nearly horizontally and pour gently down the side.

Turn the glass upright when one quarter remains and continue pouring.

The head should measure about three inches.

HOW TO POUR A PILSNER

Hold the glass vertically and pour the beer straight down the middle.

Wait for the foam to settle and continue pouring it.

The head should be about one to two inches.

TASTING BEER

Condition is often used interchangeably with the word "carbonation" to describe the amount of carbon dioxide in the beer, although breweries often refer to carbonation as the injection of carbon dioxide by artificial means. Proper conditioning brings out the complex elements of a beer and gives it a lively quality. Too much conditioning will often mask the beer's overall taste and homogenize the flavor profile. Too little conditioning can make a beer seem overly sweet, unbalanced, or dull.

Mouthfeel applies to the perception of body in the beer, its apparent lightness or weight created by the proteins and dextrins in the beer.

Flavor is perhaps the most subjective and yet the most obvious indicator of enjoyment. Particular beer styles should have certain common taste elements, and a well-balanced beer should have carefully orchestrated flavors of malt sweetness and hop bitterness.

Aftertaste is the lingering taste that remains after the beer has been swallowed. Proper aftertaste is as style-specific as the other qualities, but is generally desired to be balanced and clean as a result of hop bitterness.

PART TWO

The Beer
Directory

There is an old Bavarian proverb which should preface this book, and particularly this section. It states, "If you ask three brewers, you will get four opinions." That astute observation of beer-related thinking is a perfect caveat for evaluations of something as subjective as the sense of taste. Bear in mind that your own sense of taste in regards to beer will change over time and should be trusted on an evolving basis. In other words, if you enjoy a beer, do so freely, regardless of what the experts say; the craft beer renaissance was born of independence, after all. Trying to distill a sampling of some of the world's best breweries into a limited number of pages, particularly in the dynamic climate of today's beer revival, is much like trying to choose the most representative still from an action-packed motion picture. Nevertheless, what follows is a snapshot of an exciting world that will introduce you to the great enjoyment that good beer has brought humankind throughout history.

Breweries are ranked in one of the following three categories:

Classics

Craft breweries that deserve special mention, regardless of size, because they are perennial award winners, have consistently been ranked among the world's best, or have created or set the standard for a classic beer style.

Laureates

Smaller or lesser-known leaders of the craft beer movement that have won major awards, have set industry standards for the styles they brew, and produce exceptional beers of consistent quality.

Rising Stars

Award-winning craft breweries of above-average quality, trendsetting new breweries, and artisanal brewers that promise to be tomorrow's leaders.

Terms

% ABV

Percentage of alcohol by volume. A relative measurement of a beer's strength, most commonly used in Britain, Europe, and by American winemakers. Many U.S. microbrewers use this designation, but others still use the "alcohol by weight" measurement, which is approximately 25% lower, e.g., 4% ABW=5% ABV.

BOTTLE CONDITIONED

Carbonation in the beer is produced naturally by the yeast left in the bottle as it consumes residual sugars and emits carbon dioxide as a waste product.

IBU'S

International Bittering Units. A measurement of the amount of hop bitterness in a beer.

DRY HOPPING

Addition of whole flower hops late in the fermentation process to supply hop aroma.

EBC

The measurement of color generally used by European breweries.

ESTER

Fruity smells produced during fermentation, most often by ale yeast.

GRIST

The grains or combinations of grain used in a beer's mash.

HECTOLITER

The international standard liquid measure used in the brewing industry. 1 U.S. barrel is equivalent to 1.643 hectoliters and 1 U.K. barrel is equivalent to 1.368 hectoliters.

LOVIBOND

A measurement of color occasionally used with brewing grains that is roughly the same as SRM.

O.G.

An abbreviation of "original gravity," the first measurement of fermentable sugars in the beer before fermentation begins. Original gravity is the prime indicator of a beer's potential strength. An o.g. of 1.040, or its equivalent of 10 degrees Plato, generally will yield a beer with roughly four percent alcohol by volume. "Final or terminal gravity" is the measurement of sugars remaining in the beer at the end of fermentation.

REINHEITSGEBOT

This so-called "beer purity law" was enacted by Duke Wilhelm IV of Bavaria in 1516—it now dictates that only malted grains, hops, water, and yeast may be used as ingredients for beer sold in Germany.

SRM

The measurement of color used in the U.S. Roughly equivalent to 40% of the EBC figure. 10 EBC equals approximately 4 SRM, the color of a typical pilsner. Dry stouts are typically 100–150 EBC/40–60 SRM.

°P

The symbol for degrees Plato, a system used mostly in continental Europe and the U.S. to measure the fermentable sugar level of beer. Degrees Plato roughly corresponds to one-fourth of the gravity measurement. Both are noted in the Directory because they are both in widespread use.

RATING SYSTEM

Needs significant improvement. Not one of this brewery's better efforts.

Good. A nice example of the style, but not exceptional enough to stand out in a crowd.

Very good. Better than most in this style category.

Excellent. A brew among the world's best in its style category.

Superlative. A flawless beer and one of the world's best.

CLASSICS

Anchor Brewing Company ● Bass Brewers ● Berliner Kindl Brauerei ● Budweiser Budvar ● Brasserie Cantillon ● Celis Brewery ● Coopers Brewery ● Privatbrauerei Diebels ● Brasserie Dubuisson Freres ● Einbecker Brauhaus ● Eldridge, Pope & Company ● Fuller, Smith & Turner ● Gabriel Sedlmayr ● Greene King & Sons PLC ● Arthur Guinness & Son Ltd ● Brouwerij Het Anker ● Brauerei Hürlimann ● Brouwerij Liefmans ● Mendocino Brewing Company ● Brouwerij Moortgat ● Brasserie d'Orval S.A. ● Paulener-Salvator-Thomas-Bräu ● Plzensky Prazdroj ● Brouwerij Rodenbach ● Abbaye de Notre-Dame de Saint-Remy ● Samuel Smith ● Brauerei G. Schneider & Sohn ● Scottish Courage Ltd ● Abbaye de Notre-Dame de Scourmont ● Sierra Nevada Brewing Company ● Brasserie de Silly ● T&R Theakston Ltd ● Traquair House Brewery ● Abdij der Trappisten van Westmalle ● Bayerische Staatsbrauerei Weihenstephan ● Young & Co's Brewery

ANCHOR
BREWING COMPANY

1705 MARIPOSA STREET, SAN FRANCISCO, CALIFORNIA 94107
(1–415) 863–8350

By now, the story of how Fritz Maytag saved the failing Anchor Brewing Company is legendary among craft beer aficionados. Although Anchor was a long-established regional brewery and not a micro when purchased by the heir to the Maytag appliance fortune, in many ways, Anchor paved the way for the microbrewery revolution by proving that beers of unusually high quality and character could succeed in the U.S. In 1965, when the idealistic young grad student decided to purchase the brewery, one of Maytag's main reasons for saving Anchor from bankruptcy was to preserve a piece of San Francisco history. In that spirit, Anchor brews are made in a traditional, handmade copper brewhouse in combination with state-of-the-art methods of sanitation and packaging to preserve their trademark freshness and consistency.

BREW FACTS	
FOUNDED:	1896
HEAD BREWER:	Fritz Maytag
ANNUAL OUTPUT:	140,904 hectoliters
BREW STYLES:	Steam beer, pale ale, porter, wheat beer, barley wine, holiday ale

Fritz Maytag, president and head brewer of Anchor Brewing Company

CONNOISSEUR'S RATING

OUR SPECIAL ALE

LIBERTY ALE

OLD FOGHORN BARLEYWINE STYLE ALE

PORTER

STEAM

WHEAT BEER

TASTING NOTES

1995 OUR SPECIAL ALE: *(Gravity varies yearly). Deep mahogany in color with a rich, tan head that leaves a heavy lace. Full of fresh, spicy aromas of cinnamon, cloves, and nutmeg. Full bodied, rich, and dry in palate with a smoky, roasted malt flavor dominated by tasteful spicing. Finishes with a lingering roast bitterness and the flavor of spice. This is the twenty-first incarnation of Anchor's holiday ale.*

LIBERTY ALE: *14.25 °P/1.057 o.g., 6.1% ABV. Straw gold in color with a huge, dry-hopped bouquet of perfumey hops. Assertively hoppy and fresh in flavor with a firm, balancing maltiness and rounded bitterness. Expertly crafted with a very big flavor married to a mature smoothness. One of America's best ales.*

OLD FOGHORN BARLEYWINE STYLE ALE: *25 °P/1.100 o.g., 65 BU, 8.7% ABV. Bright mahogany in color with a fruity aroma reminiscent of orange-flavored hard candy. Brewed from the first runnings of an all-malt mash, this top-fermented, dry hopped barley wine has a very English character with a blend of fruitiness, maltiness, and hop bitterness to balance. Although this renowned ale has been around since 1975, it has recently been rereleased in 7-ounce nips.*

PORTER: *17 °P/1.068 o.g., 6.3% ABV. Black in color with a rich, creamy head and aromas of roasted malt and some hops. Like all of Anchor's products, this is nicely crafted with a balanced mixture of hops and malt, but more adventurous than many American porters, offering a mellow roasted malt flavor profile and medium body beneath richly mingled flavors of sweet fruit, caramel, licorice, smoke, and hops.*

STEAM: *12.5 °P/1.050 o.g., 33 BU, 5% ABV. Deep amber in color with a generous, rocky head. Firmly malty, faintly fruity, and fresh with a crisp, refreshing hop dryness developing toward the finish. Very rounded and full of character, the cornerstone of this classic American brewery.*

WHEAT BEER: *First introduced in 1984, this was perhaps the first wheat beer brewed in the U.S. since Prohibition. Aromatic of honey, ripe fruit, and vanilla. The high percentage of wheat malt gives this honey-colored beer a very dry, clean, lagerlike character, with a firm hop presence and a fruity, dry finish.*

BASS BREWERS

137 HIGH STREET, BURTON-ON-TRENT, STAFFORDSHIRE DE14 1JZ, ENGLAND (44-1283) 511000

This classic producer of pale ale, founded by William Bass in 1777, now produces nearly a quarter of all the beer brewed in the U.K. Its Draught Bass is that nation's top-selling cask-conditioned ale. One of the most interesting and unique aspects of Bass' brewing is its Museum Brewery at Burton-on-Trent. The active plant dates from the 1920s and features two copper squares for open fermentation, one of which dates from 1850. Although the copper, steam-heated brewhouse is the centerpiece of the busy Museum, head brewer Steve Wellington churns out 1972 hectoliters per year of limited edition commemorative, seasonal, and specialty ales.

BREW FACTS

FOUNDED: 1777

HEAD BREWERS: Steve Wellington (Bass Museum Brewery), Mike Jenkins (Draught Bass), Gilbert Wilson (Pale Ale), Steve Nuttall (Highgate Dark)

ANNUAL OUTPUT: Figures not available

BREW STYLES: Pale ale, mild, old ale, strong ale

CONNOISSEUR'S RATING

DRAUGHT BASS
10.75°P/1.043 o.g., 4.4% ABV

EXPORT PALE ALE
12°P/1.048 o.g., 5% ABV

HIGHGATE DARK
8.5°P/1.035 o.g., 3.2% ABV

BERLINER KINDL BRAUEREI

WERBELLINSTRASSE 50, 12006 BERLIN, GERMANY
(49-30) 6-89-92-0

Although this large brewery offers a wide selection of beers—including an assortment of bocks, pils, and more familiar styles—it is most noteworthy as one of the last two producers of the classic Berliner weisse style. The low-gravity low-alcohol "Champagne of the North," as it was dubbed by Napoleon's conquering army, is often served like champagne, in a wide-mouthed goblet. These light, spritzy wheat beers are fermented with ale yeast and a dose of lactic acid–producing bacteria called *lactobacillus delbrückii*, which gives them a tart, slightly sour character making them ideal as a summer refresher. In Germany, they are served with a dash of either raspberry or woodruff syrup in order to cut the acidity.

BREW FACTS

FOUNDED: 1872

HEAD BREWER:
Berndt Neumann

ANNUAL OUTPUT:
Figures not available

BREW STYLES: Berliner weisse, pils, maibock, bock, diät pils, alcohol-free, low-calorie, alt, weizen

CONNOISSEUR'S RATING

BERLINER KINDL WEISSE
7.5°P/1.030 o.g., 2.5% ABV

BUDWEISER BUDVAR

KAROLINY SVELTÉ 4, 370–21 CESKÉ BUDEJOVICE-BUDWEIS,
CZECH REPUBLIC (42–38) 7705111

The growing fame of the pale lager beer from southern Bohemia had already resulted in many small brewery consolidations in 1895, when Budweiser Budvar was founded as a joint-stock brewery. In their first year of operation Budweiser brewed an impressive 51,000 hectoliters—proof of the enormous popularity of the style.

BREW FACTS

FOUNDED: 1895

HEAD BREWER:

Milos Heide

ANNUAL OUTPUT:

422,895 hectoliters

BREW STYLES: Lager, low-calorie, alcohol-free

This classic Czech "premium lager" is available worldwide, but has been kept out of the American market because of a trademark dispute involving the use of the name "Budweiser," which was for centuries a generic term for beers produced in the Bohemian city of Budweis (Ceské Budejovice). Budweiser was adopted as a brand name by Anheuser-Busch in the 1870s, some two decades before this world-renowned Czech brewery was founded. At the time of this writing, Anheuser-Busch is seeking an ownership stake in Budweiser Budvar, much to the trepidation of craft beer connoisseurs worldwide. Worth seeking out when travelling abroad, Budvar is available throughout Europe.

CONNOISSEUR'S RATING

BUDWEISER BUDVARS
12°P/1.048 o.g., 22 IBU, 5% ABV

BRASSERIE CANTILLON

GHEUDESTRAAT 56, ANDERLECHT, 1070 BRUSSELS, BELGIUM
(32-25) 21-49-28

This brewery has been family-owned and operated since the Cantillons came to Brussels from Lembeek as lambic merchants in 1900. The Cantillon family began brewing its own products in the 1930s, and its current operator defiantly produces what are arguably Belgium's best examples of traditional gueuze. Cantillon has been called "the supreme lambic brewery and gueuze blender" by Belgian beer authority Tim Webb, and "a classic example of a lambic brewery" by Michael Jackson. There is little one can add to accolades like those.

BREW FACTS
FOUNDED: 1900
HEAD BREWER: Jean-Pierre Van Roy
ANNUAL OUTPUT: 700 hectoliters
BREW STYLES: Lambic gueuze, fruit gueuze, faro

CONNOISSEUR'S RATING	
KRIEK LAMBIC *5% ABV*	🍾🍾🍾🍾🍾
ROSÉ DE GAMBRINUS *11.4°P/1.046 o.g., 5% ABV*	🍾🍾🍾🍾🍾
SUPER GUEUZE *5% ABV*	🍾🍾🍾🍾🍾

CELIS BREWERY

2431 FORBES DRIVE, AUSTIN, TEXAS 78754
(1–512) 835–0884

After a particularly hot summer in Hoegaarden, Belgium, in 1965, a forty-year-old dairy farmer named Pierre Celis began to crave the refreshing witbiers of his youth. Pierre homebrewed a small batch of the traditional Belgian beer using reconfigured dairy equipment. His friends liked it so much that Celis sold his dairy business and opened a small artisanal brewery named De Kluis, or "Cloister," to honor the Trappist monks who first brought brewing to the region. Word of the quality and freshness of this brewery spread and Celis was soon exporting to France and the Netherlands.

BREW FACTS
FOUNDED: 1991
HEAD BREWER:
Peter Camps
ANNUAL OUTPUT:
27,360 hectoliters
BREW STYLES: White beer, pale ale, strong ale, fruit-wheat, pilsner

In the fall of 1985, tragedy struck when Pierre Celis' De Kluis brewery burnt to the ground. Underinsured, Pierre entered into association with brewing giant Stella Artois and, later, Interbrew to rebuild. This association proved agreeable for a time, but Celis was eventually ordered to take shortcuts to increase profits. It was then that Pierre decided to sell his brewery to the megabrewers and start fresh in the home of independent pioneers, Texas. The waters in the vibrant city of Austin proved to be as limestone-rich as the waters of Pierre's hometown. When Celis' brewery began selling beer in 1992, there were no American breweries producing Belgian white: today there are ten.

Pierre Celis—renowned microbrewer

CONNOISSEUR'S RATING

CELIS GOLDEN

CELIS GRAND CRU

CELIS PALE BOCK

CELIS WHITE

CELIS RASPBERRY

TASTING NOTES

CELIS GOLDEN: *11.5 °P/1.049 o.g., 20–25 BU, 2 SRM, 5% ABV. A European-style pilsner finished with Saaz hops from the Czech Republic. Bright golden color, aromatic in the nose, with a hoppy balance leading to a dry finish. Aged six weeks before bottling. The refreshing flavor brings out the best in a wide-ranging choice of foods, including fried chicken and fish, pizza, Cajun, Chinese, and sushi.*

CELIS GRAND CRU: *17.5 °P/1.080 o.g., 15–20 BU, 3.5 SRM, 5% ABV. Brewed in small quantities, Grand Cru (special vintage) ales were originally brewed for special occasions such as weddings or for village dignitaries. Celis Grand Cru is based on a traditional recipe of pale lager malts, orange peel, and other spices, as well as Saaz and Cascade hops. Subtle, creamy, and slightly sweet, this golden strong ale is best served at cellar temperatures with hearty foods such as beef tenderloin, smoked sausage, wild game, and Mexican food, and is also good as an aperitif.*

CELIS PALE BOCK: *12.5 °P/1.050 o.g., 20–25 BU, 8.7 SRM, 5% ABV. Not*

Belgian-style pale ale (peculiarities of Texas liquor law require the "bock" designation). Reddish gold with a fruity-berry aroma. Spicy, sharply intense and dry in the mouth, but with a pronounced caramel malt finish. Full of flavor and highly recommended with hearty fare such as roasted fowl, smoked ham, venison, and Southwestern cuisine.

CELIS WHITE: *11.5 °P/1.048 o.g., 12–15 BU, 1.5 SRM, 5% ABV. Brewed from 50% raw Texas winter wheat and 50% barley malt, hopped with Willamette and Cascade. The beer that resurrected the white beer style in Belgium and instigated the Belgian witbier craze in the U.S. Features a fruity, aromatic banana, orange, and coriander aroma. Recommended with fruits, salads, delicate sauces, fish, and poultry or as an aperitif.*

Celis White won Great American Beer and Festival gold medals in 1992, 1993, and 1995, and a silver medal in 1994.

CELIS RASPBERRY: *12 °P/1.048 o.g., 12–15 BU, 5% ABV. 60% barley malt/40% raw winter wheat from Luckenbach, Texas, and a blend of Cascade, Willamette, and Goldings hops. Natural raspberry is added during secondary fermentation. A terrific seasonal summer refresher or aperitif, but also a great complement to fresh raspberry ice cream, frozen yogurt, and raspberry-chocolate desserts.*

COOPERS BREWERY

9 STATENBOROUGH STREET, LEABROOK, ADELAIDE, SOUTH AUSTRALIA
5068, AUSTRALIA (61-8) 332-5088

In the south Australian town of Adelaide there is unique style of beer called "sparkling ale" that has survived the lager revolution and the other conformities that followed. Sparkling ale is produced by a few brewers only and bears many similarities to a fruity, bottle-conditioned English pale ale. The premier example is brewed by Coopers, a traditionalist family brewery founded by Thomas Cooper, a Yorkshireman who immigrated to Australia in 1852. With a heavy sediment of yeast, Coopers ale is actually quite cloudy. It is hopped with the Australian Pride of Ringwood hops.

BREW FACTS

FOUNDED: 1862

HEAD BREWER: Ched Bojic

ANNUAL OUTPUT: 900,000 hectoliters

BREW STYLES: Sparkling ale, lager, stout

CONNOISSEUR'S RATING

COOPERS SPARKLING ALE
11.5°P/1.046 o.g., 5.8% ABV

PRIVATBRAUEREI DIEBELS

BRAUEREI-DIEBELS-STRASSE 1, 47661 ISSUM, GERMANY
(49–2835) 30146

With an annual production of more than 1.7 million hectoliters, it is hard to think of the brewing giant Diebels in the traditional sense of a "craft brewery;" it is certainly not a microbrewery by any definition. Nevertheless, this Rhineland powerhouse has helped keep the classic Düsseldorf-style German ale very much alive in a land increasingly threatened by mass-market pilsners and brewery consolidation.

When the Privatbrauerei was founded in 1878 by thirty-two-year-old master brewer Josef Diebels, the Rhine Province had a mind-boggling 1,569 breweries already in operation. Amidst this fierce competition, the Diebels family carved out a niche, and in twenty years they were producing an amazing 10,000 hectoliters per year. A fourth generation of the Diebels family now manages the brewery, which produces its flagship brand, Diebels Alt, as well as low-alcohol and low-calorie beers, using the traditional method of a warm top ferment followed by weeks of cold lagering at near freezing temperatures.

BREW FACTS

FOUNDED: 1878

HEAD BREWER:
Franz Schiessl

ANNUAL OUTPUT:
1.7 million hectoliters

BREW STYLES: Alt, low-calorie, low-alcohol

CONNOISSEUR'S RATING

ALT *11.6 °P/1.046 o.g.,
38 BU, 4.8% ABV*

BRASSERIE
DUBUISSON
FRERES

CHAUSSEE DE MONS 28, 7904 PIPAIX, BELGIUM
(32-69) 66-20-85

This small, independent, family-run brewery in the province of Hainaut produces just two beers, both in the Belgian strong category and both world renowned not only for their strength, but for their uniqueness of character. Their basic product is dry hopped to create a Christmas version subtitled "Noël," and both are renamed "Scaldis" for the American market, in the unlikely event the Belgian designation "Bush Beer" would cause confusion with Anheuser-Busch's product. "Bush" is the English translation of Dubuisson.

BREW FACTS	
FOUNDED: 1769	
HEAD BREWER: Vincent Dubuisson	
ANNUAL OUTPUT: 15,000 hectoliters	
BREW STYLES: Strong ale, strong Christmas ale	

CONNOISSEUR'S RATING

SCALDIS (BUSH BEER)
24.5°P/1.098 o.g., 12% ABV

SCALDIS NOËL
24.5°P/1.098 o.g., 12% ABV

EINBECKER BRAUHAUS

PAPEN STRASSE 4–7, 3352 EINBECK, LOWER SAXONY, GERMANY
(49–5561) 7970

In the Middle Ages, the 700 citizens of the town of Einbeck in northern Germany all brewed their own beer using a communal brew kettle; any excess not used for personal consumption was bought up by the town council for export. Einbeck's membership in the Hanseatic League facilitated the sale of the renowned "Einpöcksche Bier" throughout the Hanseatic trade routes, causing Martin Luther to remark, "The best draught is called Einbeck beer." The popularity of this beer among the German order of knighthood, high-ranking bishops, and kings prompted Bavarian dukes in 1612 to entice an Einbeck brewmaster to brew Einpöcksche Bier for the Hofbräuhaus in Munich. The Bavarian dialect quickly transformed "Einpöcksche" into "Oanpock," then into "Bock."

In the seventeenth century, the 742 house breweries of Einbeck were merged into a single company. In 1844, in the midst of the Industrial Revolution, this company became known as the Städtische Dampfbierbrauerei and continued to utilize steam power for nearly 100 years. In 1967, it became a joint-stock company and is now the only surviving brewery in this birthplace of one of the world's great beer styles.

BREW FACTS

FOUNDED: 1967

HEAD BREWER: Lother Gross

ANNUAL OUTPUT: 670,000 hectoliters

BREW STYLES: Bock, helles bock, maibock, export pils

TASTING NOTES

BRAUHERREN PILS: *12 °P/1.048 o.g., 4.9% ABV. Very pale gold in color with a pungent fresh hops and lightly fruity aroma and a dry, well-attenuated palate. Develops into a bittersweet blend of rounded hops and mineral-tinged malt flavors. Finishes dryly with a slightly sour hop aftertaste. A good example of your average dry northern pils. Serve as a thirst quencher, aperitif, or to cleanse the palate when enjoying a spicy entrée.*

UR-BOCK DUNKEL: *16.5 °P/1.066 o.g., 6.5% ABV. Deep, golden amber with aromas of roasted malt and some hops. Malty in flavor with a strong hop presence and more pronounced dryness than typical Bavarian versions. Finishes dry and clean with a lingering hop flavor. Serve with robust seafood dishes such as fish stew or with deli cuts on pumpernickel.*

CONNOISSEUR'S RATING

BRAUHERREN PILS

UR-BOCK DUNKEL

ELDRIDGE, POPE & COMPANY

WEYMOUTH AVENUE, DORCHESTER, DORSET DT1 1QT, ENGLAND
(44–305) 251251

Dorchester has been regarded as a great brewing center since at least 1760, inspiring mapmaker Emmanuel Bowen to write, "Tis also famous for brewing the best and finest beer in England, whereof great quantities have been of late years exported and consigned to London." This reputation is no less true today, thanks in large part to the products of the family-run, independent brewery, Eldridge Pope, and particularly its strong classic, Thomas Hardy's Ale, brewed in memory of the novelist, who hailed from Dorchester.

BREW FACTS

FOUNDED: 1837

HEAD BREWER: Roger Wharton

ANNUAL OUTPUT: Figures not available

BREW STYLES: Barley wine, bitter, pale ale, porter, lager

The Dorchester Brewery in 1880.

ROYAL OAK PALE ALE: *12.2 °P/1.048 o.g., 30 BU, 4.8% ABV. Deep reddish golden color and thick creamy head. Herbal, woody English hops bouquet and rich, buttery caramel candy aroma. Malty toffee and cooked fruit tastes provide a sweetish flavor overall, with just enough hop bitterness to finish cleanly. Smooth, full bodied, and fruity.*

THOMAS HARDY COUNTRY BITTER: *10.2 °P/ 1.041 o.g., 25 BU, 4.2% ABV. Deep orange copper in color with a massive fresh hops aroma. Features malty and well-balanced flavors of malt and fruit, but with a strong base of hop bitterness. Finishes dry and light with a gentle hop flavor. The only detriment to this bottle-conditioned beer is that it is meant to be enjoyed fresh and, therefore, sometimes suffers with age and the rigors of travel. Store and serve at 50–55°F.*

THOMAS HARDY'S ALE: *29.9 °P/1.125 o.g., 70 BU, 11.7% ABV. Beer authorities alternately define this as an old ale or as a barley wine, but all agree that it is a major classic. Young samples have an assertive pungency and syrupy sweetness with a strong, dry-hopped aroma; older versions seem to have more of a fruity-winey nose with an amazing depth of nutty flavors and a more organized, woody mellowness. In either version, you are likely to encounter elusive notes of wine, wood, leather, hazelnuts, golden raisins, or prunes, to name but a few. This bottle-conditioned masterpiece is individually numbered and dated and is suitable for laying down for twenty-five years or more. It has been suggested that it is better if aged five or more years before sampling in order to mellow the intense, cloying malt sweetness. Store and serve at 50–55°F.*

ROYAL OAK PALE ALE

THOMAS HARDY COUNTRY BITTER

THOMAS HARDY'S ALE

FULLER, SMITH & TURNER

GRIFFIN BREWERY, CHISWICK LANE SOUTH, LONDON W4 2QB,
ENGLAND (44–181) 996–2000

Although there has been a brewery on the current site of this London independent for more than 300 years, Fuller's notoriety has no doubt been bolstered recently by CAMRA's Great British Beer Festival, in which Fuller's ESB has consistently dominated the strong ale category. In fact, Fuller's ESB, Chiswick Bitter, and London Pride together have taken the Champion Beer of Britain award five times between 1979 and 1993. Fuller's also offers a full range of seasonal selections and an excellent Christmas barley wine called Golden Pride at 1.089 o.g., 8.5% ABV.

BREW FACTS

FOUNDED: 1845

HEAD BREWER:

Reg Drury

ANNUAL OUTPUT:

410,750 hectoliters

BREW STYLES: Bitter, barley wine, mild, IPA, winter warmer

CHISWICK BITTER: *8.5 °P/1.034 o.g., 3.5% ABV. A light-bodied, hoppy session beer with a more toned-down character than the ESB or London Pride. Features a nice, thirst-quenching balance of hops and malt and a lingering aftertaste of rounded hop bitterness.*

ESB: *13.25 °P/1.053 o.g., 5.5% ABV (1.060 o.g., 6% ABV in bottled form). A massive floral hops and fruity malt aroma persists to the last drop of this bold ale. The first sip reveals wonderfully rich flavors of* *fruity, full-bodied malt sweetness and rounded hop bitterness. Immensely complex and layered, with a smooth hoppiness in the finish.*

LONDON PRIDE: *10 °P/1.040 o.g., 4.1% ABV (1.046 o.g., 4.5% ABV in bottled form). Assertive malty flavor beneath balancing hop bitterness and flavor. Smoother and less aromatic than the ESB, London Pride emphasizes a complex, fruity malt character. Finishes with lingering fruity-hoppy flavor.*

CHISWICK BITTER

ESB

LONDON PRIDE

GABRIEL SEDLMAYR
SPATEN-FRANZISKANER-BRAU

SPATEN-FRANZISKANER-BRÄU, MARSSTRASSE 46–48, 80335 MÜNCHEN,
GERMANY (49–89) 51220

Spaten holds a special place in my heart because it was at a restaurant near the Hauptbahnhof in Munich that I had my first liter of Münchner dunkel. I fell hopelessly in love with real, fresh Bavarian beer and have never been the same. Spaten is the acknowledged birthplace of modern lager brewing techniques and, in 1872, of the traditional märzen beer.

Munich's oldest brewery lists its official founding as 1397, but the Franziskaner brewery has roots that go back to 1363. The most important dates in Spaten's history, however, began when the thirty-five-year-old brewmaster for the Royal Court of Bavaria, Gabriel Sedlmayr, took over the brewery in 1807, beginning a long legacy of innovation and expansion. After Gabriel's death in 1839, his son, Gabriel II achieved even greater success, introducing to Munich brewing methods he had learned in his extensive travels around Europe. Sedlmayr's most influential achievements were his use of refrigeration and steam power in the 1870s, which, by his death in 1891, were in use worldwide.

Today's corporation is the product of a 1922 merger of Gabriel Sedlmayr's Brewery and his brother Josef's Franziskaner Weissbier brewery. Spaten is now Bavaria's second largest beer exporter and the top seller in the U.S., but is fairly traditional in many of its brewing methods and is still largely family owned.

BREW FACTS	
FOUNDED:	1397
HEAD BREWER:	Georg Balk
ANNUAL OUTPUT:	1.2 million hectoliters
BREW STYLES:	Weissbier, helles, premium lager, dunkel, doppelbock, märzen, pils, maibock

CONNOISSEUR'S RATING

DUNKEL EXPORT

FRANZISKANER CLUB-WEISSBIER

FRANZISKANER HEFE-WEISSBIER DUNKEL

FRANZISKANER HEFE-WEISSBIER

PREMIUM LAGER

UR-MARZEN

TASTING NOTES

DUNKEL EXPORT: *5% ABV. Deep ruby brown with an aromatic and fluffy head of foam when served on draft. Surprisingly light-bodied and dangerously quaffable with subtly balanced flavors of sweetness, roasted malt, and hops. The essential match for* schweinebraten *and* semmelknödel, *or for any hearty German meal and rich dessert. Regrettably, this classic example of the style is not available in the U.S. at the present time.*

FRANZISKANER CLUB-WEISSBIER: *5% ABV. Pale golden in color with the trademark weissbier head of billowy white foam. Very spicy, tart, and dry, and with more depth of flavor than most kristall-weizens,which are often an attempt to please the pils crowd.*

FRANZISKANER HEFE-WEISSBIER DUNKEL: *5% ABV. Hazy, ruby brown with aromas of bittersweet fruit and bread. Yeasty, malty, and almost oily in mouthfeel, developing into a tart, grainy dryness in the finish. Pair with spicy foods and hearty meat dishes. Serve at 42–46°F.*

FRANZISKANER HEFE-WEISSBIER: *5% ABV. Deep, hazy gold in color with a huge, fluffy head throwing a bouquet of fruity, spicy aromas of bananas, apples, and cloves. Spicy, tart, and fruity in palate with a nice rounded softness and a dryish finish. Understandably, this is the world's best-selling Bavarian weissbier. Pair with light dishes such as salads, fruit, pasta, and grilled foods. Serve at 42–46°F.*

PREMIUM LAGER: *5.2% ABV. Pale gold in color with a large head of creamy, small bubbles. Features profound aromas of herbally hops and malty sweetness. Dry and bittersweet with a dry, lingering hop finish and a faintly bitter aftertaste.*

UR-MARZEN: *5.6% ABV. Reddish amber in color with a candyish malt aroma and an unapologetic malt sweetness from start to finish. Although this beer may have followed the other Märzens in lowering gravity over recent years, it has always been one of the maltiest and most full-bodied. Balanced with just enough Bavarian hops not to be cloying, it finishes clean, smooth, and mellow. Goes well with grilled steaks and traditional German cuisine.*

GREENE KING
& SONS PLC

WESTGATE STREET, BURY ST. EDMUNDS, SUFFOLK IP33 1QT, ENGLAND
(44–1284) 763222

This venerable old brewery in East Anglia produces a wide range of traditional ales and is one of England's largest independent breweries, with an estate of 900 pubs. Greene King is also one of the most commercially-minded regional breweries, and is now exporting its Abbot Ale to the U.S.

BREW FACTS

FOUNDED: 1799

HEAD BREWER:

Alistair Heeley

ANNUAL OUTPUT:

Figures not available

BREW STYLES: Mild, bitter, old ale, barley wine, winter warmer, strong ale, IPA

CONNOISSEUR'S RATING

ABBOT ALE
12.25°P/1.049 o.g., 5% ABV

STRONG SUFFOLK
14.5°P/1.058 o.g., 6% ABV

ARTHUR GUINNESS & SON LTD.

ST. JAMES GATE, DUBLIN 8, IRELAND
(353-1) 453-6700

On December 31, 1759, the thirty-four-year-old Arthur Guinness paid £100 for a 9,000-year lease on an abandoned brewery at St. James Gate in Dublin. Guinness began with the intention of brewing Dublin-style brown ales, but he was soon taken by new black beers called "Entire" coming from London, and decided to brew his own. The fame of his strong ale spread slowly at first along Ireland's network of canals. Ten years later, the first casks were exported. In the early nineteenth century, steam age advances soon catapulted Guinness into worldwide prominence.

An Irish Dragoon convalescing after the Battle of Waterloo wrote of Guinness' Extra Stout Porter: "When I was sufficiently recovered to be permitted nourishment I felt the most extraordinary desire for a glass of Guinness, which I knew could be obtained without difficulty. I am confident that it contributed more than anything else to my recovery." Today, Guinness is undeniably the world's most popular stout, with sales in more than 150 countries and breweries in fifty far-flung locales such as Jamaica, Malaysia, and Vietnam. The arm of Guinness Brewing Worldwide known as "Guinness Ireland" produce the brands detailed here.

BREW FACTS

FOUNDED: 1759

HEAD BREWER: David Holmes

ANNUAL OUTPUT: 25.6 million hectoliters

BREW STYLES: Stout, low-caloric, alcohol-free, lager, barley wine, Irish ale, strong ale

CONNOISSEUR'S RATING

DRAUGHT GUINNESS

DRAUGHT GUINNESS (CANNED)

EXTRA STOUT (U.S.)

HARP LAGER

KALIBER

KILKENNY IRISH BEER

TASTING NOTES

DRAUGHT GUINNESS: *4.1–5.1% ABV. Opaque black in color, with a massive head of tan foam induced by a carbon dioxide/nitrogen mixture. Full of chocolatey, dry roasty character and the trademark sourness, but it seems somewhat thinner in body and less fruity than the bottled versions.*

DRAUGHT GUINNESS (CANNED): *4.1–5.1% ABV. The gas widget in the bottom of the can intended to produce the draft head creates a dense mass of draft-like foam that seems to accentuate the lightly carbonated beer below. Possesses some of the rich qualities of its bottled counterpart, but with more evidence of pasteurization and little of the roasted malt character.*

EXTRA STOUT (BOTTLED): *(Varies by country from 4.1% ABV in Ireland to 7.7% ABV in Belgium). The version available in the U.S. contains 6% ABV. Deep black in color with a dense tan head of foam that lasts until the last sip and provides a very creamy texture to the brew. Features a surprisingly fruity aroma amidst the massive roasted malt nose. Deep, rich, and bitter with tinges of sourness and flavors of dark roasted coffee, bittersweet chocolate, and malt.*

HARP LAGER: *3.6–5% ABV. Deep straw in color with a mildly pungent aroma of hops and sweet malt. Refreshingly bitter with a nice malty base and a respectable amount of body, if somewhat one-dimensional in flavor development. Finishes dryly with a faintly bittersweet aftertaste.*

KALIBER: *0.5% ABV. Pale gold in color with a full, but loose head of white foam. Like its cousin Harp Lager, it is hard to compare this beer favorably with the more famous stout, but, nevertheless, this is one of the better non-alcoholic brews available. Light to medium bodied, with a nicely balanced malt sweetness and drying hop bitterness. Finishes bittersweet with a lingering, slightly astringent aftertaste.*

KILKENNY IRISH BEER: *5–5.5% ABV. Deep reddish amber in color with an aroma of caramel candy, fruit, and roasted malt. Soft, malty, and faintly sweet in the classic Irish and Scottish tradition of subdued hop usage. The strain of yeast used provides a slightly earthy, buttery quality that gives this medium-bodied ale a warming, satisfying quality. A very good all-round accompaniment to many foods, but especially traditional boiled Irish fare.*

BROUWERIJ HET ANKER

GUIDO GEZELLELAAN 49, B-2800 MECHELEN, BELGIUM
(32-15) 20-38-80

The success of Brouwerij Het Anker is due in large part to the fact that the town of Mechelen has been a renowned center of brown ale brewing for six centuries. Beer has been brewed on the site of the present day Anker brewery itself since at least 1500. Anker's most prestigious product by far is its legendary Gouden Carolus (meaning "Golden Charles"), alluding to the golden coin depicting Mechelen's native and Holy Roman Emperor Charles V. Anker formed a partnership with the Riva Group in the early 1990s in order to broaden their worldwide distribution.

BREW FACTS

FOUNDED: 1873

HEAD BREWER: Charles Lecles

ANNUAL OUTPUT: 4,000 hectoliters

BREW STYLES: Strong brown ale, Belgian pale ale

CONNOISSEUR'S RATING

GOUDEN CAROLUS
19°P/1.076 o.g., 7% ABV

BRAUEREI HURLIMANN

150 BRANDSCHENKE STRASSE, 8002 ZURICH, SWITZERLAND
(41-1) 288-2626

Hürlimann's flagship beer, Samichlaus, is truly a world classic. Brewed just once a year on December 6, St. Nicholas' Day, this strong Christmas lager is aged for ten to twelve months before it is bottled, which accounts for its incredible smoothness and subtlety. Brewed from two-row Pilsener and Munich malts, two Hallertau hop varieties, and a special strain of yeast capable of withstanding the high alcohol level, Samichlaus is made in accordance with the Reinheitsgebot and lays claim to being the strongest lager in the world.

BREW FACTS

FOUNDED: 1836

HEAD BREWER:
Hans Sonderegger

ANNUAL OUTPUT:
670,000 hectoliters

BREW STYLES: Strong lager, dunkel, pale bock, alcohol-free

CONNOISSEUR'S RATING

CAESARUS IMPERATOR HELLER BOCK	🍾🍾🍾
HEXEN BRAU	🍾🍾🍾
SAMICHLAUS BIER	🍾🍾🍾🍾🍾

TASTING NOTES

CAESARUS IMPERATOR HELLER BOCK:
*24.5 °P/1.103 o.g., 25 BU, 12.5% ABV.
Brewed from Pilsener and Munich malts, and
Hallertau and Super-Styrer hops. This new offering
from Hürlimann is richly malty and spicy, but
smooth and mature. A great accompaniment to
robust foods and desserts, or as an after-dinner drink
served at 45°F. Cellar for three or more years at
55–60°F.*

HEXEN BRAU: *13.25 °P/1.053 o.g., 23 BU,
5.4% ABV. Offers an explosion of molasses and
warm biscuits aroma above a fluffy, tan head.
Lagered for three months, Hexen Bräu is malty,
smooth, and slightly sweet, with subtle notes of
chocolate and rich flavors of caramel and fruit.
Excellent with chocolate desserts or German and
Mexican fare. Serve at 42–50°F. Cellar for up to
eighteen months at 55–60°F.*

SAMICHLAUS BIER: *28.74 °P/1.127 o.g., 32
BU, 14.7% ABV. Indefinite shelf life if stored at
55–60°F. Serve with robust foods and desserts,
especially chocolate, and as an after-dinner
cordial, or perhaps with a cigar.*

BROUWERIJ LIEFMANS

200 AALST STRAAT, 9700 OUDENAARDE, BELGIUM
(32-55) 31-13-92

For more than 300 years, this East Flanders brewery has made the town of Oudenaarde synonymous with classic Belgian ales. Their stock-in-trade is a range of variations on the tart, wine-like oud bruin, including basic old browns for the local market and blends with stronger, older beer for the Goudenband, Frambozen, and Kriek beers. Liefmans also has an interesting spiced winter specialty called "Glühkriek," which is is meant to be mulled and served at 158°F, not unlike the German glühwein (it is also very good served chilled).

Liefmans was absorbed into the Riva Group based in Dentergem, West Flanders, in 1990, Two years later, Liefmans beers were being brewed in Dentergems then shipped to Oudenaarde for fermentation and conditioning. Riva's intention is to update the Liefmans brewery and return all production there once renovation is complete. Liefmans beers, especially the more heavily sedimented Goudenband, are ideal for cellaring with the bottles laid on their sides, like wine, to preserve the cork.

BREW FACTS
FOUNDED: 1679
HEAD BREWER: Roland Decaluwe
ANNUAL OUTPUT: 13,000 hectoliters
BREW STYLES: Oud bruin, cherry oud bruin, raspberry oud bruin

TASTING NOTES

FRAMBOZENBIER: *14 °P/1.057 o.g., 21 BU, 5% ABV. First introduced in Belgium in October 1985, in little more than ten years this has come to be considered a classic. Features a massive raspberry aroma and the fresh, lively character of champagne. Fresh, dry, and smooth, with a teasing fruit sweetness balanced by a full-bodied tart sourness. Can be cellared two to three years at 55–60°F. Serve in place of champagne at brunch, as an opening aperitif, and with fresh, light-bodied foods.*

GOUDENBAND: *14 °P/1.057 o.g., 21 BU, 5% ABV. Brewed with four hop varieties including Hallertau, Brewers Gold, Saaz, and Tettnang, and a 100-year-old yeast strain. Warm-conditioned for eight to ten months, then bottle-conditioned for a further three to twelve months. Infinitely complex in aroma and flavor with notes of acidity, maltiness, and tartness throughout. An unsurpassed old brown with the richness and complexity of a vintage wine. Serve this "Burgundy of Belgium" with beef, game, and cheeses or with smoked salmon and shellfish.*

Suitable for cellaring five to seven years at 55–60°F.

KRIEKBIER: *17.2 °P/1.067 o.g., 24.5 BU, 5.8% ABV. Deep, cloudy reddish brown color; frothy, light tan head of foam exudes a soft aroma of cherry lozenges. Features a sweet-tart blend of sharp fruit sourness, lactic tang, and hop bitterness. Somewhat thin body and spritzy mouthfeel finishes fairly anticlimatically, but is nonetheless a respectable summer refresher. Excellent with Sunday brunch, crêpes, warm fruit compote, mellow cheeses, and French bread, or as an aperitif. Cellar three to four years at 55–60°F.*

CONNOISSEUR'S RATING

FRAMBOZENBIER	🍺🍺🍺🍺
GOUDENBAND	🍺🍺🍺🍺
KRIEKBIER	🍺🍺🍺🍺

MENDOCINO
BREWING COMPANY

13551 SOUTH HIGHWAY 101, HOPLAND, CALIFORNIA 95449
(1-707) 744-1361

Mendocino grew out of a multitude of adverse circumstances facing five men. For dedicated homebrewers Michael Laybourn and Norman Franks, the adversity was a downturn in the construction industry in which they were employed. For Michael Lovett and Don Barkley, it was the closure of America's first modern microbrewery, New Albion in Sonoma, where they were brewers. But like all great achievers in human history they, along with their friend John Scahill, pulled together and turned crisis into opportunity. Barkley and Lovett moved north, bringing New Albion's equipment and unique yeast culture to the little town of Hopland, ninety miles north of San Francisco. The end result was California's first brewpub since Prohibition.

Mendocino grew quickly from an 1,094-hectoliters-a-year pub into a 13,680-hectoliters microbrewery with wholesale distribution coming in 1987. Mendocino is now in the midst of a major expansion fueled by a direct public offering in order to build a 273,600 hectoliters brewhouse in nearby Ukiah that is scheduled for completion in late 1997. Mendocino employs the age-old brewing methods of infusion mashing, gravity-flow transfer of wort, and bottle conditioning, but their beers represent the new classic American microbrewery style and character.

BREW FACTS

FOUNDED: 1983

HEAD BREWER
Don Barkley

ANNUAL OUTPUT:
20,520 hectoliters

BREW STYLES: Stout, pale ale, scotch ale, strong ale, holiday ale, porter

TASTING NOTES

BLUE HERON PALE ALE: *13.5 °P/1.054 o.g., 6.3% ABV. Hazy yellow gold in color with a creamy and light mouthfeel and a tart, fruity palate developing quickly into a dry, fruity finish. Its complexity grows with every sip, revealing lemony, hoppy flavors and a long, resiny hop aftertaste. Serve with light vegetarian dishes and fresh seafood.*

EYE OF THE HAWK SELECT ALE: *16.25 °P/1.065 o.g., 7.6% ABV. Peachy amber gold in color. Fruity and liqueur like in aroma and equally fruity and winey in palate with a soft, smooth mouthfeel. Develops slowly to a cleansing hoppiness toward the end. Finishes dryly with a lingering fruity aftertaste.*

RED TAIL ALE: *13.5 °P/1.054 o.g., 6.5% ABV. Peachy copper in color and well blessed with a cap of perfumey foam throughout. Flowery and fruity in flavor and aroma, with a cleansing hop bitterness and flavor over a rounded maltiness. Finishes fruity and dry with tangy, mellow aftertastes of pears and hops. Well suited for pairing with fresh fruits, crudités, and soft cheeses.*

CONNOISSEUR'S RATING

BLUE HERON PALE ALE

**EYE OF THE HAWK
SELECT ALE**

RED TAIL ALE

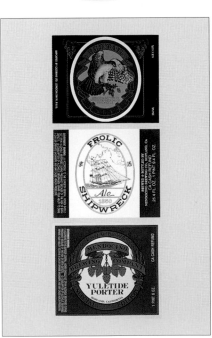

BROUWERIJ MOORTGAT

BREENDONKDORP 58, 2870 BREENDONK-PUURS, BELGIUM
(32-3) 886-7121

This famous independent brewery is most noted for its classic strong, golden ale called Duvel (pronounced "Doov'l") and for having their own maltings, a practice now almost extinct among small breweries. Duvel, from the Flemish word for Devil, began life as a strong, dark ale inspired by McEwan's Scotch Ale. The post-world War II explosion of pale lagers prompted Moortgat to change the recipe in the late 1960s to produce a golden ale and the rest is history. Since its release, Duvel has been regarded as an instant classic, spurring the creation of dozens of imitators, all with similarly "devilish" names.

BREW FACTS

FOUNDED: 1871

HEAD BREWER:
Fons Van Regenmortel

ANNUAL OUTPUT:
250,000 hectoliters

BREW STYLES: Dubbel, tripel, strong ale, pils, pale ale, low-alcohol

TASTING NOTES

DUVEL: *7% ABV. Brewed from Danish summer barley and whole flower Styrian and Saaz hops. Bottle-conditioned warm for five weeks. This is truly one of the world classics, just below the Trappist beers in stature, and a must for any well-stocked beer cellar. Bright and richly gold in color, this beer must be served with a full head of foam to appreciate its aromatic qualities of fruit, hops, and peppery spiciness. Complexly fruity in the mouth with alternating waves of hops and malt. A great accompaniment to fish, shellfish, chicken stew, roast pork with fruit sauces, and dishes served in a cream sauce and, of course, by itself as you admire its personality.*

BEL PILS: *5.3% ABV. It is often hard to think of drinking pils from a land so full of the world's best ales, but this is still a very convincing version of a pilsner. Very pale gold in color, but with a much more exciting aroma that is gently flowery. Nicely balanced with the sweetness of the malt just edging out the hop bitterness for dominance. Light, clean, and soft, if not somewhat of a wallflower. A nice diversion from the many rough and astringently bitter versions on the market, Bel Pils is very good with seafoods that have a mellow sweetness, such as crab and lobster.*

CONNOISSEUR'S RATING

DUVEL	
BEL PILS	

BRASSERIE
D'ORVAL S.A.

6823 VILLERS-DEVANT-ORVAL, BELGIUM
(32-61) 31-10-60

In 1076, as the legend goes, Countess Matilda, Duchess of Tuscany and suzerain of the Orval region, came to visit the courageous Benedictine monks from Calabria, Italy, who had settled there. As she sat at the end of a spring near the monastery, her wedding ring accidentally fell into the water. As it was a treasured keepsake of her late husband, the Countess ardently prayed to the Virgin Mary to help her. Suddenly, a trout rose up from the water with the ring in its mouth and returned it to the stunned countess. She cried out, *"This is truly a val d'or!"* (golden valley). The abbey has since been named Orval, and the image of a fish with a ring in its mouth is the brewery logo. Like many abbeys across Europe, Orval was plundered, sacked, burned, and beset with tragedy many times before its latest incarnation was completed in 1948. The new brewhouse was intended to help finance the extensive renovations and maintenance of the monastery.

The golden orange Orval is brewed with spring water and French, Dutch, and German barley malts. Pale lager malt comprises 86.5% of the grist; caravienne caramel malt constitutes the remaining 13.5%. A single yeast strain is used in the primary fermentation and again in the bottle refermentation. A blend of five yeast strains is employed in the secondary fermentation. Hops, including German Hallertau and Slovenian Styrian, are generously added in the kettle as well as the lagering tanks.

BREW FACTS

FOUNDED: 1931

HEAD BREWER:
Jacques Petre

ANNUAL OUTPUT:
38,000 hectoliters

BREW STYLE:
Trappist ale

Chipped candy sugar is used in the boil; liquid invert candy sugar is added for bottle fermentation to produce the trademark voluminous head of foam.

TASTING NOTES

ORVAL TRAPPIST ALE: *13.4 °P/1.055 o.g., 32 BU, 6% ABV at bottling; after ten months, 7.1% ABV. Unlike most Trappist ales, Orval is unique in its powerful hop presence. Served in a wide-mouthed goblet, this classic offers an explosion of herbal hop aromas and dry, rich flavors of fruit and hops on the palate. Recommended serving temperature is 57°F. Stored at cellar temperatures, Orval can be laid down for up to five years.*

CONNOISSEUR'S RATING

ORVAL TRAPPIST ALE

PAULENER-SALVATOR-THOMAS-BRAU

HOCHSTRASSE 75, 8000 MUNCHEN 95, GERMANY
(49–89) 480050

The Paulaner brewery derives its name from the monks of Order of Saint Francis of Paula who first brewed beer at their monastery in 1631. They began selling their beer to the grateful people of Munich around 1780, and became a secular lager brewery in the early part of the nineteenth century. Owner Franz Zacherl capitalized on the popularity of a strong beer brewed for the Lenten fasts by creating his own version, which he dubbed "Salvator," now the benchmark of the Bavarian doppelbock style.

BREW FACTS
FOUNDED: 1631
HEAD BREWER: Peter Hellich
ANNUAL OUTPUT: 2 million hectoliters
BREW STYLES: Dunkel, pils, weissbier, doppelbock, helles

Today's corporation is the result of the acquisition of, the old Thomas brothers' brewery in 1923 and, more recently, of Hacker-Pschorr, making it Munich's largest. Paulaner operates two notable establishments in Munich, the Paulaner Bräuhaus brewpub at Kapuzinerplatz 5, and the Salvator Keller at Hochstraße 77 near the brewery, which features a "Starkbierfest" in March to herald the first Salvator of the season and, secondarily, the arrival of spring.

TASTING NOTES

HEFE-WEIZEN: *5.4% ABV. Bright, hazy yellow in color with snow white head that exudes lively aromas of vanilla, cloves, bananas, and apple. The body is medium-light with a smooth, fluffy texture and a rounded maltiness. A modern weissbier intended for wide appeal no doubt, but eminently enjoyable with fresh fruity flavors and a light lemony tartness towards the dry finish. Very refreshing as a summer picnic libation and with hot and spicy ethnic cuisine.*

PREMIUM LAGER: *4.9% ABV. Rich, golden color and a nice lacy head that is full of the classic Munich helles aromas of vanilla-tinged malt and mellow hops. Malty and slightly fruity in flavor with a very dry finish developing slowly into a piney aftertaste of hops. A quintessential beer hall favorite meant to be enjoyed with traditional Bavarian fare or alone as a session beer.*

SALVATOR: *7.5% ABV. The originator and undisputed champion of the doppelbock style. Deep ruby brown in color with a mouthwatering aroma of rich maltiness, dark fruit, chocolate, and caramel. The same endless depth of character carries through into the robust taste which is superbly kept from being cloying by a good base of Bavarian hop bitterness. Smooth, mature, and well organized, this Bavarian classic ends cleanly with a warm, fruity aftertaste.*

CONNOISSEUR'S RATING

HEFE-WEIZEN

PREMIUM LAGER

SALVATOR

PLZENSKY PRAZDROJ

30497 PLZEN, CZECH REPUBLIC
(42-19) 7061111

Frustrated with the inconsistent outcome of their top-fermented beer after having to dump thirty-eight barrels in the town square, the burghers of Pilsen decided in 1838 to switch to brewing the popular new bottom-fermented beer. Joseph Grolle, a gifted twenty-nine-year-old Bavarian brewmaster was hired and, in 1842, after completion of the brewhouse, the first pilsen lager was brewed. Unlike their Bavarian counterparts, who produced dark or auburn hued lagers, the pilsner version, produced with exceptionally pale Bohemian malt, was deep golden and crystal clear, the world's first light lager. On September 1, 1994, brewers of Pilsner Urquell officially merged with their next-door neighbor and the brewers of another Czech classic, Gambrinus, the Czech Republic's biggest seller.

Malt for these beers is produced in the brewery's own malting house from choice Moravian barley. The Saazer hops used come exclusively from the Zatec region, thirty-seven miles north of Pilsen.

BREW FACTS

FOUNDED: 1838

HEAD BREWERS:
Jaroslav Rous and
Pavel Zitek

ANNUAL OUTPUT:
3.3 million hectoliters

BREW STYLES:
Czech pilsner

CONNOISSEUR'S RATING

PILSNER URQUELL *10 and 12° Balling
(1.040 and 1.048 o.g.), 4.4/4.7% ABV*

GAMBRINUS *10 and 12° Balling
(1.040 and 1.048 o.g.), 4.4/4.7% ABV*

BROUWERIJ RODENBACH

SPANJESTRAAT 133–141, 8800 ROESELARE, BELGIUM
(32–51) 22–34–00

The legendary "Belgian red" style of beer of West Flanders is sometimes considered to consist solely of the products of Brouwerij Rodenbach, a testament to the exemplary quality of these brews. Rodenbach's "racy" beers, as the brewery dubs them, begin life in a very conventional way in cylindro-conical fermenters. They gain their character, however, from the eighteen months to two years they spend in Rodenbach's famous uncoated oak maturation vats, where they obtain their trademark sourness from microorganisms residing in the wood. Aged ale direct from the massive tuns is filtered and bottled to become the individualistic Rodenbach Grand Cru. Freshly fermented beer is blended with well-aged beer to create the ale called simply "Rodenbach." A third beer, called Alexander, is a blend of the Grand Cru with cherry essence. In their promotions, Rodenbach proudly quotes the beer writer Michael Jackson, who called Belgian reds, "the world's most refreshing beer."

BREW FACTS

FOUNDED: 1836

HEAD BREWER: Rudi Ghequire

ANNUAL OUTPUT: 100,000 hectoliters

BREW STYLES: Belgian red, cherry-flavored Belgian red

CONNOISSEUR'S RATING

GRAND CRU
14.5°P / 1.058 o.g., 6.5% ABV

ABBAYE
DE NOTRE-DAME
DE SAINT-REMY

5430 ROCHEFORT, BELGIUM
(32-84) 22-21-32

The origins of the Saint-Rémy Abbey can be traced back to 1230, when the monastery was first inhabited by nuns who had to endure severe Ardennes weather and poor soil conditions. In 1464, they were replaced in the abbey by monks, who remained until 1794. The abbey was then reinhabited in 1887. Monastery records show that Saint-Rémy had a brewery as far back as 1595, with barley and hops being grown in the grounds. The small brewery used today was built in 1899, modernized in 1960, and renovated in 1974. It produces what are perhaps the least publicized of all the Trappist beers, despite its Rochefort 10 being regarded as one of the world's greatest beers. The 8 and 10 are particularly suitable for laying down. Store at 59–61°F and serve at 54–61°F.

BREW FACTS

FOUNDED: 1794

HEAD BREWER:
Frère Antoine

ANNUAL OUTPUT:
15,000 hectoliters

BREW STYLES: Dubbel, tripel, strong

CONNOISSEUR'S RATING

ROCHEFORT 6 (RED CAP)
7.5% ABV

ROCHEFORT 8 (GREEN CAP)
9.2% ABV

ROCHEFORT 10 (BLACK CAP)
11.3% ABV

SAMUEL SMITH

THE OLD BREWERY, TADCASTER, N. YORKSHIRE LS24 9SB, ENGLAND
(44–1937) 832225

This tiny brewery is the oldest in Yorkshire and remains fiercely traditional, independent, and family owned. Their use of Yorkshire stone square fermenters, wooden casks, and horse-drawn drays for local delivery have earned them legendary status among beer connoisseurs the world over. I can only fault this brewery for its stubborn use of clear glass bottles to package their world-class brews and for being prohibitively expensive for American admirers of Yorkshire ales.

BREW FACTS

FOUNDED: 1758

HEAD BREWER:

Steve Barrett

ANNUAL OUTPUT:

Figures not available

BREW STYLES: Pale ale, porter, oatmeal stout, imperial stout, brown ale, lager

TASTING NOTES

NUT BROWN ALE: *12.5 °P/1.050 o.g., 5.4% ABV. The walnut color is well matched to the nutty malt flavor and gentle sweetness of this mellow and comforting ale. Earthy, full bodied, and multilayered, but reserved and mature in its restrained malt flavors. Glides easily to a dry, fruity finish. Serve at 55°F with a ploughman's lunch, roasted wild game, or pepper steak.*

OLD BREWERY PALE ALE: *11.75 °P/1.047 o.g., 5% ABV. Bright mahogany in color with the densely creamy, off-white head that is the trademark of fine Yorkshire ales. Malt dominated from start to finish, with a gentle hop bitterness holding all the robust earthiness and faint butteriness perfectly in check. The prime example of a classic Yorkshire bitter and the embodiment of Samuel Smith's traditional brewing.*

THE FAMOUS TADDY PORTER (NOURISHING STRONG STOUT IN THE U.K.): *12.5 °P/ 1.050 o.g., 5% ABV. Deep brownish black in color with only faint glimmers of red shining through. Immensely aromatic with layers of roast malt, fruit, licorice, and minty herbs. Medium bodied, dry, roasty, and rich in character with a hint of sweetness and a lingering malt dryness in the finish. Serve at 55°F with fresh shellfish, particularly raw oysters, and with dark chocolate desserts.*

WINTER WELCOME: *14 °P/1.056 o.g., 5.4% ABV. Hazy, peachy amber in color with a tight, long-lasting collar of foam. Spicy, fruity, and dry in aroma. Assertively bitter in front with fruit,*

malt, and crystal malt notes developing toward the finish. Ends fruity and dry with a good lingering taste of hops. Not spiced or particularly alcoholic as are many winter brews, this strong pale ale is nonetheless a great match for hearty holiday feasts featuring roasted fowl, Virginia ham, and baked vegetables of the season.

CONNOISSEUR'S RATING

NUT BROWN ALE

OLD BREWERY PALE ALE

THE FAMOUS TADDY PORTER

WINTER WELCOME

BRAUEREI
G. SCHNEIDER
& SOHN

1-5 EMIL-OTT-STRASSE, 8420 KELHEIM, GERMANY
(49-9441) 7050

In 1856, Georg Schneider was granted the exclusive right to brew wheat beer in Germany by the Royal Court, making his brewery the world's oldest brewer of Bavarian weissbier. Because of the wild success of the new lager beers, wheat beer's popularity began to sharply decline in the late 1800s after two centuries of being the preferred drink of the aristocracy. The Schneider's have tenaciously kept the style alive for six generations and are now able to savor weissbier's amazing comeback in the last few years, with weissbier now accounting for as much as half of all sales at some lager brewing giants in Munich.

BREW FACTS

FOUNDED: 1856

HEAD BREWER:

Dieter Drecksler

ANNUAL OUTPUT:

Figures not available

BREW STYLES: Weissbier, weizenbock

TASTING NOTES

SCHNEIDER WEISSE: *13.5 °P/1.054 o.g., 13 IBU, 5.4% ABV. Brewed from 60% wheat malt; bottle-conditioned. Its dark color should encourage the homebrewers who struggle in vain to achieve very pale weissbiers, for this is the true traditional wheat beer of Munich that does not simultaneously try to be a pils. Gold medal winner in the 1995 World Beer Championships. Complements German sausages, smoked meats, zesty cheeses, pizza, and a host of spicy ethnic dishes.*

AVENTINUS: *18.5 °P/1.074 o.g., 11 IBU, 8% ABV. Brewed from pale, crystal, and dark malts; unpasteurized, unfiltered, bottle-conditioned. This one-of-a-kind wheat doppelbock possesses infinite character, melding the spicy fruitiness of a weizen with the dense, malty complexity of a doppelbock without being overwhelmed or cloying. Platinum medal winner in the 1995 World Beer Championships. A great accompaniment to roasted fowl, pâtés, terrines, and rich desserts.*

CONNOISSEUR'S RATING

SCHNEIDER WEISSE

AVENTINUS

SCOTTISH COURAGE LTD.

ABBEY BREWERY, 111 HOLYROOD ROAD, EDINBURGH EH8 8YS, SCOTLAND (44–131) 552 9191

An historic deal that has created a new force in British brewing was completed in August 1995 when Courage Ltd became part of Scottish & Newcastle plc. Both companies boast a rich tradition in the beer industry and the new company, Scottish Courage Ltd is the U.K.'s biggest brewer.

Scottish Courage has leading local and regional brands in most areas of Britain together with the big-selling national and international lagers and ales. Two of the company's most highly acclaimed bottled beers are Newcastle Brown Ale and Imperial Russian Stout.

First brewed in 1927, Newcastle Brown Ale was heralded by the press as "the one and only" when it was declared Champion Beer at the International Brewers Exhibition just one year later. Today Newcastle Brown Ale is the biggest-selling bottled ale in the U.K.

Brewed by the Courage satellite brewery John Smith's of Tadcaster, Yorkshire, Imperial Russian Stout single-handedly created its own beer style, which has spawned a score of imitators in the craft beer renaissance. Alcoholically strong, this classic brew flirts with being a barley wine. It gained the designation "Imperial Russian" from its popularity at the court of czarist Russia in the eighteenth and nineteenth centuries.

BREW FACTS

FOUNDED:
Scottish & Newcastle 1749
Courage Ltd 1787

HEAD BREWER:
John Gore

ANNUAL OUTPUT:
Figures not available

BREW STYLES: bitter, imperial stout, lager, ale

TASTING NOTES

IMPERIAL RUSSIAN STOUT: *25 °P/1.102 o.g., 10% ABV. Ingredients include: pale, amber, and black malts; brewing sugar; and huge quantities of English hops. Bottle conditioned and unpasteurized. Rich aromas of spicy hops and smoky roasted malt precede intensely rich, warming, and deep flavors of malt and chocolate. One of the world's classic "laying-down" beers, suitable for cellaring indefinitely. Excellent as a nightcap, digestif, or with a fine, medium-to-robust cigar such as a Punch Double Corona.*

NEWCASTLE BROWN ALE: *1.044 o.g., 4.7% ABV. Ingredients include: Newcastle Brown Ale yeast, pale and crystal malts, hops, brewing sugar, and liquor. This stylish premium ale has a distinctive reddish brown color with a thick creamy head and a rich mellow flavor.*

CONNOISSEUR'S RATING

IMPERIAL RUSSIAN STOUT

NEWCASTLE BROWN ALE

ABBAYE DE NOTRE-DAME DE SCOURMONT

294 ROUTE DU ROND-POINT, 6464 FORGES-LEZ-CHIMAY, BELGIUM
(32–60) 21-03-11

Better known as Chimay, the name of a small town six miles away, Our Lady of Scourmont Abbey has the most commercially successful and well known of the Trappist breweries. The abbey was founded in 1850 at Forges, but it eventually became apparent that the poor yields of its Ardennes farmland would not be sufficient to support the monastery. This realization led to the opening of a brewery in 1862, which has since greatly helped the local economy.

Chimay's three ales are sold in corked, bordeaux-type bottles (75 cl (27 fl. oz/1.35 pint) as Première, Cinq Cents, and Grand Réserve, and in 33 cl (13 fl. oz/0.65 pint) bottles identified as red, white, and blue cap, respectively. The blue cap is most suitable for laying down, where it will develop a velvety barley wine/port character. The white cap is best drunk at a relatively young age. The red cap is lighter in character than the blue cap and is best drunk within a two year period.

BREW FACTS

FOUNDED: 1850

HEAD BREWERS:
Paul Arnott, Marc Habran

ANNUAL OUTPUT:
120,000 hectoliters

BREW STYLES: Dubbel, tripel, strong

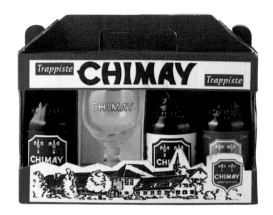

PREMIERE: *(red cap) 7% ABV. Rich, reddish brown in color with a foamy head exuding complex aromas of hops, fruit, and powerful fermentation esters. The most accessible of the three, with a very fruity, rounded quality and an earthy, spicy sweetness balanced by hop bitterness. Serve with hearty roasted or grilled meats and vegetables or as a full-bodied libation instead of red wine.*

CINQ CENTS: *(white cap) 8% ABV. Golden amber in color with an expansive head of rich foam with a massive hoppy and faintly sweet aroma. Robust, fruity maltiness and peppery hop flavor characteristic of a good tripel develop to an exceptionally rounded, dry, and acidic finish. Wonderful as an appetite stimulator or with roasted white meats, fish in cream sauces, and lemony-garlicky Italian cuisine.*

GRAND RESERVE: *(blue cap) 9% ABV. Bold, complex, and rich with fruity, yeasty esters, offering the most evidence of Chimay's use of high fermentation temperatures. The palate features complex acidic, almost minerally notes above a base of fruity, spicy malt flavors and sherry-like sweetness. Finishes with a long, mature taste reminiscent of port wine. Most foods would prove no match for this complex and strong ale, except perhaps a strong Trappist cheese or a dark holiday dessert such as mince pie. Best enjoyed slowly as an after-dinner drink or nightcap.*

PREMIERE

CINQ CENTS

GRAND RESERVE

SIERRA NEVADA
BREWING COMPANY

1075 EAST 20TH STREET, CHICO, CALIFORNIA 95928
(1-916) 893-3520

Situated in the foothills of the Sierra Nevada Mountains in northern California, the largest craft brewery on the West Coast began humbly as a do-it-yourself project for founders Ken Grossman and Paul Camusi. The two constructed the original brewery in their spare time over a period of eighteen months; shaping used soft drink, dairy, and other scrap equipment into a workable brewery.

BREW FACTS

FOUNDED: 1978

HEAD BREWER
Steve Dresler

ANNUAL OUTPUT:
342,000 hectoliters

BREW STYLES: Pale ale, porter, stout, barley wine, pale bock, pilsner, strong holiday ale

For years, the pair performed all duties of the brewery themselves. Using the experience he had gained as a homebrewer, Ken brewed and performed plant development and maintenance; Paul tackled fermentation, microbiology, and administrative duties. By 1987, a new brewery was needed to keep up with the demand of this increasingly popular brewery that has grown steadily at the rate of fifty percent per year. Sierra Nevada typifies the meteoric success of America's best craft breweries in that what began as the dream child of a twenty-two-year-old homebrew store owner now includes a premier brewery and restaurant with a staff of more than ninety and an enviable collection of sixteen medals from the Great American Beer Festival.

TASTING NOTES

BIGFOOT BARLEYWINE STYLE ALE: *23 °P/ 1.092 o.g., 10.6% ABV. Brewed from two-row barley and caramel malts; Nugget hops for bittering, Cascade for finishing, and Centennial and Cascade for dry hopping. The perennial Great American Beer Festival gold medal winner in the Barley Wine category (1987, 1988, 1992, and 1995). Sports a complex, fruity aroma and deep, reddish brown appearance. Rich, intense, and mature with well-organized flavors of candied fruit, bitter hops, and sweet malt under it all. Dangerously drinkable in its smoothness and balance.*

CELEBRATION ALE: *16 °P/ 1.064 o.g., 6.4% ABV. Brewed from two-row barley, caramel, and dextrin malts; Chinook hops for bittering, Cascade for finishing, with Centennial and Cascade used for dry hopping. Full-bodied, rich, and well balanced. A now-legendary holiday beer anxiously awaited each year by beer devotees in the U.S.*

PALE ALE: *13 °P/ 1.052 o.g., 5.5% ABV. Brewed from two-row barley, caramel, and dextrin malts; Perle hops for bittering and Cascade for finishing. Deep amber in color with the distinctive aroma of Cascade hops and caramel malt. Perfectly balanced, fresh tasting, and full-bodied*

with a lingering hop flavor finish. Should be considered a classic pale ale on either side of the Atlantic. Wonderful as a session beer.

PORTER: *14.5 °P/1.058 o.g., 5.9% ABV. Brewed from two-row barley, caramel, chocolate, black, and dextrin malts; Nugget hops for bittering and Willamette for finishing. Rich, smooth, and mellow medium-bodied porter in the classic London tradition and largely considered to be one of America's best.*

STOUT: *16 °P/1.064 o.g., 6% ABV. Brewed from two-row barley, caramel, black, and dextrin malts; Chinook hops for bittering and Cascade for finishing. Creamy, full bodied, dark, and rich with an assertive roasted malt flavor. Great American Beer Festival silver medal winner in 1988 and 1989. Try with smoked shellfish, herbed cheeses, and salmon.*

CONNOISSEUR'S RATING

BIGFOOT BARLEYWINE	🍺🍺🍺🍺
CELEBRATION ALE	🍺🍺
PALE ALE	🍺🍺🍺🍺
PORTER	🍺🍺🍺
STOUT	🍺🍺

BRASSERIE DE SILLY

VILLE-BASSE, 141. 7830 SILLY, BELGIUM
(32-68) 55-16-95

The village of Silly is situated in the Hainault region of Belgium near the river Sylle, from which the family-owned brasserie derives its name. The current brewery was founded in 1850 as a farmhouse brewery, but in 1947 brewing eclipsed farming as a commercial enterprise. It is now devoted solely to producing craft beers and managing its estate of cafés. In 1975, Silly purchased the Tennstedt Decroes brewery at Enghein, allowing them to add Double Enghien to their product range. The year 1990 saw the creation of Titje, an entry into the bière blanche market.

BREW FACTS

FOUNDED: 1850

HEAD BREWER: Jean Paul Van Der Haegen

ANNUAL OUTPUT: 12,000 hectoliters

BREW STYLES: Old brown, white beer, strong ale, abbey ale, Scotch ale

The brewery in the village of Silly, Belgium

~ 88 ~

TASTING NOTES

TITJE BLANCHE: *4.7% ABV. A delicate and delicious bottle-conditioned summer refresher in the white beer style with subtle flavor notes of orange, coriander, wheat, and oats. Serve at 41°F.*

SCOTCH SILLY: *8% ABV. Brewed with malt, brewing sugar, and English hops, this most famous of the Silly line is bottle conditioned and suitable for laying down. True to Scotch style, strong with a smooth velvety taste, and subdued bitterness for balance. Serve at 46–54°F.*

DOUBLE ENGHIEN: *8% ABV (Brune)/7.5% ABV (Blond). Available in two versions, this strong, bottle-conditioned ale is predominantly sweet in flavor and well suited for aging. The "blond" version is spicy, mellow, and much subtler in flavor than the "brown." Serve at 48–54°F.*

LA DIVINE: *9.5% ABV. Ingredients for this deep brown abbey-style ale include malt, caramel malt, brewing sugar, and English hops. Like its counterparts, it is bottle conditioned and suitable for cellaring. Serve at 46–54°F.*

SAISON DE SILLY: *5.3% ABV. Not actually a "Saison" in the French country meaning of the word, but rather a classic in the old brown style. Top-fermented, vinous, and balanced with a slight lactic tang from fermentation in wood. Serve at 43–50°F.*

CONNOISSEUR'S RATING

TITJE BLANCHE	🍶🍶🍶🍶🍶
SCOTCH SILLY	🍶🍶🍶🍶🍶
DOUBLE ENGHIEN BLOND	🍶🍶🍶
LA DIVINE	🍶🍶🍶🍶
SAISON DE SILLY	🍶🍶🍶

T&R THEAKSTON LTD.

WELLGARTH, MASHAM, RIPON, N. YORKSHIRE HG4 4DX, ENGLAND
(44-1765) 689544

This old North Yorkshire brewery has been brewing at the same site for more than 120 years, producing a wide range of popular session bitters and seasonal beers. Since being bought out by Scottish and Newcastle, Theakston has undergone an expensive brewery renovation in an attempt to increase production and make the Theakston brands more national in scope. Its claim to brewing fame, however, is its singular old ale, called Old Peculier. The "peculiar" spelling refers to the Peculier of Masham, a parish granted an exemption from the ordinary jurisdiction of the church.

BREW FACTS

FOUNDED: 1827

HEAD BREWER:
Hugh Curley

ANNUAL OUTPUT:
Figures not available

BREW STYLES: Old ale, mild, bitter

CONNOISSEUR'S RATING

OLD PECULIER
14.25°P/1.057 o.g., 5.6% ABV

TRAQUAIR HOUSE BREWERY

INNERLEITHEN, PEEBLESSHIRE, THE BORDERS EH44 6PW, SCOTLAND
(44–1896) 830323

I n the mid-1960s, Peter Maxwell Stuart, twentieth Laird of Traquair, discovered an ancient brewery while cleaning out the old stable buildings of the 1,000-year-old manor house he had recently inherited. Because of his background in the distillery business, Stuart immediately recognized the pristine equipment as belonging to an eighteenth-century brewery and was fired with the desire to brew with it again. A recipe based on a traditional old Scottish ale was concocted with Sandy Hunter, formerly of the Belhaven Brewery, and a classic was born. Since Peter Maxwell Stuart's death in 1990, the brewery has been managed by his daughter Catherine. Head brewer Ian Cameron brews twice a week, using the same equipment that had lain unused for at least 150 years. In addition to the Traquair House Ale, Cameron also brews a limited-edition Festival Ale at 1.055 o.g., 6% ABV; a Fair Ale at 1.060 o.g., 6.5% ABV; a Bear Ale at 1.050 o.g., 5% ABV; and a coriander-spiced Traquair Jacobite Ale at 1.075 o.g., 8% ABV, brewed to commemorate the 1745 Jacobite rebellion.

BREW FACTS

FOUNDED: 1965

HEAD BREWER:
Ian Cameron

ANNUAL OUTPUT:
652 hectoliters

BREW STYLES: Scottish ale

CONNOISSEUR'S RATING

TRAQUAIR HOUSE ALE
18.75 °P/1.075 o.g., 7.2% ABV

ABDIJ DER TRAPPISTEN VAN WESTMALLE

ANTWERPSESTEENWEG 496, 2390 MALLE, BELGIUM
(32-3) 312-05-35

Our Lady of the Sacred Heart Abbey at Westmalle was founded in 1794 by monks from the La Trappe monastery in France. From 1794 until 1836, the monks of Westmalle drank nothing but water. While this may have been healthy, it was not always very tasty. On April 22, 1836, in an act that has been greatly appreciated by the outside world, Abbot de Rancé graciously decreed that the monks would be allowed to switch from drinking water to drinking beer.

BREW FACTS

FOUNDED: 1794

HEAD BREWER:
Information not available

ANNUAL OUTPUT:
125,000 hectoliters

BREW STYLES: Dubbel, tripel

Adhering to the rule of Saint Benedict, who preached self sufficiency, the monks decided not to buy their beer from outside the abbey, but rather to brew their own. For that purpose, they built a brewery and on December 10, 1836, the first beer was tasted within the abbey walls. Around 1860, the monks gradually began to sell their beer to the Flemish locals. Over the years, the two beers offered for sale became very popular and, to meet increasing demand, a completely new brewery was built in 1934. The brewery underwent further changes in 1956 and 1991 to keep pace with brewing technology. The monks also produce a variety of dairy products, but their mainstay for abbey upkeep and charitable work is their brewery. Westmalle's beers are brewed from a blend of summer barleys and Hallertau, Poperinge, Austrian, and Slovenian hops. They are top fermented and bottle conditioned, and undergo three months of aging. They are suitable for laying down for at least two years, and should be served cool in a wide-mouthed goblet.

CONNOISSEUR'S RATING

WESTMALLE DUBBEL

WESTMALLE TRIPEL

TASTING NOTES

WESTMALLE DUBBEL: *15.7 °P/ 1.063 o.g., 83 EBC, 7% ABV. Although much darker than many in the style, this is the dubbel by which secular versions should be judged. Features a massive, deeply layered aroma of fruitiness and hops and an equally assertive palate of dark fruit, malt, chocolate, and spicy hops. Finishes with a gentle aftertaste of dry roasted malt and fruit.*

WESTMALLE TRIPEL: *19.8 °P/ 1.079 o.g., 12 EBC, 9% ABV. The original Belgian tripel, it is richly golden in color with a big, fluffy head. Impressively aromatic with notes of hops and fruit and a bold, but balanced maltiness and cleansing hop dryness. Finishes exceptionally smooth and mellow with a slowly fading taste of honeyish malt and hops.*

BAYERISCHE STAATSBRAUEREI WEIHENSTEPHAN

8050 FREISING-WEIHENSTEPHAN, GERMANY
(49-81) 61-30-21-24

The Bavarian State Brewery at Weishenstephan may not only be the oldest, but also the world's most resilient brewery. Founded as a monastery in 725 by Saint Corbinian of the Benedictine order, what is now the Weihenstephan State Brewery was destroyed in 746 by Svevian King Marsillo, burned once in 955 by Barbarian invaders from the east, then four more times over the next ten years. In the fourteenth century, the abbey was shut down by knights of the emperor and was later reduced to rubble by an earthquake. The centuries that followed saw the abbey wrecked by plague, famine, plundering, and burning, but it has somehow survived to be the world's most prestigious brewing school, producing scores of head brewers not only for Germany, but for America's microbreweries as well.

Brewing has been documented here since 1040, but probably extends back much further. In fact, the first mention of hop cultivation was recorded here in Freising in the year 768. In 1803, the abbey was taken over by the Bavarian government and has since ceased to be operated by monks.

BREW FACTS

FOUNDED: 1040

HEAD BREWER: Alois Fischer

ANNUAL OUTPUT: 190,000 hectoliters

BREW STYLES: Weissbier, dunkel, bock, pils, helles, alcohol-free, light weissbiers

TASTING NOTES

EXPORT DUNKEL: *12.8 °P/1.051 o.g., 24 BU, 5.2% ABV. Dark reddish brown in color with a roasty, malty nose that offers some hints of hops and fruit. A nicely balanced and easy drinking Dunkel, featuring medium-bodied, chocolatey maltiness and dryish hops in back. Finishes somewhat blandly with a touch of bittersweetness in the aftertaste that takes something away from an otherwise clean profile.*

KORBINIAN: *18.3 °P/1.073 o.g., 32 BU, 7.4% ABV. A nicely crafted deep amber red bock featuring a weighty, but balanced blend of rich, multilayered malts and ripe fruit with a persistent, rounded hop bitterness. Concludes with an equally malty and hoppy finish and smooth, coffeeish aftertaste.*

HEFE-WEISSBIER: *12.7 °P/1.051 o.g., 14 BU, 5.4% ABV. What might be regarded as a prime example of a classic Bavarian weissbier, it certainly possesses all of the hallmarks of banana/clove aroma and hearty flavor. Big and robust in body, with an enormous head of billowing foam and a tart, refreshing palate of fruit, spice, and drying wheat.*

CONNOISSEUR'S RATING

EXPORT DUNKEL

KORBINIAN

HEFE-WEISSBIER

YOUNG & CO'S
BREWERY

THE RAM BREWERY, WANDSWORTH, LONDON SW18 4JD, ENGLAND
(44–181) 8700141

A family-operated brewery since partners Charles Allen Young and Anthony Fothergill Bainbridge purchased the seventeenth-century Ram Brewery on November 23, 1831. Young's went public in 1898, but is still chaired by a member of the Young family. Young's was the only London brewer not to switch to kegs in the 1970s, and still makes some of its deliveries with horse-drawn drays. Young's great emphasis on tradition has repaid them with countless awards for their quality beers, which now number twelve brands.

BREW FACTS

FOUNDED: 1831

HEAD BREWER:
J.K. Don

ANNUAL OUTPUT:
Figures not available

BREW STYLES: Pale ale, bitter, winter warmer, oatmeal stout, lager, barley wine, low-alcohol, brown ale

TASTING NOTES

OATMEAL STOUT: *5% ABV. Introduced in the late 1980s, this very popular stout was not released in Britain until 1993. Deep ruby black in color with a firm, tan head of foam. A very well rounded example of the style, combining rich, malty depth with the smooth, chewy softness of oats. Finishes dry with a lingering roasted malt taste.*

OLD NICK: *6.8% ABV. Ruby brown in color with an enticing aroma of fruit and sweet malt. Considered to be a quintessential sample of the style, featuring deep, vinous fruitiness, malt sweetness, and intense hop bitterness for balance. Finishes surprisingly dry, with all of its flavors lingering in the aftertaste.*

RAM ROD: *11.5 °P/ 1.048 o.g., 4.8% ABV. The slightly stronger bottled cousin of the superlative cask-conditioned Special. (Young's dry-hopped draft Ram Rod, introduced in 1995, is an entirely different brew, made with 100% Maris Otter malt and Fuggles and Goldings hops.) A very full-bodied ale with a vigorous hop bitterness carefully balanced by rich malt character. Concludes with a smooth and rounded hoppy dryness. The 1980 Great British Beer Festival Best Strong Ale; 1985 Great British Beer Festival Best Premium Bitter.*

SPECIAL LONDON ALE: *15.75 °P/ 1.063 o.g., 6.4% ABV. Known in the U.K. as Strong Export, this pale ale features a massive fresh hops aroma, a firm hop bitterness, and an astringent dryness. Full bodied, rich, and thirst quenching, with a definite hop character lingering in the finish. The 1990 gold medal award winner chosen by the British Bottlers' Institute.*

WINTER WARMER: *13.75 °P/1.055 o.g., 5% ABV. This legendary example of the style is deep, ruby brown with complex aromas of dark malt and fruit. Roasty, fruity, and malty with a very rounded, smooth mouthfeel. Lightly carbonated, this sophisticated and reserved ale glides easily to a bittersweet end with hints of molasses, caramel candy, and malt in the aftertaste. Winner of the Championship Trophy in the traditional draft beer category at the 1992 Brewing Industry International Awards. Enjoy alone or with rich holiday desserts.*

CONNOISSEUR'S RATING

OATMEAL STOUT			
OLD NICK			
RAM ROD			
SPECIAL LONDON ALE			
WINTER WARMER			

LAUREATES

Brasserie d'Achouffe ● Adnams & Co. ● Alaskan Brewing & Bottling Company ● Anderson Valley Brewing Company ● August Schell Brewing Company ● Brauerei Aying ● George Bateman & Son Ltd ● Bitburger Privatbrauerei Th. Simon ● Brouwerij Frank Boon ● Caledonian Brewing Co. ● Brasserie Castelain ● Catamount Brewing Company ● Abdij Corsendonk ● De Dolle Brouwers ● Brouwerij de Gouden Boom ● Brouwerij de Kluis ● Brouwerij de Smedt ● Brasserie Dupont ● Erdinger Weissbrau ● Felinfoel Brewing Co. Ltd. ● Frankenmuth Brewery ● D.L. Geary Brewing Company ● Gebrüder Maisel's Brauerei ● George Gale & Co. Ltd. ● Privat Brauerei Georg Modschiedler ● Gibbs Mew ● Hacker-Pschorr Bräu ● Hart Brewing Company ● Heckler Brewing Company ● Hook Norton Brewery Co. Ltd. ● Sudwerk Privatbrauerei Hübsch ● Ind Coope Burton Brewery Ltd. ● Friesches Brauhaus Zu Jever ● Abdij Kongingshoeven ● Kulmbacher Reichelbrau AG ● Lindemans ● Mansfield Brewery Co. ● Marston, Thompson & Evershed ● F.X. Matt Brewing Company ● La Cerveceria Modelo ● Birra Moretti ● Morrells Brewery Ltd. ● Pennsylvania Brewing Company ● Pike Place Brewery ● Portland Brewing Company ● Redhook Brewery ● Broujerij Riva ● Riverside Brewing Company ● Rogue Ales ● Shepherd Neame ● Brouwerij Slaghmuylder ● Brouwerij St. Bernardus ● Bierbrouwerij St. Christoffel ● St. Stan's Brewery ● Brasserie St. Sylvestre ● Staropramen Brewery ● Stoudt's Real Beer ● Straffe Hendrik ● Furstliche Brauerei Thurn und Taxis ● Unertl Weissbier ● Warsteiner Brauerei ● Charles Wells Ltd. ● Yakima Brewing & Malting Company

BRASSERIE D'ACHOUFFE

RUE DU VILLAGE 32, B-6666 ACHOUFFE, BELGIUM
(32-61) 28-81-47

In a scenario familiar to students of the microbrewery movement in the U.S., two family members decided at the end of the 1970s that they wanted to create their own beer in their own brewery. With a small investment of 200,000 Belgian Francs spread over two years, Pierre Gobron and Chris Bauweraerts ran their brewery as a part-time hobby. In 1984, however, the success of this tiny farmhouse brewery forced Pierre to quit his job as production manager at an ice cream plant. Four years later, Chris quit his job as a computer engineer and joined his brother-in-law in what had become one of Belgium's most highly regarded new artisinal breweries, located just a few miles from Belgium's border with Luxembourg. Over the years, Chris and Pierre have continuously updated and improved this self-proclaimed "craft brewery of the twenty-first century" and now have a popular restaurant specializing in beer-friendly cuisine.

BREW FACTS

FOUNDED: 1982

HEAD BREWERS:

Pierre Gobron,
Chris Bauweraerts

ANNUAL OUTPUT:

8,000 hectoliters

BREW STYLES: Spiced ale,
pale ale, brown ale

TASTING NOTES

LA CHOUFFE: *17.64 °P/ 1.071 o.g., 15.3 EBC, 8% ABV. Ingredients include: ale yeast, Ardennes spring water, Pilsener malt, white candy brewing sugar, one spice, and Slovenian and Czech hops. Amber brown in color. Features a full, spicy hop and fruit aroma. Well hopped and lightly spicy in palate with a full malt character and a dry, hoppy finish with just a hint of malt sweetness. Bottle-conditioned and suitable for cellaring at least two years. Excellent with spicy holiday desserts or as an after-dinner drink.*

MCCHOUFFE: *17.97 °P/ 1.072 o.g., 29.3 EBC, 8.5% ABV. Ingredients include: ale yeast, spring water, Pilsner malt, brown candy sugar, Slovenian and Czech hops. Brewed to approximate the Scotch Ale style, this magnificent brew is cloudy reddish brown with the intense, woody aroma of hops. Despite a solid hop bitterness, McChouffe is richly flavored with sweetish notes of dried fruit, chocolate, raisins, and complex malt sweetness. Absolutely wonderful. Bottle-conditioned, this beer will also age nicely at cellar temperatures for at least two years.*

CONNOISSEUR'S RATING

LA CHOUFFE

MCCHOUFFE

A D N A M S & C O.

SOLE BAY BREWERY, SOUTHWOLD, SUFFOLK IP18 6JW, ENGLAND
(44–1502) 727200

George and Ernest Adnams established this independent brewery in 1872 on a site where brewing had been going on for five centuries. The brewery went public in 1890, but has remained in the same location and under the ownership of the same family to this day. All of Adnams' ales are brewed from East Anglian barley malt that reportedly lends a lusher, fruity flavor; Fuggles and Goldings hops; and a closely-guarded house yeast. It is said that this brewery's location near the sea is responsible for a subtle taste of salt in its brews. Deliveries in the Southwold area are still made with horse drays drawn by Percherons, the battle horses of medieval times.

BREW FACTS

FOUNDED: 1890

HEAD BREWER:
Mike Powell Evans

ANNUAL OUTPUT:
Figures not available

BREW STYLES: Pale ale, nut brown, dark mild, old ale

CONNOISSEUR'S RATING

BROADSIDE
12.25 °P/ 1.049 o.g., 4.7% ABV

SUFFOLK EXTRA ALE
10.75 °P/ 1.043 o.g., 4.3% ABV

ALASKAN
BREWING & BOTTLING
COMPANY

5429 SHAUNE DRIVE, JUNEAU, ALASKA 99801
(1-907) 780-5866

Husband and wife Geoff and Marcy Larson were in their mid-twenties when they decided to leave their mainstream jobs and actively pursue brewing careers. An avid homebrewer since college, Geoff's friends had long nudged him and Marcy toward opening a brewery for years, if only jokingly, as they sampled their homemade beers. The decision to turn the "joke" into a reality required four long years of preparation, with Geoff studying brewing at the Siebel Institute in Chicago and Marcy combing through mountains of historical documents about Alaska's pre-Prohibition breweries.

Marcy's research uncovered a turn-of-the-century recipe from a defunct Alaskan brewery that is the basis for their award-winning flagship brew, Alaskan Amber Beer. The success of that beer led to ten years of rapid growth and expansion, as well as an outpouring of critical acclaim. Alaskan Brewing's three year-round selections have garnered a total of thirteen gold and four silver medals in major national competitions since 1987. Its seasonal Smoked Porter has taken the gold in the Rauchbier category of the Great American Beer Festival every year since 1991.

BREW FACTS

FOUNDED: 1986

HEAD BREWER

Geoff Larson

ANNUAL OUTPUT:

34,200 hectoliters

BREW STYLES: Alt, American amber ale, golden ale, porter, bock, wheat beer, stock ale

TASTING NOTES

AMBER BEER: *14.25 °P/ 1.057 o.g., 5.25% ABV. Ingredients include: two-row Klages pale and crystal malts; Cascade and Czech Saaz hops. Top-fermented at cooler lager temperatures. Luminescent dark amber in color with a spicy malt aroma. Lightly carbonated with a soft mouthfeel and unique maltiness. Comforting flavors of malt and sweet, ripened fruit persist through to a gently lingering, honeyish aftertaste. An immensely rich and satisfying beer. Best savored by itself or with rare beef tenderloin, swordfish steaks, or broiled lobster.*

PALE ALE: *12 °P/ 1.048 o.g., 4.6% ABV. Ingredients include: two-row Klages and Munich malts; Tettnanger, Willamette, and Chinook hops. Dry hopped for aroma. Bright amber colored, lightly carbonated, soft and smooth, this is a solid version of an aromatic Pacific Northwest pale ale. Malty, fruity, and full of rich, fresh hop flavors above a mellow bed of hop bitterness. Finishes fresh and on the malty side with a long fruity aftertaste.*

SMOKED PORTER: *13.75 °P/ 1.055 o.g. Ingredients include: two-row Klages, chocolate, black patent, and two crystal malts; Chinook and Willamette hops. The malts are cold smoked over an alder wood fire at the local fish smokehouse in Juneau prior to mashing, resulting in an intense smoke flavor and aroma. Smoky and malty in the mouth, but also very expertly hopped for a clean, dryish finish that leaves a fresh smoky aftertaste. Recommended for pairing with smoked meats, fish, and cheeses, as well as zesty deli sandwiches.*

CONNOISSEUR'S RATING

AMBER BEER

PALE ALE

SMOKED PORTER

ANDERSON VALLEY BREWING COMPANY

14081 HIGHWAY 128, BOONVILLE, CALIFORNIA 95415
(1-707) 895-2337

Situated on the site where the original Buckhorn Saloon was opened in 1873, the Anderson Valley Brewing Company and its modern incarnation of the Buckhorn is an impressive three-story structure of cedar, redwood, and glass. Originally purchased by Dr. Kenneth and Kimberly Allen as a site for Dr. Allen's chiropractic office, the Allens soon discovered that they were sitting on a reservoir of especially fine brewing water. This fact greatly influenced their decision to open a brewpub and brewery producing ales labelled with allusions to the local "Boontling" dialect, a sort of secret code developed by the locals for amusement (Mendocino County was once more isolated than it is today).

The amazingly hoppy Belk's Extra Special Bitter was my introduction to Anderson Valley Brewing Company when insistently thrust upon me by Hercules Dimitratos, the proprietor of Fancy Grocery in Greenwich Village. I didn't understand his hard sell at the time, but I am now eternally grateful.

BREW FACTS

FOUNDED: 1987

HEAD BREWER: David Towne

ANNUAL OUTPUT: 6,195 hectoliters

BREW STYLES: American amber ale, porter, oatmeal stout, wheat beer, seasonals, pale ale, IPA

TASTING NOTES

BARNEY FLAT'S OATMEAL STOUT: *15.75 °P/1.063 o.g., 28 BU, 5.1% ABV. Black, rich, and creamy in the sweet stout style with a complex layering of chocolate, roast, and wheat qualities and the smooth softness of oats. The Great American Beer Festival gold medal winner and Michael Jackson's favorite American version of the style.*

BELK'S EXTRA SPECIAL BITTER: *15.5 °P/1.062 o.g., 87 BU, 5.8% ABV. Don't expect too many similarities with its English namesake; this firm-bodied ale is bursting with Eroica, Nugget, Northern Brewer, and Mt. Hood bitterness, flavor, and aroma, which is nicely complemented by a smooth maltiness. The 1994 and 1995 Great American Beer Festival gold medal winner.*

BOONT AMBER ALE: *13.75 °P/1.055 o.g., 30 BU, 5.1% ABV. Coppery gold in color with rich aromas of sweet malt, resiny hops, and ripe fruit. Robust and rich in flavor with a smooth, slightly sweet maltiness on a base of fresh hop bitterness and flavor. Ends rounded and dryish with a hoppy aftertaste. The 1995 Great American Beer Festival bronze medal winner in the increasingly crowded American amber ale category.*

DEEP ENDER'S DARK PORTER: *13 °P/1.052 o.g., 35 BU, 5% ABV. Dark brown in color with a rich, velvety head and an aroma of dark chocolate, caramel, and fruit. Medium bodied and smooth in palate with a mellow, easy drinking flavor of hops, roasted malt, and fruit with a dry finish.*

HIGH ROLLER'S WHEAT BEER: *12.75 °P/1.051 o.g., 66 BU, 5% ABV. Deep straw in color with a definite tart, spicy dryness provided by 40% wheat in the grist. Lightly hopped with a clean, rounded maltiness. Serve as a summer refresher and with lighter seasonal vegetables or spicy Mexican food.*

POLEEKO GOLD PALE ALE: *13 °P/1.052 o.g., 50 BU, 5% ABV. Rich amber gold with a fresh, floral hop aroma. Light and dryish overall despite its relatively high gravity, developing to a hoppy, bitter finish and aftertaste of hops. A solid dinner beer suitable for pairing with roasted chicken, grilled fish, and spicy pub grub.*

CONNOISSEUR'S RATING

BARNEY FLAT'S OATMEAL STOUT	🍾🍾🍾
BELK'S EXTRA SPECIAL BITTER	🍾🍾🍾
BOONT AMBER ALE	🍾🍾🍾
DEEP ENDER'S DARK PORTER	🍾🍾🍾
HIGH ROLLER'S WHEAT BEER	🍾🍾🍾
POLEEKO GOLD PALE ALE	🍾🍾🍾

AUGUST SCHELL
BREWING COMPANY

SCHELL'S PARK, NEW ULM, MINNESOTA 56073
(1-507) 354-5528

Family owned and operated for more than 135 years, this famous midwest regional brewery was founded by German immigrant August Schell soon after his arrival in the U.S. in 1858. He had seen the great potential for a brewery in this largely German community, but there was fierce competition. Schell's business was helped considerably in 1862, when the town of New Ulm was burned to the ground during the Dakota uprising. Because of the family's friendship with the Dakotas his brewery was spared, and, by 1880, it dominated beer sales in the region.

Today, August Schell is one of the nation's strongest regional breweries and is rapidly attracting an even larger audience in the wake of the craft beer movement. Schell's products are synonymous with the revered style of pre-Prohibition American lagers, and it has consistently had strong showings at the Great American Beer Festival.

BREW FACTS

FOUNDED: 1860

HEAD BREWER:

Ted Marti

ANNUAL OUTPUT:

54,720 hectoliters

BREW STYLES: Pilsner, weizen, bock, doppelbock, Octoberfest, alt, lager, dunkel, maibock, low-calorie

TASTING NOTES

OCTOBERFEST: *13.2 °P/1.053 o.g., 5.3% ABV. Ingredients include pale, caramel, cara-pils, and black malts; Cascade and Nugget hops. Deep reddish brown in color with a lush malt and hops aroma. Smooth but firm bodied, with a solid malt foundation balanced by a pronounced hop bitterness. Silver medal, 1991 Great American Beer Festival Seasonal.*

PILS: *13.5 °P/1.054 o.g., 5.3% ABV. Ingredients include 100% barley malt, imported Hallertau, and domestic Cascade hops. Naturally krausened for a smooth, creamy mouthfeel. Full of rounded hop flavors and aromas with a perfect malt sweetness underneath. Gold medal, 1988 Great American Beer Festival; silver medal, 1987 Great American Beer Festival.*

SCHMALTZ'S ALT: *6% ABV. Ingredients include two-row pale ale, Munich, black, chocolate, and caramel malts; Chinook, Mt. Hood, and imported Hallertau hops. Aromatic of spicy hops and chocolate. Darker and maltier than the average alt, Schell's strong version features faint licorice and chocolate notes followed by a wonderfully creamy finish.*

WEIZEN: *11 °P/1.044 o.g., 4.4% ABV. Ingredients include 60% wheat/40% barley malt, imported Hallertau, and domestic Cascade hops. Light, dry, and refreshing with a distinctive citric tanginess. Natural krausening gives it the fluffy, voluminous head of a true Bavarian wheat. Garnered gold and silver medals at the Great American Beer Festival in 1988 and 1993, respectively.*

CONNOISSEUR'S RATING

OCTOBERFEST

PILS

SCHMALTZ'S ALT

WEIZEN

BRAUEREI AYING

FRANZ INSELKAMMER KG, 85 653 AYING, GERMANY
(49–8095) 8–80

Six generations of the Inselkammer family have lived in the tiny Bavarian village of Aying, ten miles from Munich, earning their living as tavern keepers, farmers, and, since 1878, as beer brewers. Brauerei Aying owner Franz Inselkammer, along with his brewmaster, constantly monitor the quality of all Ayinger brews. They also employ the technical expertise of Bavaria's famous Staatsbrauerei Weihenstephan. An infusion mash is used for Ayinger's lighter-colored beers, the more traditional decoction mash for their darker products.

This small brewery has garnered an impressive array of awards. It was named small brewery of the year in 1994 at the World Beer Championships in addition to receiving gold medals for its Oktober Fest-Märzen and Altbairisch Dunkel, and silver medals for its Maibock, Bräu-Weisse, Jahrhundert Bier, and Celebrator Doppelbock. Its Ur-Weisse dark wheat beer took a bronze medal in the World Beer Championships, and, in the same year, the Oktober Fest-Märzen and Altbairisch Dunkel also won gold medals from the German Agricultural Society.

BREW FACTS

FOUNDED: 1878

HEAD BREWER:
Jörgen Iwan

ANNUAL OUTPUT:
100,000 hectoliters

BREW STYLES:
Dortmunder-export, dunkel, weizen, doppelbock, maibock, märzen

TASTING NOTES

ALTBAIRISCH DUNKEL: *12.8 °P/ 1.051 o.g., 5% ABV. A great example of the Münchener dunkel style. Malty, rounded, and well balanced by hops without being too bitter and without any roasted malt harshness. A must with roast pork, sausages, kraut, pumpernickel bread, and other Bavarian delights. Serve at 45°F.*

BRAU-WEISSE: *11.8 °P/ 1.047 o.g., 5.1% ABV/ 60% wheat/ 40% barley. Pale color in the helles hefe-weizen style, tart in palate with a complex fruitiness. Garnished with a slice of lemon, Bräu-Weisse makes a spritzy champagne-like accompaniment to brunch of lobster, crab, or vegetable pâtés and herbed cheeses.*

CELEBRATOR: *18.5 °P/ 1.074 o.g., 7.2% ABV. Ingredients include 100% two-row barley malt and Hallertau hops. Lagered six months to become richly malty, infinitely complex, and bold. Complements dessert pastries, wild mushrooms, roasted fowl, smoked meats, and prime beef dishes. Serve in a stemmed tumbler or earthenware stein at 50°F.*

JAHRHUNDERT-BIER: *12.8 °P/ 1.051 o.g., 5.5% ABV. Originally brewed to celebrate the brewery's 100th anniversary, this is one of the rare imported examples of a quality Dortmunder-Export style lager. Moderately strong, hoppy, and bitter with a recognizable sweetish malt presence. A great Bavarian lager. Serve at 45°F.*

MAIBOCK: *16.5 °P/ 1.066 o.g., 7.2% ABV. Brewed to celebrate May Day, this lager is fruity and malty in aroma, with a smooth, soft palate and balancing spicy dryness. Recommended with roasted lamb, barbequed ribs, Szechuan and Mexican dishes, and seafood. Serve at 45°F.*

OKTOBER FEST-MARZEN: *13.5 °P/ 1.054 o.g., 5.8% ABV. Fruity malt nose and full body. Softly rounded from the traditional long maturation period, from March to September. Serve with spicy ethnic dishes or with its traditional accompaniments of wurst, pretzels, bread dumplings, and roast chicken. Serve at 45–50°F.*

UR-WEISSE: *13.3 °P/ 1.053 o.g., 5.8% ABV, 60% wheat/ 40% barley. The name means "original wheat beer" and Ur-Weisse is in the tradition of the slightly dark weissbiers of the past. Amber colored with a dry palate from the wheat malt and a fruity apple, clove, and banana flavor and aroma. Serve "mit hefe" at 45–50°F with hearty meat and potatoes or roasted vegetarian fare.*

CONNOISSEUR'S RATING

ALTBAIRISCH DUNKEL	🍾🍾🍾🍾
BRÄU-WEISSE	🍾🍾🍾
CELEBRATOR	🍾🍾🍾
JAHRHUNDERT-BIER	🍾🍾🍾
MAIBOCK	🍾🍾🍾
OKTOBER FEST-MÄRZEN	🍾🍾🍾
UR-WEISSE	🍾🍾🍾

GEORGE BATEMAN & SON LTD.

SALEM BRIDGE BREWERY, WAINFLEET, SKEGNESS, LINCOLNSHIRE
PE24 4JF, ENGLAND (44-1754) 880317

In 1874, when Edwin Crowe decided to retire from the brewery business, he sold his lease and brewing equipment to Lincolnshire farmers George and Suzanna Bateman. Crowe stayed on until the young, upstart owners got on their feet. He also left behind a blind masterbrewer who, as the story goes, checked mash temperatures with his elbow and controlled quality with highly developed senses of smell and taste. From these humble beginnings—producing just one beer that farmers paid for twice a year on "Fair Day," and often by barter—grew one of England's finest craft breweries.

Bateman's faced economic extinction in the face of the popularity of brewery-conditioned keg beer in the 1970s, until England's Campaign for Real Ale renewed the country's interest in their cask-conditioned heritage. With advertising slogans like "good, honest ales" and "beer is best," Bateman's intended to be a simple brewery to serve the hard-working farmers around the small village of Wainfleet. However, the attention to quality and independent family brewing traditions quickly gained them a wider appeal that now stretches to North America, Scandinavia, and Japan.

BREW FACTS

FOUNDED: 1874

HEAD BREWER:

Martin J. Cullimore

ANNUAL OUTPUT:

40,925 hectoliters

BREW STYLES: Mild, porter, bitter, pale ale

TASTING NOTES

DARK MILD: *8.25 °P/ 1.033 o.g., 3% ABV. A creamy dark mild with a light, soft body, a fruity palate with some roast character, and a hoppy finish. The Great British Beer Festival's Champion Mild Ale of Britain in 1988; Runner-Up to the Champion Mild Ale of Britain, 1990 and 1991.*

SALEM PORTER: *12.25 °P/ 1.049 o.g., 4.9% ABV. This recent, medium-bodied addition to the Bateman's range has a dry, roasty, nutty flavor with a rich, creamy malt aftertaste. Winner in the Porter-Stout category of the 1992 and 1993 Great British Beer Festival.*

VICTORY ALE: *14.75 °P/ 1.059 o.g., 6% ABV. A full-flavored pale ale, predominantly fruity in palate with malty overtones. Moderate hop character and light carbonation give this strong pale ale a delicate, candyish overall palate, but it is deceptively powerful. Great British Beer Festival Runner-Up to the Champion Strong Ale of Britain in 1989 and 1990.*

XXXB ALE: *12.25 °P/ 1.049 o.g., 5% ABV. A superb strong bitter with a complex palate consisting of a delicate aroma of hops delightfully balanced by a prominent malt character. CAMRA's Beer of the Year in 1986; Great British Beer Festival Champion Special Bitter of England in 1987, 1988, 1989, and 1990.*

CONNOISSEUR'S RATING

DARK MILD

SALEM PORTER

VICTORY ALE

XXXB ALE

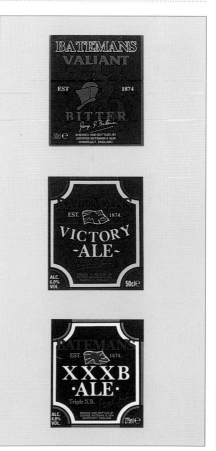

BITBURGER
PRIVATBRAUEREI
TH. SIMON

RÖMERMAUER 3, POSTFACH 189, D-5520 BITBURG, GERMANY
(49–6561) 140

The Bitburger brewery was originally founded in 1817 by Johann Peter Wallenborn as a brewpub producing traditional German ales. In 1876, his grandson, Theobold Simon, began to enlarge and promote the humble operation, and switched from altbier to the new lager style of brewing. For decades, Bitburger was well known throughout the Rhineland and the rest of Germany, and is easily one of the country's most popular brands, but it has now become equally well known and highly regarded worldwide. A very complete fermentation results in an exceptionally dry beer with a clean finish aided by an extended lagering.

BREW FACTS

FOUNDED: 1817

HEAD BREWER:

Rodolf Habel

ANNUAL OUTPUT:

8 million hectoliters

BREW STYLES: Pils

CONNOISSEUR'S RATING

PREMIUM PILS
11.3 °P/1.045 o.g., 4.9% ABV

BROUWERIJ FRANK BOON

65 FONTEIN STRAAT, 1520 LEMBEEK, BELGIUM
(32-2) 356-66-44

For nearly two decades Frank Boon (pronounced "Bone") has been regarded in Belgium as a pioneer and a traditionalist at the same time. When he took up the old traditional business of blending lambics in a market increasingly overrun with pils, many considered the young upstart either out of touch with beer industry realities or insane. Today, Boon is highly regarded as a brewer maintaining traditional lambic styles and one of a new crop of craft brewers creating their own unique signature. Brouwerij Frank Boon was named "Micro/Craft Brewery of the Year" by the Beverage Testing Institute. Boon's most traditional blends of lambic are sold with the "Mariage Parfait" moniker attached; the others tend to be fruitier and less dry.

BREW FACTS

FOUNDED: 1977

HEAD BREWER: Frank Boon

ANNUAL OUTPUT: 1,500 hectoliters

BREW STYLES: Lambic, fruit lambic, gueuze, faro

CONNOISSEUR'S RATING

FRAMBOISE
6.2% ABV

GUEUZE
6% ABV

KRIEK
5% ABV

PERTOTALE FARO
16% ABV

CALEDONIAN

BREWING CO.

42 SLATEFORD ROAD, EDINBURGH, LOTHIAN EH11 1P4, SCOTLAND
(44–131) 337–1286

Saved from extinction by a management buyout led by the former chief chemist for Chivas Regal and current head brewer Russell Sharp, Caledonian is emerging as one of the U.K.'s, and the world's, best independent breweries. As the last of Edinburgh's thirty great Victorian-era breweries, Caledonian exists as a veritable museum of Scottish beer brewing, turning out very traditional brews in direct-fired, open copper kettles; one of which dates to 1869 and is the last of its kind in Britain.

This prolific craft brewery was founded in 1869 by Robert Clark and George Lorimer. The brewery was subsequently bought out and operated by Vaux of Sunderland from 1919 until 1987. When imminent closure threatened, a group of loyal Caledonian drinkers intent on keeping it open bought the brewery. Caledonian now has the largest cask and bottled range of beers in Britain and was voted "1996 British Brewery of the Year" by the World Beer Guide.

BREW FACTS
FOUNDED: 1869
HEAD BREWER: Russell Sharp
ANNUAL OUTPUT: 42,380 hectoliters
BREW STYLES: 60/-, 70/-, 80/-, IPA, strong ale, pale ale, porter

TASTING NOTES

80/- EXPORT ALE: *4.1% ABV. Deep, coppery gold in color, this full-bodied brew is reminiscent of the great 80 Shilling brews that were exported in great numbers to the U.S. in colonial times. Well hopped, but with Caledonian's trademark rounded, soft maltiness. It has a firm and creamy body and a malty taste that finishes with a faintly sweet fruitiness.*

DEUCHAR'S EXPORT STRENGTH IPA: *4.4% ABV. The bottled version of the award-winning cask ale called Deuchar's IPA. Pale gold in color with an intense hop aroma and a solid bitterness that typifies the pale, well-hopped ales of the IPA style. A hop head's delight, but that traditional Caledonian malt flavor is still in evidence. Glasgow and West of Scotland Beer of the Year, 1991–1994. Great British Beer Festival award winner, 1993 and 1994.*

GOLDEN PROMISE: *5% ABV. An orangey gold brew of incredible softness and complexity. Fruity, malty, and fresh from start to finish with a subtle hop bitterness in back. Finishes dry and fruity with a teasing hint of bittersweetness in the aftertaste. Produced from organically grown malt and hops.*

MACANDREWS: *6.5% ABV. Rosy amber gold with an aroma of caramel malt. Velvety smooth and lightly carbonated with a faint hint of buttery caramel candy in its flavor. Not the sweet, black concoction often equated with the term "Scotch ale," this beer features Caledonian's wonderful fruity malt character and a subdued hop dryness. Finishes dry and fruity.*

MERMAN XXX: *4.8% ABV. Brewed from a recipe that dates from 1890, Merman is subtitled "East India Pale Ale" and features ample amounts of crystal and roasted malts to give it a creamy, lasting head; a rich, full-bodied maltiness; a touch of malt sweetness; and a rounded finish full of fruit and malt. An impressively complex brew with robust, interwoven malt and hop flavors that persist well past the last swallow.*

CONNOISSEUR'S RATING

80/- EXPORT ALE	🍾🍾🍾🍾
DEUCHAR'S EXPORT STRENGTH IPA	🍾🍾🍾
GOLDEN PROMISE	🍾🍾🍾🍾
MACANDREWS	🍾🍾🍾
MERMAN XXX	🍾🍾🍾🍾🍾

BRASSERIE
CASTELAIN

13 RUE PASTEUR, BÉNIFONTAINE, 62410 BENIFONTAINE, FRANCE
(33) 21-40-38-38

W hat began in 1926 as the Delomel Brewery was taken over in 1966 by Monsieur and Madame Roland Castelain, grandparents of today's pioneering master brewer, Yves Castelain. In 1978, Yves became determined to raise this tiny brewery above the 5,000-hectoliter-a-year level and make it a major artisanal brewer.

Castelain is now a dynamic force in the Bière de Garde revival in France, where the vast majority of beer is still produced by large industrial brewers. Bière de garde producers use either top or bottom fermentation, Castelain uses lager yeast for its primary brands, Blond and Ambrée; ale yeast for its St. Armand French Country Ale. Castelain's bières de garde are fermented for ten to twelve days at 57°F, then lagered for six weeks at 32°F. For the sedimented beers, a dose of yeast is added at bottling.

BREW FACTS

FOUNDED: 1966

HEAD BREWER:
Yves Castelain

ANNUAL OUTPUT:
26,000 hectoliters

BREW STYLES: Bière de garde, bière de mars, Christmas beer

TASTING NOTES

CASTELAIN BLOND: *15 °P/ 1.060 o.g., 6.5% ABV. Brewed from two-row spring malt; Flemish, Hallertau, Saaz, and Tettnang hops. Deep gold in color with a malty-sweet, grassy nose. Sweet and malty in flavor with a definite fruity character and an extended malty finish, but with a nice, mellow hop bitterness to balance. Filtered but unpasteurized. Suggested pairings include goat cheese, quiche, roasted duck, and Thai cuisine.*

CH'TI AMBRÉE: *14 °P/ 1.056 o.g., 6% ABV. The maltier, amber cousin of the Castelain Blond available in the U.S. Fuller in roasted malt character than the Blond with more musty cellar notes typical of Bières de Garde.*

JADE: *12 °P/ 1.048 o.g., 4.8% ABV. Ingredients include: artesian well water; organically raised Tremois barley malt from Flanders; and Perle and Aurora hops from Austria. The only certified organic beer brewed in France. Yellow gold in color with subtle, grassy aromas. A pale, medium-bodied, fruity ale well suited to drink with meals, especially light summer fare. Finishes refreshingly clean and tart.*

CONNOISSEUR'S RATING

CASTELAIN BLOND 🍾🍾🍾🍾

CH'TI AMBRÉE 🍾🍾🍾🍾

JADE 🍾🍾🍾

CATAMOUNT
BREWING COMPANY

58 SOUTH MAIN STREET, WHITE RIVER JUNCTION, VERMONT 05001
(1-802) 296-2248

When Catamount President and co-founder Steve Mason decided to open a microbrewery in the northeastern U.S., he was blazing a trail. Vermont had not had an operating brewery since the 1890s. In 1983, there was scant information, let alone affordable brewing equipment, available to homebrewers turned head brewers, so Mason traveled to England to apprentice at the Swannell Brewery in Hertfordshire, where he learned the craft and fell in love with English ales.

BREW FACTS

FOUNDED: 1984

HEAD BREWER
Tony Lubold

ANNUAL OUTPUT:
20,000 hectoliters

BREW STYLES: American amber ale, pale ale, bock, porter, Oktoberfest, wheat beer, Christmas ale

In 1985, Mason formed the Catamount Brewing Company with partners Alan Davis and Steve Israel. By early 1987, their first brews, Catamount Gold and Catamount Amber, rolled off the bottling line and into stores. Catamount has since become a perennial award winner and a veritable school of microbrewing, with many of its alumni going on to auspicious head brewer positions across America. In recent years, Catamount has ventured quite successfully beyond its pale ale roots into bock, porter, and Oktoberfest styles. Catamount also contract-brews several beers, including Pike Place ales for the East Coast market and Post Road Pale Ale, which is distributed in Massachusetts.

TASTING NOTES

AMBER: *12 °P/1.048 o.g., 5% ABV. Deep amber, with dense, lasting head. Faint caramel malt and floral hoppy aroma. A light-bodied, caramel-accented beer with dominant hop flavor and bitterness followed by a clean, bitter finish. A good session beer to pair with solid American fare.*

BOCK: *14.5 °P/1.058 o.g., 5.5% ABV. One of the best American "single" bocks. Dangerously easy to drink with just the right amount of malt sweetness and elegant hop bitterness, accented by clean flavors of chocolate malt and Hallertau hops. Seasonal.*

GOLD: *10.5 °P/1.042 o.g., 4.5% ABV. Patterned after golden American ales popular before Prohibition, Catamount Gold reminds me of the bold Midwest microbrews in its attack of hops, grainy malt character, and dry complexity in the middle. Finishes long with a lingering tanginess and faint malt sweetness. The 1989 Great American Beer Festival gold medal winner.*

OKTOBERFEST: *13 °P/1.052 o.g., 5% ABV. Light amber color and a long-lasting creamy head, but somewhat reserved in roasted malt flavor. A fine, malty beer in keeping with many modern Oktoberfests (American and German) in its crisp, dry flavor, but not as malty sweet as the strong, traditional Bavarian Märzens. Seasonal.*

PALE ALE: *13 °P/1.052 o.g., 5.3% ABV. Deep copper in color with a profound aroma of herbally hops, sweet malt, and ripe fruit. Predominantly bitter with hints of smooth, malty sweetness and notes of a minerally Burton Ale sharpness. Finishes cleanly with a dry, hoppy aftertaste and just a trace of caramel. Given Catamount's link with English brewing tradition, this excellent new beer has been a long time coming. An excellent English-style pale ale.*

PORTER: *13 °P/1.052 o.g., 5.3% ABV. Full of traditional rich, roasty malt aroma and chocolatey flavor, but much smoother and more mellow than the average porter. Well balanced flavors of dark malt and hops with a bittersweet finish could easily make this your regular beer due to its exceptional drinkability. Serve with (or in) hearty stews, Irish mixed grill, or by itself.*

CONNOISSEUR'S RATING

	Rating
AMBER	2
BOCK	4
GOLD	3
OKTOBERFEST	3
PALE ALE	4
PORTER	4

ABDIJ
CORSENDONK

2360 OUD-TURNHOUT, BELGIUM
(32-14) 45-33-11

Monks of Corsedonk Abbey brewed happily from the year 1400 until 1784, when the abbey was closed by Austrian Emperor Jozef II during a time of revolt against the wealth and power of the monastic communities. In 1906, Antonius Keersmaekers adopted the Corsendonk name for his secular brewery and began producing ales in the abbey tradition. The Corsendonk brews today include Agnus Dei, meaning "Lamb of God," and Pater Noster, meaning "Our Father." These beers have been renamed for the American market "Monk's Pale Ale" and "Monk's Brown Ale," respectively. The Agnus, which is now brewed by Du Bocq of Purnode, Belgium, is said to be closely based on the Namur brewery's Triple Moine. The Pater is brewed by Van Steenberge in Flanders and is similar to their Bornem Dubbel. Despite their "contract-brewed" pedigree, these fine Belgian ales are some of the most accessibly flavored beers available on the American market and have lured legions of craft brew neophytes into the world of artisanal Belgian brewing.

BREW FACTS

FOUNDED: 1906

HEAD BREWER:

Gef Geer Smaekirs

ANNUAL OUTPUT:

20,000 to 25,000 hectoliters

BREW STYLES: Dubbel, tripel

TASTING NOTES

MONK'S PALE ALE (AGNUS DEI): *17.36 °P/1.072 o.g., 7.8% ABV. A bottle-conditioned Belgian tripel. This luscious, golden ale has a woody, fruity aroma with hints of cinnamon, coriander, and citrus. Dry, delicate, and distinctive, gently sweet in the finish with a soft balance of malt and hops. Will become drier with age. Serve at 45–55°F in a tulip glass. Complements creamy pasta and shellfish, as well as a host of fruit-based desserts. Matures up to three years at 55–60°F.*

MONK'S BROWN ALE (PATER NOSTER): *15.7 °P/1.064 o.g., 24 BU, 7.5% ABV. Deep, ruby brown with a fluffy, long-lasting head and full aroma of chocolate and spice. Complex flavors reminiscent of chocolate and raisins conclude with a fairly dry, clean hop bitterness. A mellow nightcap or digestif. Suitable for laying down for up to five years at 55–60°F.*

CONNOISSEUR'S RATING

MONK'S PALE ALE

MONK'S BROWN ALE

DE DOLLE
BROUWERS

ROESELARESTRAAT 12B, 8600 ESEN-DIKSMUIDE, BELGIUM
(32-51) 50-27-81

The story of "The Mad Brewers" is not unlike that of many artisanal brewers. However, when the three Herteleer brothers became successful homebrewers, they did not immediately quit their jobs and go into brewing full-time. They moved into professional brewing on a small scale and have stayed there. The Mad Brewers brew primarily on weekends and in limited quantities, despite the growing reputation and popularity of their strong, bottle-conditioned ales.

BREW FACTS

FOUNDED: 1980

HEAD BREWER:
Kris Herteleer

ANNUAL OUTPUT:
1,000 hectoliters

BREW STYLES: Strong blond ale, Belgian pale ale, brown ale, holiday seasonals

TASTING NOTES

ARABIER: *20 °P/1.080 o.g., 8% ABV. A pale, seasonal summer beer that is heavily aromatic of fruit esters and the Kent Goldings used in dry hopping. The body is light and well attenuated with the mellow, rounded bitterness of the Saaz hops used in the boil. Fruity, hoppy, and complex, with its alcoholic strength adding a smooth, warming character. Finishes very fruity and dry with an earthy aftertaste of hops.*

OERBIER: *25 °P/1.100 o.g., 7.5% ABV. Brewed from six malts and candy sugar; Goldings for bitterness; and Spalt and Saaz hops for aroma. Features huge, fruity-herbal aromas. Because the wort is boiled for three hours in the kettle, the resulting color is a dark brown with auburn highlights. The palate is smooth and creamy with a sweet, vinous quality over a complex layering of tart fruit and sweet malt flavors. Oerbier is available year-round.*

STILLE NACHT: *30 °P/1.120 o.g., 8% ABV. Deep, reddish brown with hints of gold. Features a powerful aroma of fruity fermentation esters. The palate is complex, with a forceful, fruity-sweet, and alcoholically strong character that evolves well in the cellar, becoming much mellower, drier, and approachable after a year or two. This most celebrated seasonal of The Mad Brewers has gained an international reputation for its strength and personality, joining the ranks of the older classics. One of the world's top ten Christmas beers.*

CONNOISSEUR'S RATING

ARABIER

OERBIER

STILLE NACHT

BROUWERIJ DE GOUDEN BOOM

LANGESTRAAT 45, B-8000 BRUGGE, BELGIUM
(32-50) 33-06-99

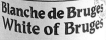

De Gouden Boom (the Golden Tree) has been the symbol for the Belgian city of Bruges (Brugge) since medieval times. This title was therefore a natural choice for a small brewery founded and renamed in 1983 on the site of the ancient 't Hamerken (the Hammer) brewery which had closed a year earlier due to competition from encroaching lager breweries. The current brewmaster's family has been involved with brewing on the site since 1889.

BREW FACTS
FOUNDED: 1983
HEAD BREWER: Paul Vanneste
ANNUAL OUTPUT: 25,000 hectoliters
BREW STYLES: Witbier, tripel, dubbel

All of the Gouden Boom beers are top fermented and bottle conditioned, primarily using Pilsner malt, with a blend of Poperinge, Kentish, and hops from the former Yugoslavia. The Steenbrugge beers are brewed more in the abbey style, using the name of Steenbrugge Abbey founded by St. Arnold, the patron saint of beer, on the outskirts of Bruges in the Middle Ages. Legend has it that St. Arnold used to prescribe beer to the local villagers as the only sure way to ward off illness.

TASTING NOTES

BLANCHE DE BRUGES *(known as Brugs
Tarwebier in Europe): 11.9 °P/1.048 o.g., 5%
ABV. Hazy, lemony yellow with a fluffy white
head. Fresh, citrusy, and bright in the mouth with
a long, enveloping earthiness of flavor layered with
hops, coriander, and sweet fruit above a wheaty
dryness. Superbly refreshing and smooth with a tart,
dry finish. A perfect summer beer. Store at
41–50°F, serve at 50°F in a wide-mouthed goblet.*

BRUGSE TRIPEL: *19.4 °P/1.078 o.g., 9%
ABV. Darkish gold in color with a sweet fruit and
hops aroma. Forceful and malty on the palate with
a big hop bitterness, this beer is full of complex
character, but should be cellared for at least a year
or two to mellow its aggressive profile. Suitable for
cellaring several years with corked bottles on their
side and capped bottles upright. Serve between
46–54°F in a weissbier-style tumber.*

STEENBRUGGE DUBBEL: *14.3 °P/1.057 o.g.,
6.5% ABV. Deep mahogany in color with a*
tremendous fluffy head. Features a classic dubbel
nose of malt, chocolate, and fruit. Features
somewhat less classic, cloying flavors of malt and
fruit brandy, and a rough base of hops. Serve
between 46–54°F in a wide-mouthed goblet.*

STEENBRUGGE TRIPEL: *17.6 °P/1.070 o.g.,
8.5% ABV. Cloudy yellow gold in color, with an
immense creamy head and powerful estery-alcohol
aromas. Thin bodied with cloying sugary flavors
that lead to an astringently bitter finish. Serve
between 46–54°F in a wide-mouthed goblet.*

CONNOISSEUR'S RATING

BLANCHE DE BRUGES

BRUGSE TRIPEL

STEENBRUGGE DUBBEL

STEENBRUGGE TRIPEL

BROUWERIJ DE KLUIS

46 STOOPKENS STRAAT, 3320 HOEGAARDEN, BELGIUM
(32-16) 76-98-11

Originally founded by Pierre Celis in the mid-1960s to resurrect Hoegaarden's classic witbier style. When fire destroyed the brewery in 1985, the Interbrew group came in with an infusion of capital and eventually gained control of the brewery. Celis soon left for greater independence in the U.S. and founded a microbrewery in Texas. Since his departure, this brewery has, to the astonishment of many, retained the high quality of its beers, and produces a highly regarded range of traditional Belgian ales. More than eighty percent of Brouwerij De Kluis' production is wheat beer, but it is also famous for its stronger brands, particularly the "Verboden Vrucht," a dark, fruity, brown ale of 9% ABV.

BREW FACTS

FOUNDED: 1966

HEAD BREWER:
Eddy Van Der Heggen

ANNUAL OUTPUT:
800,000 hectoliters

BREW STYLES: Witbier, strong brown ale, tripel, strong golden ale, spiced ale

CONNOISSEUR'S RATING

HOEGAARDEN
12 °P/1.048 o.g., 4.8% ABV

BROUWERIJ
DE SMEDT

RINGLAN 18, B-1745 OPWIJK, BELGIUM

(32-52) 35-99·11

This skilled, family-owned brewery uses the name of the oldest abbey in Flanders, Affligem, on several of its more popular brews. Monks from the nearby Affligem Abbey (founded 1074) turned to the De Smedt family to brew their beers when their brewhouse was destroyed in World War II, so that local devotees could still enjoy this "Belgian Burgundy." De Smedt now produces about a dozen beers based on the Abbey dubbel and tripel styles, in addition to Pierre Celis' White Beer under license.

BREW FACTS	
FOUNDED:	1790
HEAD BREWER:	Petrus Van Der Elst
ANNUAL OUTPUT:	40,000 hectoliters
BREW STYLES:	Dubbel, tripel, holiday ale, pale ale

CONNOISSEUR'S RATING

AFFLIGEM DOBBEL
7% ABV

AFFLIGEM SUPER NOEL
9% ABV

BRASSERIE DUPONT

5 RUE BASSE, 7904 TOURPES-LEUZE, BELGIUM
(32–69) 67–10–66

Brasserie DuPont is one of Europe's last farmhouse breweries and one of the greatest producers of styles of ale from the French-speaking province of Hainaut. Besides producing a full range of uniquely Wallonian beers, Dupont has boldly ventured into producing a superb range of organic beers. The flagship of this artisanal brewery is its Saison, a style of beer traditionally brewed in winter and matured until summer, when it plays the role of warm-weather thirst-quencher—much like wheat beers in other parts of the world. The long conditioning leaves Saison well attenuated and deceptively high in alcohol.

BREW FACTS

FOUNDED: 1850

HEAD BREWER:
Marc Rosier

ANNUAL OUTPUT:
5,500 hectoliters

BREW STYLES: Strong ale, winter ale, pils, spiced ale, Scotch ale

TASTING NOTES

FORET: *5% ABV. Belgium's only certified organic ale. Rich golden in color with a dense, rocky head that explodes with hoppy and yeasty aroma. A bold, hoppy version of the Saison style featuring a crisp attack of herbally-peppery hops. Dry in character with underlying flavors of malt and fruit. Great with fresh whole-grain breads, sharp cheeses, roasted meats, fowl, and seafood.*

MOINETTE: *8.5% ABV. Pale gold in color with a huge fluffy head. Massively aromatic with interlaced spice, fruit, and herbal hops. Full bodied and rounded in the mouth with a rich spicy, fruitiness. Finishing equally fruity and well organized, it is no wonder this is Dupont's best selling beer. Suitable for cellaring, this beer is slightly sweeter and heavier than the Saison, and can be served before meals or with marinated meats and barbeques.*

SAISON DUPONT: *6.5% ABV. Hoppy, herbal, and fresh, with strong notes of peppery hops and a lively fruitiness. Features a big, refreshing fruity flavor that develops to a finish that is clean, smooth, and dry, with a lingering earthy aftertaste. The classic example of the style. Bottle-conditioned and cork finished, this is a wonderful laying-down ale whose earthy spiciness will mellow over one or two years, becoming less fruity and more vinous. Excellent with Belgian, Cajun, and French country cuisine, as well as fresh summer salads and steamed shellfish. Gold medal winner, 1995 World Beer Championships.*

CONNOISSEUR'S RATING

FORET	🍾🍾🍾🍾
MOINETTE	🍾🍾🍾🍾
SAISON DUPONT	🍾🍾🍾🍾🍾

ERDINGER WEISSBRAU

1–20 FRANZ BOMBACH STRASSE, 8058 ERDING, BAVARIA, GERMANY
(49–8122) 4090

This utilitarian brewery on the outskirts of the Munich suburb of Erding brews wheat beer exclusively. Its commitment to specialize in Europe's fastest-growing beer style has been handsomely rewarded, making it Germany's favorite wheat beer.

BREW FACTS

FOUNDED: 1853

HEAD BREWER:

Friederich Abei

ANNUAL OUTPUT:

3 million hectoliters

BREW STYLES: Hefe-weizen, kristall-weizen, weizenbock, dunkelweizen

CONNOISSEUR'S RATING

HEFE-WEISSBIER
12.75°P/ 1.051 o.g., 5.2% ABV

KRISTALL
1.75°P/ 1.051 o.g., 5.2% ABV

PIKANTUS
17.3°P/ 1.070 o.g., 7.3% ABV

FELINFOEL

BREWING CO. LTD.

FARMERS ROW, FELINFOEL, LLANELLI, DYFED SA14 8LB, WALES
(44–1554) 773356

Much like the many American brewpubs whose popularity forced them to open a proper brewery, Felinfoel operated as a tiny village brewpub until 1878, when David John built a new brewery across the road from the Union Inn. In 1905, the name was changed to the Felinfoel Brewery. It has the distinction of being the first European brewery to package beer in cans (1935). Felinfoel's recent acclaim, fostered by the success of its Double Dragon, has made it an inviting target for takeover, but it has doggedly managed to remain independent. Felinfoel prefers three varieties of hops: Challenger, Bramling Cross, and Goldings. It uses a small portion of flaked wheat for a balancing dryness, and Invert No. 1 sugar, which is similar to raw sugar, for color, higher fermentability, and a unique, subtle flavor. The beers are open fermented in traditional squares.

BREW FACTS	
FOUNDED:	1878
HEAD BREWERS:	John Keddie
ANNUAL OUTPUT:	Figures not available
BREW STYLES:	Bitter, dark mild, Christmas ale

CONNOISSEUR'S RATING

WELSH ALE (DOUBLE DRAGON)
11 °P/1.044 o.g., 4.2% ABV

WELSH BITTER ALE
8.5°P/1.034 o.g., 3.4% ABV

FESTIVE ALE
15.25°P/1.061 o.g., 6% ABV

FRANKENMUTH BREWERY

425 SOUTH MAIN STREET, FRANKENMUTH, MICHIGAN 48734
(1-517) 652-6183

Frankenmuth was founded in 1845 by immigrants from the rural region of Franconia in northern Bavaria. Franconians are known for their independence, their tradition, but perhaps mostly for their beer. Modern Franconia has the largest density of breweries per capita in the world and is particularly noted for its rauch and keller bier styles. Situated on the Cass River in the rolling farmland of the Saginaw Valley, Frankenmuth is sometimes called "Little Bavaria," and is one of America's most popular tourist attractions, particularly around Christmas.

Frankenmuth Brewery's current operation began in the late 1980s as a remodeling and updating of a regional brewery that had served the area since 1862. In recent years, Frankenmuth has garnered critical acclaim as one of the growing number of Midwestern craft brewers producing exceptional German-style beers.

BREW FACTS

FOUNDED: 1987

HEAD BREWER: Fred Scheer

ANNUAL OUTPUT: 68,400 hectoliters

BREW STYLES: Pilsner, bock, Munich dark, amber ale

TASTING NOTES

BOCK: *16.6 °P/1.067 o.g., 6.4% ABV. Deep ruby brown in color with enticing aromas of malt and candied fruit. Although the head is somewhat fast fading, this bock is otherwise exceptional. A very well crafted bock that does not try to overpower, but develops gently and intricately with hints of caramel, fruit, and drying hops. The flavors of sweet malt and balancing hops are subtly intertwined very much in the German tradition, finishing tangy and faintly sweet. Great American Beer Festival silver medal winner in 1989 and gold medal winner in 1991 and 1992.*

DARK: *13.5 °P/1.054 o.g., 5.2% ABV. Deep ruby red with golden brown highlights and a dense lasting head. Soft, smooth, and well balanced, this is an exceptional example of the Münchner dunkel style and is one of America's best German-style darks. Clean, rounded, and full of character. Gold medal winner in 1989 and silver medal winner in 1990 at the Great American Beer Festival.*

PILSNER: *11.5 °P/1.046 o.g., 5.2% ABV. Pale gold in color with a light, but long-lasting head. Features subdued aromas of hops and mellow malt with a character mainly of hop bitterness and a backdrop of mildly sweet maltiness. Finishes dry and bitter with a slight sourness in the aftertaste.*

OLD DETROIT AMBER ALE: *13.8 °P/1.055 o.g., 5.9% ABV. A copper gold ale with a solidly pleasing, rich, fruity malt character featuring hops underneath it all and a fruity, sweet aftertaste. Very satisfying and fresh. Silver medal, 1995 World Beer Championships; winner of the Brewmaster's Best Award of Excellence in 1993; and two-time Chicago Beer Society Best of Show winner.*

CONNOISSEUR'S RATING

BOCK	🍺🍺🍺
DARK	🍺🍺🍺🍺🍺
PILSNER	🍺🍺🍺
OLD DETROIT AMBER ALE	🍺🍺🍺🍺

D.L. GEARY
BREWING COMPANY

38 EVERGREEN DRIVE, PORTLAND, MAINE 04103
(1-207) 878-2337

When David and Karen Geary founded their tiny brewery in Maine in the mid-1980s there were scarcely more than a dozen microbreweries on the East Coast. To achieve a solid grasp of the brewing arts, David trained and researched in Scotland and England with the assistance of Peter Maxwell Stuart of Traquair House fame. This study gave him a strong foundation in the British brewing tradition. That British influence is greatly evident in Geary's selection of highly praised ales, relying heavily on traditional English malts and hops to achieve their authentic character.

BREW FACTS	
FOUNDED:	1983
HEAD BREWER:	David Geary
ANNUAL OUTPUT:	8,208 hectoliters
BREW STYLES:	Porter, pale ale, holiday ale

TASTING NOTES

GEARY'S LONDON PORTER: *11.25 °P/1.045 o.g., 4.2% ABV. Brewed from two-row English pale, crystal, black, and chocolate malts; Cascade, Willamette, and Goldings hops. A dark, coffee-colored brew with a husky black malt aroma. The dry, roasted malt theme is carried through in the flavor profile which is robust and smoky against a subtle background of malt sweetness and hop bitterness. Finishes cleanly with hints of molasses and tobacco in a dryish aftertaste. Seems a natural for fish and chips or meat pies, but is equally at home with the succulent "down-east" crustacean that graces the label. Seasonal.*

GEARY'S PALE ALE: *11.75 °P/1.047 o.g., 4.5% ABV. Brewed from two-row English pale, crystal, and chocolate malts; Cascade, Mt. Hood, Tettnang, and Fuggles hops. Deep amber in color with a very tantalizing head of rocky foam. Typically British in all aspects except one: its massive hop flavor. The wonderfully fresh and rounded taste upstages the other ingredients, but provides quite a feast for the hop head.*

1995 HAMPSHIRE SPECIAL ALE: *17.5 °P/ 1.070 o.g., 7% ABV. Brewed from two-row English pale, crystal, and chocolate malts; Cascade, Mt. Hood, and East Kent Goldings hops. A New England legend, the 1995 version charges at you with a robust attack of spicy hops over a firm and rounded malty base. Assertive, but fresh and well balanced, with neither malt sweetness nor hop bitterness and flavor gaining the upper hand. Seasonal.*

CONNOISSEUR'S RATING

GEARY'S LONDON PORTER

GEARY'S PALE ALE

HAMPSHIRE SPECIAL ALE

GEBRÜDER MAISEL'S BRAUEREI

HINDENBURGHSTRASSE 9, 95445 BAYREUTH, GERMANY
(49-921) 4010

The name means "Maisel Brothers' Brewery" after the founders Hans and Eberhardt Maisel. Today, the brewery is still in the hands of two brothers, Hans and Oscar Maisel, descendants of the founders. The brewery's trademark is a six-pointed alchemist's star that symbolized the production of beer in medieval times. In the Middle Ages, a brewer earned the privilege of displaying this symbol if his "homebrew" met rigid standards of taste and quality. The original brewery building has now been remodeled into what the Guinness Book of Records calls the world's largest brewery museum. All of Maisel's beers are brewed from fresh mountain spring water from the nearby Fichtel Mountains, Hallertau hops, two-row barley, malted wheat, and ale yeast.

BREW FACTS

FOUNDED: 1887

HEAD BREWER

Hans Holländer

ANNUAL OUTPUT:

514,000 hectoliters

BREW STYLES: Weissbier, dampfbier

CONNOISSEUR'S RATING

HEFE WEISSE
13 °P/1.052 o.g., 5.7% ABV

GEORGE GALE
& CO. LTD.

THE BREWERY, HORNDEAN, PORTSMOUTH, HAMPSHIRE, PO8 0DA,
ENGLAND (44–1705) 571212

In 1847, Richard Gale bought the Ship & Bell Hotel in Horndean and its associated brewery near the English Channel and the great naval center of Portsmouth. The Ship & Bell flourished until it was destroyed by fire in 1869, after which a Victorian tower brewery was constructed. That charming old building still houses today's operation, which is run by the Bowyer family, who purchased the brewery in 1896.

BREW FACTS

FOUNDED: 1847

HEAD BREWER:
Derek Lowe

ANNUAL OUTPUT:
57,505 hectoliters

BREW STYLES: Bitter, old ale, dark mild, winter ale

George Gale is now the largest family-owned independent brewery in Hampshire, with more than 130 pubs spread across the south of England. Gale's is best known for its Premium Bitter, dubbed "HSB" (Horndean Special Bitter), and especially for its bottle-conditioned Prize Old Ale. The brewery primarily uses Fuggles, Goldings, and Challenger hops, and Marris Otter malt. Their beers are open-fermented in traditional, round wooden vessels and have garnered numerous awards across Britain in the past decade. George Gale is currently planning to enter the U.S. market.

HSB: *12.75 °P/ 1.051 o.g., 4.8% ABV. Gale's beers are generally malt accented with hops playing a secondary role, and this is a prime example of their range of beers. It features a moderate head with good lace. HSB is rich mahogany in color with deep gold highlights and a subtle malty aroma of fruit compote and some resiny hops. A sweet, soft caramel candy taste and a good smack of hops is well married to a malty, nutty sweetness and a dryish, hoppy finish. Silver medal, 1994 International Brewing Awards.*

PRIZE OLD ALE: *23.75 °P/ 1.095 o.g., 9% ABV. Matured in bulk for up to one year, then hand bottled, corked, and labeled. Fruity, rich, and dry with ample evidence of alcoholic strength. Full-bodied, complex, and acidic with a woody, vinous taste you'll never forget. This is a beer to be slowly savored on a winter evening, perhaps with a Griffin's Prestige cigar. This is one of the world's great cellaring beers, with a life span of at least five and possibly even twenty years. The 1992 Great British Beer Festival Champion bottle-conditioned ale. Slowly decant off yeast sediment and serve at room temperature.*

HSB

PRIZE OLD ALE

PRIVAT-BRAUEREI GEORG MODSCHIEDLER

MARKT STRASSE 12, BUTTENHEIM, BAVARIA, GERMANY
(49–9545) 4460

When lager beer displaced top-fermented brews as the preferred drink of Germany, many smaller breweries such as Modschiedler began to produce the popular new lagers while maintaining the centuries-old traditions and methods of ale brewing. Unfiltered, unpasteurized, unkrausened, this version of the rarely bottled Bavarian "brewery tap" lager has a wonderfully fresh, homebrewed character. Intentionally cloudy, heavily hopped, and lightly carbonated, kellerbier is a supreme refresher.

BREW FACTS

FOUNDED: 1624

HEAD BREWER:
Information not available

ANNUAL OUTPUT:
Figures not available

BREW STYLES: Kellerbier, pils, märzen

CONNOISSEUR'S RATING

ST. GEORGEN BRAU
12.5°P/1.049 o.g.,
35 BU, 25 EBC, 4.9% ABV

GIBBS MEW

ANCHOR BREWERY, SALISBURY, WILTSHIRE SP1 2AR, ENGLAND
(44–1722) 411911

The Gibbs family began with a brewpub called The Swan in the mid-1700s, but moved to the Anchor Brewery site a century later, constructing a classic Victorian tower brewery in 1890. The Gibbs family still retains a substantial stake in the brewery.

Defiantly intent on remaining a quality independent, Gibbs Mew bought out Charrington's interest in the brewery in the 1970s and fought off a hostile takeover with the aid of CAMRA's "Hands off our Tipple" campaign in the early 1990s. Ironically, Gibbs Mew had been one of the first brewers to keg beer in Britain, with its entire draft range being kegged during the 1960s. In 1973, they introduced the award-winning The Bishop's Tipple in cask-conditioned form. Its success has since spurred them to add half a dozen real ales to their line. Gibbs currently uses Halcyon and Pipkin barley malts; Goldings, Fuggles, Challenger, and Target hops; water from their own bore hole; and a yeast strain that they have employed since 1982.

BREW FACTS

FOUNDED: 1858

HEAD BREWER:
Richard Hamley

ANNUAL OUTPUT:
47,647 hectoliters

BREW STYLES: Bitter, barley wine, seasonals, brown ale, mild

CONNOISSEUR'S RATING

THE BISHOP'S TIPPLE
16.5 °P / 1.066 o.g., 6.5% ABV

HACKER-PSCHORR BRÄU

SCHWANTHALERSTRASSE 113, D-8000 MÜNCHEN 2, GERMANY
(49–89) 51-06-8-00

Hacker-Pschorr is one of the "Big Six" breweries that dominate Munich's brewing industry, along with Spaten, Augustiner, Paulaner, Löwenbräu, and Hofbrähaus. Hacker-Pschorr is now owned by Paulaner but retains its own brand identity and, as one of the Big Six, its tent is one of the major draws at Munich's yearly Oktoberfest. With the wheat beer revival of the past decade in Bavaria, Hacker-Pschorr has increasingly promoted its traditionalist Pschorr Weisse brands in addition to its pale lagers. The next time you are in Munich, visit the brewery's tap/shrine at the Altes Hackerhaus near the Marienplatz for a bit of brewing history.

BREW FACTS

FOUNDED: 1417

HEAD BREWER:
Peter Hellich

ANNUAL OUTPUT:
Figures not available

BREW STYLES: Weizen, märzen, helles, pils, dunkel, mai bock, doppelbock

TASTING NOTES

EDELHELL EXPORT: *12.7 °P/1.051 o.g., 5.5% ABV. Pale gold in color with a fluffy white head of foam. Offers gentle aromas of hops and malt esters, and a nice balance of maltiness and mellow hops in the palate, but it is generally a mass-market beer. Best served as a "quaffing" summer thirst-quencher.*

OKTOBERFEST MÄRZEN (ORIGINAL OKTOBERFEST): *13.6 °P/1.054 o.g., 5.6% ABV. Features a full, rocky, but fast-fading head. Rich, dark amber in color with golden highlights. Heavy caramel in aroma with just a hint of hops. Malty sweet with a nice balance of hops developing to a mix of hop flavor and roasted malt. Finishes malty with a sweet aftertaste in back.*

PSCHORR WEISSE: *12.7 °P/1.051 o.g., 5.4% ABV. Bearing the stern image of founder Georg Pschorr on its label, this pale, unfiltered weissbier is a robust full-bodied version of the style, with more assertive esters and phenols than many of its Munich rivals. Rusty and turbid in color, Pschorr Weisse has a nice yeasty presence and is sturdier and more reserved than some of its peers, but is nonetheless a well-crafted beer that can accompany most hearty foods long after the end of summer.*

PSCHORR WEISSE DUNKEL: *12.5 °P/1.050 o.g., 5% ABV. Unfortunately, the dunkelweizen style is downplayed for the export market by many breweries; this is one of a few great examples that is widely available. Malty and rich, but not cloying, and nicely balanced by a zesty fruitiness and a dryish finish*

CONNOISSEUR'S RATING

EDELHELL EXPORT

OKTOBERFEST MÄRZEN

PSCHORR WEISSE

PSCHORR WEISSE DUNKEL

HART
BREWING COMPANY

110 WEST MARINE DRIVE, KALAMA, WASHINGTON 98625
(1–360) 673–2121

This most prolific of American craft breweries was founded in a turn-of-the-century general store by Beth Hartwell in 1984. Today, Hart Brewing actually consists of three entities in three separate locations: Pyramid Ales Brewery in Kalama, Thomas Kemper Brewery in Poulsbo, and the Hart Brewery and Pub in Seattle. Pyramid primarily brews Hart's ales, Kemper concentrates on the lagers, and the Hart Brewery brews both and serves as the brewery's tap and restaurant. Over the past decade, Hart has emerged as one of America's most important microbreweries, although their annual output now places them outside of the technical definition of the term. They are famous for creating unique names for their beers, such as "Wheaten Ale," and for consistently taking top honors at the Great American Beer Festival.

BREW FACTS
FOUNDED: 1984
HEAD BREWERS:
Rande Reed and
Clay Biberdorf
ANNUAL OUTPUT:
95,760 hectoliters
BREW STYLES: Wheat, brown ale, Christmas beer, stout, weizenbock, pale ale, fruit beers, lager, witbier, Oktoberfest, porter, kölsch

TASTING NOTES

APRICOT ALE: *11.25 °P/ 1.045 o.g., 5% ABV. Hazy yellow in color with a stunningly lush apricot aroma appearing instantly from the bottle. Equally full of apricot flavor and aroma in the glass with a fresh, fruity palate and a persistently tart dryness developing in the finish. Features a long, lingering aftertaste of apricots. Gold medal, 1994 Great American Beer Festival.*

BEST BROWN ALE: *13 °P/ 1.052 o.g., 5% ABV. Brownish gold in color with an intense malty, citrus aroma. Big, fruity, and hoppy in flavor with a rich malty base underneath. Develops a tart dryness over the gentle sweetness, but finishes with a slightly sour aftertaste. A very good example of an American brown ale. Gold medal, 1990 Great American Beer Festival.*

HART ESPRESSO STOUT: *15.5 °P/ 1.062 o.g., 5.6% ABV. Deep black in color with a rich, deeply layered aroma of roasted malt, ground coffee beans, fruit, and chocolate. The flavor is also very complex, deep, and layered with a very dry, roasted malt character overall and a creamy smoothness in the finish. You've got to live up to your word when you give a beer a name like this in a coffee-loving town like Seattle: this one keeps its promises.*

PYRAMID WHEATEN ALE: *10.5 °P/ 1.042 o.g., 4% ABV. Bright bronze in color with a spicy, fruity aroma. Very pale ale-ish in character with an impressively clean, fresh, and light-bodied palate. Nicely balanced between the lively dryness of wheat and the rich roundness of malt. Finishes*

dry and clean. A beer with a very "cheerful" personality. Recommended with seafood or as a summer refresher. Silver medal, 1990 Great American Beer Festival.

CONNOISSEUR'S RATING

APRICOT ALE	🍺🍺🍺🍺
BEST BROWN ALE	🍺🍺🍺🍺
HART ESPRESSO STOUT	🍺🍺🍺
WHEATEN ALE	🍺🍺🍺

HECKLER
BREWING COMPANY

P.O. BOX 947, TAHOE CITY, CALIFORNIA 96145
(1-916) 583-2728

Like many successful American microbrewers, Heckler founder/head brewer Keith Hilken Jr. began as a homebrewing college student. After stints in several California breweries and brewpubs, Keith served a tour of duty as a brewers' apprentice at the Paulaner brewery in Munich and at Bavarian Prince Luitpold's "Kleine Brauhaus im Luitpold Park." As a graduate of The Doemens Techikum's International Course in Brewing Science and Technology in Grafelfing-München, the styles of beer Keith would brew upon his return to California would be quite obvious. Heckler Bräu produces only Bavarian-style lagers in strict accordance with the Reinheitsgebot, brewed with the traditional pilsner malts, specialty malts, and Hallertauer, Tettnanger, Northern Brewer, and Saazer hop varieties. All the beers employ a step infusion mash and a minimum of four weeks of lagering. After only two years in business, Heckler has proven the benefits of employing traditional brewing methods by winning a gold medal with its Hell Lager in the 1995 Beverage Testing Institute's World Beer Championships, and a silver medal for its Oktoberfest.

Heckler's brews are currently being brewed under contract at the August Schell Brewing Company in New Ulm, Minnesota.

BREW FACTS

FOUNDED: 1993

HEAD BREWER:
Keith "Heckler" Hilken Jr.

ANNUAL OUTPUT:
20,520 hectoliters

BREW STYLES: Helles, fest bier, doppelbock

TASTING NOTES

DOPPEL BOCK: *18.5 °P/1.074 o.g., 7.2% ABV. Inspired by the double bocks of the Bavarian monasteries, Heckler's version features rich, roasty flavors with a hint of smokiness. Its deep ruby black color warns of its strength, but its subtle fruity, malt aroma belies the intense flavors that follow. Sweet, malty, and dense, but extremely well balanced with mellow bittering hops.*

OKTOBERFEST: *13.5 °P/1.054 o.g., 6% ABV. Features warm toasted malt aromas and the traditional sweet, nutty taste of a true Oktoberfest beer. Its bold, malty taste develops slowly toward hops in the finish and concludes with a rounded malt sweetness and long aftertaste of mellow hops. This is the epitome of the traditional fest biers being faithfully kept alive far from their homeland, where pale lagers now dominate the market.*

HELL LAGER: *12.5 °P/1.050 o.g., 4.9% ABV. The brewery flagship is based on the traditional quaffing beers of Munich, and, like its golden counterparts of the Bavarian beerhalls, Heckler Hell Lager nails the helles style on the nose. Gentle malt aromas of honey, vanilla, and hops lead subtly to perfectly balanced flavors of hops and malt and a gentle, bittersweet finish. Flawless.*

CONNOISSEUR'S RATING

DOPPEL BOCK

OKTOBERFEST

HELL LAGER

HOOK NORTON
BREWERY CO., LTD.

BANBURY, OXFORDSHIRE OX15 5NY, ENGLAND
(44-1608) 737210

Not unlike the craft brewers of today, twenty-five-year-old John Harris received such a favorable response after he began brewing in 1849 that he was encouraged to rapidly expand his cottage brewery/malthouse in the Cotswolds. The success of this family-run independent culminated in the construction of a classic "tower brewery" at the turn of the century, which still operates today with much of the original machinery and traditional brewing techniques.

The pride and joy of this Victorian-era brewery is its c. 1900 steam engine that still very efficiently pumps water from the wells beneath the brewery and hot wort to the flat cooler on the fourth floor.

BREW FACTS

FOUNDED: 1849

HEAD BREWER:
David Clarke

ANNUAL OUTPUT:
Figures not available

BREW STYLES: Bitter, pale ale, mild, winter warmer

CONNOISSEUR'S RATING

JACKPOT BEST BITTER
9 °P/1.036 o.g., 3.3% ABV

OLD HOOKY STRONG ALE
12.25 °P/1.049 o.g., 4.6% ABV

SUDWERK PRIVATBRAUEREI HUBSCH

2001 SECOND STREET, DAVIS, CALIFORNIA 95616
(1-916) 756-2739

Hübsch has the distinct and unfair advantage of being strategically located near the brewing school at the University of California, Davis, where it can recruit the candidates who survive the torturous brewer training programs offered there. Hübsch's "Brew Crew" quite possibly produces California's best selection of true German lagers, and that's saying something. Hübsch is also widely praised for its brewpub, expansive German biergarten, and authentic Bavarian cuisine.

BREW FACTS

FOUNDED: 1989

HEAD BREWER: David Sipes

ANNUAL OUTPUT: 8,208 hectoliters

BREW STYLES: Maibock, doppelbock, dunkel, hefe-weizen, lager, märzen, pilsner

TASTING NOTES

DUNKEL: *13 °P/1.052 o.g., 5.5% ABV. Brewed from Munich, chocolate, and caramel malts; and Hallertau and Tettnang hops. Deep ruby brown in color with the subtle hop aroma and mellow, balancing bitterness that are the trademarks of the style. Gentle caramel, roast, and chocolate flavors make this an equal of the best Munich darks. Perfectly matched with roasted pork, pumpernickel bread, and rotkraut.*

DOPPELBOCK: *18.5 °P/1.074 o.g., 7.5% ABV. Rich, reddish brown in color with ruby highlights. Features deeply woven flavors of rich, dark chocolate and ripe fruit on a bed of mellow, sustained hop bitterness. Mature, silky smooth, and infinitely complex. Seasonal.*

HEFE-WEIZEN: *12.5 °P/1.050 o.g., 5% ABV. A clean, Bavarian-style wheat beer that has a fruity-malty palate and a cleansing wheat dryness. Finishes fruity, mellow, and soft. World Beer Championships silver medal winner. A great summer refresher as an aperitif, for brunch, or with fresh summer vegetables.*

LAGER: *11.8 °P/1.047 o.g., 4.5% ABV. Brewed from a blend of three malts and Bavarian hops, this is a great representation of the mellow Münchener helles style. Malty with a definite sweet edge, but balanced with a hop bitterness that plays a nice supporting role. The 1994 Great American Beer Festival gold medal winner.*

MARZEN: *13.5 °P/1.054 o.g., 5.5% ABV. Aromatic of malt and some spicy hops. The use of five roasted specialty malts gives this beer a deep, coppery-amber color and complex, sweet maltiness above a hoppy base. Richly herbal, full bodied, and assertive with a slowly fading aftertaste of hops and caramel malt. The 1990 Great American Beer Festival bronze medal winner.*

PILSNER: *12.5 °P/1.050 o.g., 5% ABV. Brewed from pale two-row malt and a blend of Bavarian Hallertau, Perle, and Tettnang hops. A perfectly balanced and authentic European pilsner. Herbal, piney, and floral in aroma. Gentle and mellow in palate with a resiny hop dryness emerged from an initial maltiness. Great American Beer Festival gold medal winner in 1995; Great American Beer Festival silver medal winner in 1990 and 1993.*

CONNOISSEUR'S RATING

DUNKEL	🍾🍾🍾
DOPPELBOCK	🍾🍾🍾
HEFE-WEIZEN	🍾🍾🍾
LAGER	🍾🍾🍾
MARZEN	🍾🍾🍾
PILSNER	🍾🍾🍾

IND COOPE
BURTON
BREWERY LTD.

107 STATION STREET, BURTON-ON-TRENT, STAFFORDSHIRE DE14 1BZ,
ENGLAND (44–1283) 531111

This flagship brewery of the Allied-Domecq group moved from Romford in 1856, as Burton's renown as a brewing center began to grow. Ind Coope merged with its next-door neighbor, Allsop's, in 1934 and is now one of England's largest breweries, just behind Bass in sales.

BREW FACTS

FOUNDED: 1845

HEAD BREWER:

Steve Topliss

ANNUAL OUTPUT:

4.1 million hectoliters

BREW STYLES: Bitter,

mild, pale ale

CONNOISSEUR'S RATING

DOUBLE DIAMOND
13.25 °P / 1.053 o.g., 5.2% ABV

FRIESCHES
BRAUHAUS
ZU JEVER

ELISABETHHUFER 17, POSTFACH 2 60, 26436 JEVER, GERMANY
(49–44 61) 130

Founded by the König family in the Frisian town of Jever, then bought by Theodor Fetköter in 1867, the brewery remained a small, family-owned business until 1923, when it was purchased by Bavaria-St. Pauli-Brauerei. The popularity Jever gained from its beer has never waned, and seems to have grown stronger in recent years. Ever since it was purchased by Herr Fetköter, Jever has always used the most advanced brewing equipment available. In 1992, they continued this tradition with the construction of the world's most sophisticated and energy-efficient brewhouse. Jever's gleaming glass fermentation towers look more like they belong to the Dallas skyline than near the North Sea in Germany, but are a well-known landmark of one of Germany's most popular Pilsener brewers. The soft spring water used in brewing Jever Pilsener allows a higher hopping rate which contributes an exceptionally clean, refreshing bitterness.

BREW FACTS	
FOUNDED:	1848
HEAD BREWER:	Hans Peter Heyen
ANNUAL OUTPUT:	1.4 million hectoliters
BREW STYLES:	Pils, low-calorie, alcohol-free

CONNOISSEUR'S RATING

JEVER PILSENER *11.4 °P/ 1.046 o.g., 40 BU, 4.9% ABV*

ABDIJ KONINGSHOEVEN

EINDHOVENSEWEG 3, 5056 RP BERKEL-ENSCHOT, 5000 AJ TILBURG,
THE NETHERLANDS (31–13) 5358147

One of only six Trappist breweries in the world, De Schaapskooi ("the Sheepfold") brewhouse of the Koningshoeven Abbey in the Netherlands is the only one outside of Belgium. Like many abbey breweries, De Schaapskooi was founded to support the financial needs of the monastery.

The La Trappe beers are brewed from hops, malt, yeast, and water from the abbey's well. All are top fermented at 64–68°F and are bottle conditioned with sugar and a fresh dose of yeast. Serve all La Trappe beers between 54–61°F in a wide-mouthed goblet. The monks of the abbey also suggest enjoying their beer as they brew it, "peacefully."

BREW FACTS
FOUNDED: 1884
HEAD BREWER: Harry Vermeer
ANNUAL OUTPUT: 30,000 hectoliters
BREW STYLES: Singel, dubbel, tripel, Belgian strong ale

TASTING NOTES

ENKEL: *14 °P/1.056 o.g., 5.5% ABV. Brewed from Pilsener and Munich malts; and Hallertauer Northern Brewer and Styrian hops. One of very few commercial beers in the style of the "single" beers brewed by monks for everyday consumption with meals, Enkel is an amber-colored pale ale with a fresh, fruity character. Silver medal winner, 1995 International Food Exhibition.*

DUBBEL: *16 °P/1.064 o.g., 6.5% ABV. Brewed from an 1884 recipe including pale ale, Munich, and Kleur aromatic malts; and Hallertauer Northern Brewer hops. Dark reddish brown in color, gently aromatic, and refreshing.*

TRIPEL: *18 °P/1.072 o.g., 8% ABV. Also brewed from an 1884 recipe including pale ale and Pilsener malts and Styrian hops. Dark, fruity, and bittersweet.*

QUADRUPEL: *21 °P/1.084 o.g., 10% ABV. Brewed from pale ale and roasted malts and Styrian hops. Reddish nut brown in color with a dense, rocky head that fades somewhat quickly. Sweet winey-woody aroma with a smooth, sweet palate. Younger versions seem to have a noticeable aftertaste of the sugar used in bottle refermentation. This strong ale was first produced in the early 1990s, but has become their most noteworthy brew. Ideal as a slowly sipped nightcap on a cold winter evening. "Vintage" dated, this is an excellent beer to cellar, evolving nicely over time, despite its recommended eighteen-month shelf life.*

CONNOISSEUR'S RATING

ENKEL
14 °P/1.056 o.g., 5.5% ABV

DUBBEL
16 °P/1.064 o.g., 6.5% ABV

TRIPEL
18 °P/1.072 o.g., 8% ABV

QUADRUPEL
21 °P/1.084 o.g., 10% ABV

KULMBACHER
REICHELBRAU A.G.

POSTFACH 1860, 8650 KULMBACH, GERMANY
(49-9221) 7050

Long before "Ice Beer" became the megabrewery flavor of the month, Franconian brewers were freezing their bock beers, removing the resultant ice, and thereby creating a beer stronger than any yeast could naturally produce. Reichelbräu's "Bayrisch G'Frorns" eisbock is the singular example of this unique style. Frozen for sixteen days, then matured for eight weeks in oak casks, this impressive "dessert bier," as it is called by its brewers, is crafted from dark, Vienna, lactic, and two pale malts, and hopped with a blend of Hallertau Brewers' Gold, Perle, and Tettnang.

BREW FACTS

FOUNDED: 1846

HEAD BREWER:
Helmut Legert

ANNUAL OUTPUT:
1 million hectoliters

BREW STYLES: Eisbock, pils

CONNOISSEUR'S RATING

REICHELBRAU EISBOCK
*24 °P/1.096 o.g., 27 BU,
130 EBC, 10% ABV*

KULMBACHER
Reichelbräu

LINDEMANS

257 LENNIKSEBAAN, 1712 VLEZENBEEK, BELGIUM
(32–2) 569–03–90

The Lindemans family began as farmers centuries ago in the village of Vlezenbeek just north of Brussels, moving gradually into brewing in the early 1800s and opening a commercial brewery half a century later. Their brewery is housed in an eighteenth-century stone barn, looking very much like an estate winery with pallets of champagne bottles filling the yard. One of this brewery's proudest moments of late was winning a gold medal for "Best Wine" at a California wine and food festival in 1992, which no doubt caused scores of oenophiles to rethink their prejudices.

Lindemans sells large quantities of its traditional lambics to gueuze blenders, choosing to concentrate mostly on a line of sweetish fruit lambics. As many artisanal producers have done in answer to a small, but vocal, consumer demand for very dry and tart lambics, Lindemans has released a more traditional line under the name Cuvée René.

BREW FACTS
FOUNDED: 1869
HEAD BREWER: René Lindemans
ANNUAL OUTPUT: 18,000 hectoliters
BREW STYLES: Lambic, fruit lambic, gueuze

FRAMBOISE: *4% ABV. Hazy, rose colored with a white, champagne-like head. Features a massive aroma of fresh raspberries and a more subdued, fruity palate of raspberries above a tart, acidic base. Refreshingly clean and lively, this is a wondrous substitute for champagne or to be served with fresh raspberries, chocolate desserts, or raw oysters and caviar. Serve in a champagne flute at 45°F.*

GUEUZE: *5% ABV. Aged for three years in oak. Brownish gold in color with a rich, vinous nose and a sprightly, winey palate. Faintly sweet, smooth, well rounded and mature with a dry finish, this is a great aperitif or accompaniment to the classic Belgian dishes of mussels cooked in Gueuze and beef carbonade. Serve it as a substitute for dry sherry or perhaps sweetened with sugar in a tall tumbler. Suitable for cellaring.*

KRIEK: *4% ABV. Rosy gold in color with a magnificent bouquet of sweet cherries. Effervescent, smooth, and fruity in palate with a cleansing, dry finish. Recommended serving partners include roasted duck with cherries and other fruit-glazed meats, cherries jubilee, and seafood salads. Equally nice as an aperitif served in a champagne flute at 45°F.*

PECHE: *4% ABV. Rich gold in color with the fresh aroma of peaches bursting forth from the open bottle. Sparkling, crisp, and refreshing with a nice balance of sweet fruitiness and acidity. Serve alongside fruit sorbet, salad Niçoise, and peach-based desserts, or with Belgian waffles.*

FRAMBOISE

GUEUZE

KRIEK

PECHE

MANSFIELD
BREWERY CO.

LITTLEWORTH, MANSFIELD, NOTTINGHAMSHIRE NG18 1AB, ENGLAND
(44–1623) 25691

Founded by William Bailey in 1855, the brewery site was chosen because of the suitability of the local water for brewing, its proximity to good malt and hop producing farmland, but also because of the large number of thirsty coal miners living in the area. Despite being listed on the London Stock Exchange for more than sixty years, Mansfield has remained largely a family-owned brewery using traditional methods such as fermenting in Yorkshire Squares. To the delight of CAMRA members, Mansfield resumed cask beer production in 1982 after a decade of kegging. Mansfield is now one of England's leading regional breweries, with an estate of nearly 500 pubs.

BREW FACTS

FOUNDED: 1855

HEAD BREWER: Robert Burton

ANNUAL OUTPUT: Figures not available

BREW STYLES: Dark mild, bitter, winter warmer, Christmas ale, seasonals

CONNOISSEUR'S RATING

MANSFIELD BITTER (DRAUGHT)
9.5 °P/1.038 o.g., 3.9% ABV

RIDING TRADITIONAL BITTER
8.75 °P/1.035 o.g., 3.6% ABV

MARSTON, THOMPSON & EVERSHED

THE BREWERY, SHOBNALL ROAD, BURTON-ON-TRENT, STAFFORDSHIRE
DE14 2BW, ENGLAND (44-1283) 531131

Brewing began in Burton-on-Trent in the thirteenth century, when medieval monks discovered the positive effect the gypsum-rich water there had on their beer. Burton is also well known as the home of England's greatest brewing achievement, pale ale. Unique to Marston's is their retention of the traditional "Burton Union System" of fermentation that has ceased to be used by other British breweries. The costly Burton Union System involves recirculating actively fermenting beer through oak casks for better utilization of the yeast strain and for a crystal clear ale.

Formed by an amalgamation of Burton breweries in 1898, and again in 1905, Marston's is now run by a fourth generation of the Hurdles family and is a frequent winner at the Brewing Industry International Awards. Marston's uses Maris Otter Barley malt, East Kent Goldings and Fuggles hops, and infusion mashing.

BREW FACTS

FOUNDED: 1834

HEAD BREWER: Paul Bayley

ANNUAL OUTPUT: 492,900 hectoliters

BREW STYLES: Bitter, porter, strong ale, oyster stout, low-calorie, old ale, IPA

TASTING NOTES

INDIA EXPORT PALE ALE: *5.5% ABV. Deep golden color and a fast-fading head. Huge resiny hop nose with faint citrus fruit and caramel malt aroma. Somewhat light-bodied and sweet for an IPA, but with enough of an English hops foundation to balance. Finishes faintly sweet with an elusive, sugar-candy aftertaste.*

OWD ROGER: *7.6% ABV. Rich and fruity up front, with a dry, nutty, and woody character developing toward the finish. Complements strong cheeses and makes an ideal nightcap or digestif. The brewery recommends pairing it with the traditional ploughman's lunch.*

PEDIGREE BITTER: *4.5% ABV. Amber gold in color with a lacy, dense head of mixed bubbles. Intense hops and estery malt aroma preface perfectly understated flavors of ripe fruit, sweet malt, and a firm hop bitterness. Finishes quickly with a clean bitterness. The quintessential Burton ale.*

CONNOISSEUR'S RATING

INDIA EXPORT PALE ALE

OWD ROGER

PEDIGREE BITTER

F.X. MATT
BREWING COMPANY

811 EDWARD STREET, UTICA, NEW YORK 13503
(1-315) 732-3181

In 1885, young Francis Xavier Matt left a promising brewing career in the Black Forest of Germany to emigrate to the U.S., with the dream of one day opening his own brewery. After several years at the Bierbaur Brewery in Utica, New York, Matt reorganized the failing brewery to create the West End Brewing Company in 1888. With F.X. Matt as its star salesman and master brewer, West End rapidly became one of the most prosperous of Utica's twelve breweries. The Saranac line was introduced in 1985, and in 1989 the brewery was sold from a family trust to the five direct descendants of the founder and renamed F.X. Matt Brewing Company. Today, F.X. Matt II, grandson of the founder, heads the family-run brewery, with his brother Nick and son Fred also in leadership roles.

This brewery in the Adirondack foothills deserves as much mention for its tenacious survival as a regional brewer as it does for the beers it produces. F.X. Matt is also noteworthy as one of America's busiest contract brewers, establishing strong reputations for a host of fledgling microbreweries including such well-known award winners as Brooklyn Brewery, Harpoon, Olde Heurich, New Amsterdam, and Rhino Chasers. The Matts give much of the credit for their success to the homebrewing community, which spread its love of Saranac very effectively via word of mouth.

BREW FACTS

FOUNDED: 1888

MASTER BREWER:

F.X. Matt II

ANNUAL OUTPUT:

342,000 hectoliters

BREW STYLES: Pale ale, pilsner, seasonal beers, premium lager, fruit beer, stout, amber lager, American amber ale

CONNOISSEUR'S RATING

SARANAC ADIRONDACK AMBER

SARANAC GOLDEN PILSNER

TASTING NOTES

SARANAC ADIRONDACK AMBER: *12 °P/ 1.048 o.g., 5% ABV. Brewed from two-row and caramel malts; and Cascade, Hallertauer, and Mt. Hood hops. The color of this Bavarian-style lager defines the word "amber," and exudes a floral, hoppy aroma and a full-bodied malt taste. Features a good balance of malt and hops that is reminiscent of a classic pilsner in taste. Finishes smoothly with a faintly bitter aftertaste. Gold medal, 1991 Great American Beer Festival.*

SARANAC GOLDEN PILSNER: *12 °P/ 1.048 o.g., 5.2% ABV. Brewed from barley and wheat malts; and Cascade, Clusters, and Tettnang hops. Bright gold in color with a massive, floral aroma. Mild, soft, with a lightly spritzy mouthfeel and a smooth maltiness above gentle hop bitterness progressing into a clean, refreshing finish. Excellent as a fresh summer refresher that is suitable for pairing with the lighter salads and entrées of the season. Silver medal, 1995 Great American Beer Festival.*

LA CERVECERIA MODELO

156 LAGO ALBERTO, MEXICO CITY 11320, MEXICO
(52-5) 280-3844

The Spanish conquistador Alonso de Herrera first introduced sun-roasted malt brewing techniques to North America in 1544, laying a strong foundation of quality brewing long before the arrival of immigrant German brewers in the 1800s. Mexican brewers gradually developed their own unique interpretation of European classics, some of which have retained their original character while their German and Austrian counterparts have grown progressively blander. A perfect example is Grupo Modelo's Negra Modelo, one of a few remaining examples of an original Vienna lager.

Ironically, after years of having its Negra Modelo a beer connoisseurs' favorite, Modelo's greatest success has been with its mass-market Corona Extra. Originally exported to the southwestern United States in the 1930s as somewhat of a blue-collar beer, the Corona brand and its spinoffs suddenly achieved wild success in the 1980s, increasing in fifteen years from 2.5 to seventy-two percent of Mexico's total beer exportation.

BREW FACTS

FOUNDED: 1925

HEAD BREWER:
Information not available

ANNUAL OUTPUT:
26 million hectoliters

BREW STYLES: Lager, Vienna lager, low-calorie

CONNOISSEUR'S RATING

NEGRA MODELO
5.3% ABV

BIRRA MORETTI

VIALE VENEZIA 9, I-33100 UDINE, ITALY
(39-432) 530253

Founded by Luigi Moretti in a tiny Italian village near the border with Austria, Birra Moretti has grown non stop since the 900 hectoliters brewed in their first year. They are now Italy's third largest brewer, with great success in the export market, perhaps because they have maintained a range of characterful brands while many of their competitors have turned entirely to the production of pale lagers. Moretti seems to have always had a keen sense of the need for good advertising and publicity, but found its famous trademark in 1942 in the form of a mustachioed man seen sipping Moretti beer one afternoon in a Udine café.

BREW FACTS

FOUNDED: 1859

HEAD BREWER:
Giovanni Maccagnan

ANNUAL OUTPUT:
1.6 million hectoliters

BREW STYLES: Lager, ice-bock, low-calorie

Period advertising posters from Moretti

MORETTI LA ROSSA: *7.2% ABV.*

Crystal clear mahogany color and a gentle, flowery aroma. Light-bodied for such a malty beer, but extremely full of character that is almost a cross between a softly conditioned bock and a Bavarian fest bier. Restrained malty sweetness develops to a very clean finish. Greatly deserving of wider recognition, this strong lager is perhaps better suited to classic Italian desserts such as tiramisù or chocolate cannoli than to northern Italian entrées. Try substituting La Rossa for your usual digestif at your next Italian feast.

BIRRA MORETTI: *4.6% ABV. Brewed from Pilsener malt, flaked maize, and German hops. Double decoction mashed and lagered for four weeks, this refreshing premium lager is very reminiscent of a helles lager. The German influence appears again in the soft, malty aroma with subdued hop notes. Malty and lightly hopped in flavor with a balancing hoppy dryness and a bittersweet finish.*

BAFFO D'ORO: *4.8% ABV. 100 percent pure malt beer with a smooth, slightly sweet malt character balanced by a rounded bitterness of German hops. Bright gold in color with a fluffy head that offers mellow aromas of malt, hops, and hints of vanilla. Malty in flavor with a good rounded bitterness emerging late. Finishes bittersweet with a lingering malt aftertaste. The name means "golden mustache" in reference to Moretti's trademark man in the fedora.*

MORETTI LA ROSSA	🍺🍺🍺🍺🍺
BIRRA MORETTI	🍺🍺🍺
BAFFO D'ORO	🍺🍺🍺

MORRELLS
BREWERY LTD.

THE LION BREWERY, ST. THOMAS' STREET, OXFORD OX 1LA, ENGLAND
(44–1865) 792013

The Morrells Brewery, in the venerable old college town of Oxford, stands on the sight of a brewhouse originally built in 1454 by the Monks of Osney Abbey. When Henry VIII dissolved the monasteries in 1542, the brewery was given to Christ Church as part of the endowment of the new college founded by the King. Over the centuries, the brewery passed through the hands of a succession of brewers before the Morrells family took over at the end of the eighteenth century.

Morrells ales are brewed using traditional infusion mashing techniques and malt, hops, and wheat products from the U.K.

BREW FACTS

FOUNDED: 1782

HEAD BREWER: David Polden

ANNUAL OUTPUT: Figures not available

BREW STYLES: Bitter, mild, barley wine, lager

CONNOISSEUR'S RATING

VARSITY
10.25 °P/1.041 o.g., 4.3% ABV

GRADUATE STRONG ALE
12 °P/1.048 o.g., 5.2% ABV

COLLEGE
18 °P/1.072 o.g., 7.4% ABV

PENNSYLVANIA
BREWING COMPANY

TROY HILL ROAD AND VINIAL STREET, PITTSBURGH, PENNSYLVANIA
15212
(1–412) 237–9402

As a descendant of the oldest German family in the U.S., Pennsylvania Brewing founder Thomas V. Pastorius had a great responsibility to produce beers worthy of that heritage. Pastorius has taken great steps toward that end at Pennsylvania's first microbrewery by employing the 1988 Bavarian State Brewing Champion as his brewmaster, installing state-of-the-art brewing equipment handcrafted in Germany, and using decoction mashing. Now, some seven years after the first Penn Pilsner rolled off the bottling line, Pennsylvania Brewing has become one of the most highly regarded pioneers of the East Coast's contribution to the craft beer renaissance.

Called "Pittsburgh's Best Kept Secret," Pennsylvania Brewing is located in Germantown, on the North Side of Pittsburgh and includes an authentic German restaurant and biergarten called the "Penn Brewery."

BREW FACTS

FOUNDED: 1986

HEAD BREWER:
Alex Deml

ANNUAL OUTPUT:
20,520 hectoliters

BREW STYLES:
Weizenbock, weizen, märzen, bock, dunkel, pils, helles, Vienna

HELLES GOLD: *11.25 °P/ 1.044 o.g., 4.5% ABV. Bright golden with a white head of foam that offers a subtle aroma of sweet malt and mellow hops. Malty, rounded, and delicately bitter toward the finish with a dryish aftertaste of hops. Winner of two Great American Beer Festival gold medals in the Munich Light category (1991 and 1993).*

OKTOBERFEST: *14 °P/ 1.056 o.g., 6% ABV. A more modern version of a Bavarian fest bier, leaning toward amber in color rather than red, but with a rich, smooth, fresh flavor of hops and sweet caramel, and a lingering, but mellow, malty finish. Seasonal.*

PENN DARK: *12.8 °P/ 1.051 o.g., 5% ABV. The classic American version of the Munich dark style. Smooth, roasty, and superbly well balanced. For a beer style that is given little notice in America, this is a flawless recreation that is comparable to many well-known Bavarian brands.*

PENN PILSNER: *12.5 °P/ 1.050 o.g., 5% ABV. Brewed from two-row barley and caramel malts, this rich, malty lager is wonderfully smooth, mellow, and full bodied with a definite European personality matched to a robust, American-style maltiness.*

CONNOISSEUR'S RATING

HELLES GOLD	🍺🍺🍺🍺
OKTOBERFEST	🍺🍺🍺
PENN DARK	🍺🍺🍺🍺
PENN PILSNER	🍺🍺🍺

PIKE PLACE BREWERY

1432 WESTERN AVENUE, SEATTLE, WASHINGTON 98101
(1-206) 622-3373

Located near the gustatory paradise that is Seattle's Pike Place Public Market, Pike Place Brewery was founded by wine merchant Charles Finkel in 1989. Finkel's Merchant Du Vin importing company has been instrumental in bringing scores of classic European beers to the U.S. and, in a broader sense, to the greater appreciation of the craft beer market. Perhaps that is why Pike Place's European-style offerings have an unfair advantage in the authenticity department. They are certainly some of America's best. Pike Place ales are brewed under contract on the East Coast by Catamount and in the Midwest by Indianapolis Brewing Company in order to keep up with the national demand for the beers of the tiny brewery in Seattle.

BREW FACTS

FOUNDED: 1989

HEAD BREWER:

Fal Allen

ANNUAL OUTPUT:

13,680 hectoliters

BREW STYLES: Pale ale, porter, stout, chili ale, Italian spiced ale, spiced winter ale, barley wine

OLD BAWDY BARLEY WINE: *23 °P/ 1.092 o.g., 9.95% ABV. Brewed from peated barley and Chinook, Bullion, Galena, and Goldings hops. Deep burnished gold in color with deep fruitiness and robust presence of peat in the mouth. Complex layers of oak, hops, and malt proceed to a bittersweet finish and an aftertaste of hops and smoky peat. This seasonal beer takes its name from the fact that the brewery is in a former house of prostitution, or "bawdy house." Serve with strong cheese, nuts, and raw oysters or by itself at 60°F in a balloon glass or brandy snifter.*

PALE ALE: *12.5 °P/ 1.050 o.g., 42 BU, 4.5% ABV. This British-influenced pale ale derives its uniquely American hop bitterness and flavor from Cluster and Northern Brewer, but employs the classic English East Kent Goldings for aroma. Deep peachy copper in color with a rocky tan head. Alive with aromas of woody hops, caramel malt, and luscious ripe fruit. Solidly fresh, bitter and hoppy in flavor with a clean, rounded maltiness to balance. A pale ale firmly steeped in the English tradition. Bold, rich, and assertively malty, this is one of the best American versions of the style. The brewery recommends pairing with seafood, caesar salad, aged cheddar, rack of lamb, pizza, barbeque food, and prime rib, but, like most great pale ales, it goes with almost everything. Serve at 55°F in a shaker sleeve or nonick pint glass.*

XXXXX STOUT: *18 °P/ 1.072 o.g., 6.25% ABV. Chocolate brown in color with an inviting head of tan foam. Creamy, smooth, and soft in the mouth with rich flavors of hops, roasted malt, and coffee leading to a long, dryish finish and a warm aftertaste of roasted malt and bitter hops. Serve at 60°F with oysters on the half shell, spicy crab dishes, smoked salmon, and roasted fowl or, better yet, by itself on a cold winter evening.*

OLD BAWDY BARLEY WINE	🍾🍾🍾🍾
PALE ALE	🍾🍾🍾🍾🍾
XXXXX STOUT	🍾🍾🍾🍾

PORTLAND
BREWING COMPANY

2730 NW 31ST AVENUE, PORTLAND, OREGON 97210
(1-503) 226-7623

This company, formed by two homebrewing friends, opened its first brewery in January 1986 on Flanders Street in Portland. Two months later, a snug pub was added, allowing customers to view the brewing process. Because of the success of their distinctively Northwestern beers, Portland Brewing Company opened a second brewery in June of 1993 on 31st Avenue, doubling its brewing capacity. The Brewhouse Taproom & Grill was opened at the new location one month later. Subsequent equipment acquisitions further increased capacity to 79,344 hectoliters. Another increase of their second brewery's capacity to 136,800 hectoliters is now in the works with the recent aid of a stock offering.

BREW FACTS

FOUNDED: 1986

HEAD BREWER: Alan Kornhauser

ANNUAL OUTPUT: 136,800 hectoliters

BREW STYLES: American amber ale, honey beer, pale ale, porter, seasonal beers

TASTING NOTES

MACTARNAHAN'S ALE: *13 °P/1.052 o.g., 40 BU, 4.8% ABV. Brewed from two-row pale, 40 Lovibond caramel malt, and Cascade hops. Inspired by the lightly hopped, malty, Scottish-style pale ales, MacTarnahan's is an exceptional, full-bodied brew. Malty with rich, but gentle, flavors of caramel on a firm base of Pacific Northwest-style hop bitterness. Extremely well rounded in flavor with the malt just edging out the hops for a sweet, satisfying character. Finishes faintly dry, clean, and hoppy with just a touch of sweetness. Gold medal winner at the 1992 Great American Beer Festival and a silver medal in the 1994 World Beer Championships.*

OREGON HONEY BEER: *11.2 °P/1.045 o.g., 17 BU, 4% ABV. Brewed from two-row malt, clover honey, and Nugget and Willamette hops. Pale gold in color with a gentle, earthy aroma of hops. Light-bodied, with a firm hop bitterness and a touch of rounded honey sweetness. This is one of the better beers using honey as an ingredient. 1995 Great American Beer Festival silver medal winner.*

PORTLAND ALE: *12 °P/1.048 o.g., 32 BU, 5% ABV. The original flagship beer of the brewery, featuring the full, citrusy aroma of Cascade hops. Medium- to light-bodied, with a backdrop of English pale ale maltiness and the assertive qualities of American bittering hops that create an overall personality that is dry, clean, and refreshing. A good session beer, with fresh fruit as an accompaniment, or cheese served with fresh bread.*

WHEAT BERRY BREW: *12 °P/1.048 o.g., 20 BU, 4.5% ABV. The fruit essence used to flavor this brew is of the marionberries that are indigenous to Oregon. The result is a crisp, soft fruit beer with a faintly sweet and tart character above a wheaty dryness that is very refreshing. Ideal as a warm weather refresher and with a summer brunch that includes fresh fruit, mellow cheeses, or poached eggs with a creamy sauce.*

CONNOISSEUR'S RATING

MCTARNAHAN'S ALE

OREGON HONEY BEER

PORTLAND ALE

WHEAT BERRY BREW

REDHOOK
BREWERY

3400 PHINNEY AVENUE NORTH, SEATTLE, WASHINGTON 98103
(1–206) 548–8000

In May of 1981, Paul Shipman and Gordon Bowker founded Redhook Brewery in the belief that the rising import beer sales in America and Seattle's high level of draft beer sales indicated an environment welcoming to brewers of quality ales brewed in the European tradition. One year after the first pint of Redhook was sold in Seattle, within a five-mile radius of the brewery, the new craft brewery was turning a profit. In 1988, Redhook moved to a new brewery in the Fremont Car Barn, a former trolley car terminal in Ballard, Seattle's Scandinavian neighborhood. With the installation of a state-of-the-art Steinecker brewhouse from Germany, Redhook became one of America's most technically advanced craft brewers. In July of 1994, Redhook opened a second brewery twenty miles away in Woodinville, Washington, to keep pace with demand. Redhook recently formed an alliance with Anheuser-Busch to distribute its products nationally, and is currently constructing an East Coast brewery in Portsmouth, New Hampshire.

BREW FACTS

FOUNDED: 1981

HEAD BREWER:

Al Triplett

ANNUAL OUTPUT:

205,200 hectoliters

BREW STYLES: Bitter, porter, rye beer, American wheat

TASTING NOTES

REDHOOK ESB: *13.5 °P/1.054 o.g., 5.4% ABV. Brewed from two-row Klages and 60°L caramel malts; Willamette and Tettnang hops; and English ale yeast. Golden amber in color. Gentle fruity nose with caramel notes and the woody hop aroma of Willamette. Smooth flavor with solid hop bitterness and an underpinning of malt. Finishes balanced and clean with a rounded hop aftertaste.*

BALLARD BITTER: *14.75 °P/1.059 o.g., 5.9% ABV. Brewed from two-row Klages, 40°L caramel, and Munich malts; Northern Brewer, Willamette, and Cascade hops; and English ale yeast. Aggressively hopped, but it offers some nice maltiness in the background followed by a dry, tight finish.*

BLACKHOOK PORTER: *12.25 °P/1.049 o.g., 4.9% ABV. Brewed from roasted barley, two-row Klages, 40°L caramel, and black malts; Willamette, Eroica, and Cascade hops; and English ale yeast. Features a highly roasted malt character balanced by a lively hop bitterness and flavor, mingled with notes of chocolate and coffee.*

REDHOOK RYE: *13 °P/1.052 o.g., 5% ABV. Brewed from Flaked Rye, two-row Klages, and Munich malts; Mt. Hood and Yakima Hersbrucker hops; and English ale yeast. Bottle-conditioned. An unfiltered, hazy, golden yellow ale with a subdued, grainy, rye character. Tangy, aromatic, and fresh, with the spicy dryness of a wheat beer and a balanced, fruity, citrus flavor.*

CONNOISSEUR'S RATING

REDHOOK ESB	🍺🍺🍺🍺
BALLARD BITTER	🍺🍺🍺🍺
BLACKHOOK PORTER	🍺🍺
REDHOOK RYE	🍺🍺🍺

BROUWERIJ RIVA

This West Flanders brewery has enlarged itself considerably in the 1990s by purchasing several classic artisanal breweries, including Liefmans, Straffe Hendrik, and Het Anker. Many craft beer watchers were understandably alarmed after seeing the results of such takeovers when carried out by international brewing conglomerates. To everyone's surprise, Riva hasn't destroyed the beers of the breweries it bought, but has made them more consistent, and, in some cases, actually improved them. Consumer action groups still remain slightly skittish about the future but, so far, Riva has greatly developed the international availability of some of Belgium's best without inflicting the usual side effects of savvy marketing.

BREW FACTS

FOUNDED: 1880

HEAD BREWER:
Roland Decaluwe

ANNUAL OUTPUT:
115,000 hectoliters

BREW STYLES: Witbier,
strong golden,
Christmas ale, brown ale

CONNOISSEUR'S RATING

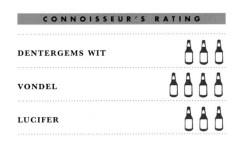

DENTERGEMS WIT	🍾🍾🍾
VONDEL	🍾🍾🍾🍾
LUCIFER	🍾🍾🍾

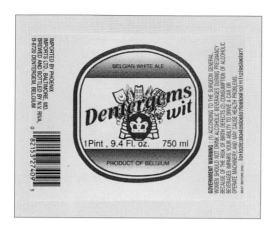

BELGIAN WHITE ALE

Dentergems wit

1 Pint , 9.4 Fl. oz.   750 ml

PRODUCT OF BELGIUM

IMPORTED BY PHOENIX IMPORTS LTD. BALTIMORE MD BREWED AND BOTTLED BY N.V. RIVA, B-8720 DENTERGEM, BELGIUM

GOVERNMENT WARNING : (1) ACCORDING TO THE SURGEON GENERAL, WOMEN SHOULD NOT DRINK ALCOHOLIC BEVERAGES DURING PREGNANCY BECAUSE OF THE RISK OF BIRTH DEFECTS (2) CONSUMPTION OF ALCOHOLIC BEVERAGES IMPAIRS YOUR ABILITY TO DRIVE A CAR OR OPERATE MACHINERY AND MAY CAUSE HEALTH PROBLEMS.

TASTING NOTES

DENTERGEMS WIT: *12 °P/1.048 o.g., 15 BU, 4.8% ABV. Emerging from the rebirth of the Belgian wit style, Riva's Dentergems Wit has become a market leader in the wheat beer category in both Belgium and the Netherlands. This bottle-conditioned Wit is noticeably drier than other examples of the style and has more of an earthy, cellarlike character with subtler notes of orange peel and coriander. Pale, hazy gold in color with a dense, creamy head. Recommended as a summer thirst quencher or as an accompaniment to seafood and chicken. Its makers suggest adding a sliver of lemon or a dash of raspberry liqueur. Recommended serving temperature is 40–45°F. Cellar at 55–60°F for twelve to eighteen months.*

VONDEL: *8% ABV. Named after the Dutch writer of the "Golden Age," Joost Van den Vondel. The piquantly aromatic, bottle-conditioned Vondel is bright amber brown in color from a generous use of roasted malts. Gently spiced with coriander and aniseed, this full-bodied, strong ale has an intense malty and tangy hop flavor with a long sweetish aftertaste that mellows considerably with aging. Vondel is brewed in small batches with an annual production limited to 3,286 hectoliters. Ideal as a nightcap. Serve at 50–55°F.*

LUCIFER: *8% ABV. Named after the play penned by Vondel and to indicate its imitation of Moortgat's Duvel, Lucifer is a nice interpretation of the style. Hazy straw colored with a warm, flowery-yeasty bouquet and a billowing head of foam. Spicy, peppery, and rich in flavor with a honeyish sweetness that tends to dominate when served at cellar temperatures. Rounded, hoppy, and becoming dryer in the finish. Can be served either cold at 45°F as a lagerlike refresher or cool at 55°F as a more aromatic accompaniment to dinner and dessert.*

RIVERSIDE
BREWING COMPANY

3397 SEVENTH STREET, RIVERSIDE, CALIFORNIA 92501
(1-909) 682-5465

Compared to some of the artisanal breweries in Europe, which have been around for centuries, Riverside's growth rate seemingly can be measured in minutes. With one gold, one silver, and two bronze medals won at the Great American Beer Festival in its first two years of operation, this craft brewery has managed to brew both ales and lagers successfully. As a testament to the success its quality has inspired, Riverside has expanded its plant three times since opening in August 1993. Alongside this first brewery to operate in the Inland Empire since Prohibition is an expansive restaurant, sidewalk café, and beer garden.

BREW FACTS
FOUNDED: 1993
HEAD BREWER: Daniel Kahn
ANNUAL OUTPUT: 34,200 hectoliters
BREW STYLES: Stout, pilsner, pale ale, cream ale

TASTING NOTES

7TH STREET STOUT: *14.5 °P/1.058 o.g., 6% ABV. Ingredients include: English and American two-row pale, special roast, Munich, 120°L caramel, chocolate, black, and carapils malts; and Bullion and Kent Golding hops. An excellent, Irish-style dry stout. Mellow, well balanced, and smooth with a hearty roast character. Bronze medal, 1994 Great American Beer Festival.*

PULLMAN PALE ALE: *12.9 °P/1.052 o.g., 5.9% ABV. Ingredients include: American two-row pale, 40°L caramel, special roast, and carapils malts; Cascade, Kent Golding, and Fuggles for dry hopping. A traditional English ale married to the American love of hops, its strongest feature is the massive, woody Fuggles aroma. Silver medal, 1994 Great American Beer Festival.*

RAINCROSS CREAM ALE: *12.5 °P/1.050 o.g., 5.4% ABV. Ingredients include: rolled oats, Carastan, and two-row pale malts; and Bullion and Kent Golding hops. Light in body and flavor with a creamy, soft texture provided by the oats. Well balanced, dry, and refreshing.*

VICTORIA AVENUE AMBER ALE: *14.9 °P/ 1.050 o.g., 5.8% ABV. Ingredients include: American two-row pale, special roast, 40°L caramel, and victory malts; and Kent Golding hops. Rich, predominantly malty, with a complex layering of flavors nicely balanced by the classic English hops. Gold medal, 1994 Great American Beer Festival in the Scottish Ale category; bronze medal, 1995 World Beer Championships.*

CONNOISSEUR'S RATING

7TH STREET STOUT

PULLMAN PALE ALE

RAINCROSS CREAM ALE

VICTORIA AVENUE AMBER ALE

ROGUE ALES

2320 S.E. OSU DRIVE, NEWPORT, OREGON 97365
(1-541) 867-3660

What began as a humble brewpub in the heartland of the craft beer renaissance has quickly grown into one of America's most influential breweries, now exporting their seventeen beers to thirty-nine states and Japan. In the short seven years since Rogue began brewing, they have garnered a total of two gold, four silver, and a bronze medal at the Great American Beer Festival, as well as a host of other honors.

Like so many successful breweries in the U.S., at the center of Rogue Ales

BREW FACTS

FOUNDED: 1988

HEAD BREWER:
John Maier

ANNUAL OUTPUT:
23,256 hectoliters

BREW STYLES: Amber ale, brown ale, Scotch ale, stout, smoked, porter, strong ale, fruit ale, pale ale, Belgian witbier

is a gifted head brewer. With a background in engineering and a history of award-winning homebrews, John Maier typifies the heart of the American microbrewery, handcrafting his works of art with a great deal of personal flair and a sense of fun. Maier's trademark is his love of hops, which he demonstrates by a liberal use of personally selected Pacific Northwest versions of European varieties and imported East Kent Goldings. Rogue has a special appeal to homebrewers and craft beer statistics lovers in that they freely publish facts and figures regarding original gravity, apparent attenuation, IBUs, degrees of color, etc. All Rogue Ales are brewed with top-fermenting yeast at 60°F, with a blend of Harrington and Klages pale as the base malts and imported Hugh Baird and Canadian specialty malts. Their ales are unpasteurized and bottled using oxygen-absorbing caps in order to avoid oxidation and to preserve the hop character.

TASTING NOTES

DEAD GUY ALE: *12 °P/1.048 o.g., 20 IBU, 5% ABV. Burnished copper in color with an earthy hop aroma. A huge, fruity sweetness is played against a sharp, dry hop bitterness that gives this big ale a dramatically robust, if not a little overwhelming amount of character. The finish is equally bittersweet, concluding in a resiny, astringent aftertaste.*

MAIERBOCK ALE: *16.5 °P/1.066 o.g., 30 IBU, 6.8% ABV. Honey colored with a honeyish, fruit, and whisky-tinged, floral hop aroma. The qualities of rich sweetness and pungent hops evident in the Dead Guy Ale are better expressed in this well-balanced brew. Wonderfully malty and fruity-sweet with a bold base of fresh hop bitterness and flavor. Finishes gently sweet, but develops a faintly bitter aftertaste when the sweetness subsides.*

MO ALE: *12 °P/1.048 o.g., 20 IBU, 5% ABV. Pale hazy gold in color, this playful version of a Belgian wheat beer begins with a very enticing resiny hop bouquet that gives way to aromas of lemon, fruit, and spice. Fruity, spicy, and softly sweet in the mouth developing lusciously tart, lemony, and refreshing qualities toward the citrusy finish.*

OLD CRUSTACEAN ALE: *26 °P/1.104 o.g., 120 IBU, 10.25% ABV. Deep, murky reddish amber with ruby highlights. Immensely complex in the nose with hints of plums, spice, flowers, and hops. Newer samples are very sweet with a rough, bitter hop edge and a somewhat chaotic fruit juice flavor and caramel sweetness. Two- or three-year-old versions are infinitely more rounded, smoother, and more organized, with an immense depth of malty, fruity flavors, and a long, resiny dryness in the finish. Give this one a few years to tame the Pacific Northwestern hops; you'll be well rewarded.*

SHAKESPEARE STOUT: *15 °P/1.060 o.g., 69 IBU, 6% ABV. Impenetrably black in color with a rich, tobacco-colored head of lace and a fruity-roasty aroma. Primarily dry and roasty in character with a persistent sourness that encroaches on much of the underlying malt richness. Ends dryly with lingering aftertaste of roasted malt and a hint of sweetness. A good accompaniment to broiled scallops, mussels, and oysters.*

CONNOISSEUR'S RATING

DEAD GUY ALE

MAIERBOCK ALE

MO ALE

OLD CRUSTACEAN ALE

SHAKESPEARE STOUT

SHEPHERD NEAME

17 COURT STREET, FAVERSHAM, KENT ME13 7AX, ENGLAND
(44–1795) 532206

From as early as the twelfth century, Cluniac monks were attracted to Faversham's brewing water and, in 1147, they built an abbey there. By the sixteenth century, eighty-four of the 250 listed trades in the town involved the production of ale. Shepherd Neame lays claim to being England's oldest continuously operating brewery. Historical records indicate that Richard Marsh was brewing long before the official founding date of 1698. A sense of cherishing brewing history persists in Shepherd Neame's use of steam engines and of unlined teak mash tuns dating from 1910. The brewery still sits atop an artesian well that has been supplying the brewery since it was built. In modern times, Kent is more famous for its hops than its water; the aromatic herb grown in this region is considered to be among the world's best. Percy Beale Neame joined the Shepherd family in 1869; today, the brewery is still family run, with Robert Neame as chairman.

BREW FACTS

FOUNDED: 1698

HEAD BREWER: Julian Herrington

ANNUAL OUTPUT: 294,000 hectoliters

BREW STYLES: Pale ale, bitter, porter, mild, lager

BISHOP'S FINGER KENTISH ALE: *12.5 °P/ 1.050 o.g., 5.4% ABV. This ruby red ale begins with a full nose of warm hop aroma. Full of intertwined flavors of hops, butter, and fruit. Clean and medium-bodied with a spritzy mouthfeel. Hop bitterness dominates, but there is a smooth, faintly sweet hint of specialty malt in the aftertaste. Gold medal, 1995 World Beer Championships; gold medal, 1994/1995 Swedish Beer Festival; gold medal, 1995 U.S. Liquor Convention.*

MASTER BREW PREMIUM ALE (KNOWN AS MASTER BREW BITTER IN U.K.): *9 °P/ 1.036 o.g., 4% ABV. Perhaps somewhat light-bodied, the beautifully amber gold Master Brew nevertheless has good hop flavors and bitterness.*

ORIGINAL PORTER: *12.25 °P/1.049 o.g., 5.2% ABV. Brewed with licorice root, it has a unique aroma of Concord grapes and roasted malt. Deep ruby brown in color, this porter is medium-bodied, well hopped, and dry, with a distinctive taste of roasted malt and the licorice root as used in porter two centuries ago.*

SPITFIRE PREMIUM ALE: *10.25 °P/1.041 o.g., 4.5% ABV. Rich, copper gold in color with a blast of hop aroma over malt. Impressively bitter and full of hop flavor, even by American microbrew standards. Finishes with a soft blend of caramel sweetness and dry bitterness. Spitfire was a gold medal winner in the 1994 Brewing Industry International Awards and at the U.S. Liquor Convention.*

BISHOP'S FINGER

MASTER BREW PREMIUM ALE

ORIGINAL PORTER

SPITFIRE ALE

BROUWERIJ SLAGHMUYLDER

DENDERHOUTEMBAAN 2, B-9400 NINOVE, BELGIUM
(32-54) 33-18-31

Situated in East Flanders near the Brabant border, the artisanal Brouwerij Slaghmuylder quietly produces a wide range of beers in limited quantities that are considered to be among Belgium's greatest. Its "Stimulo" is perhaps the best secular version of an Abbey pale ale. Its other abbey style beers are highly praised and are equally intricate and characterful.

BREW FACTS

FOUNDED: 1860

HEAD BREWER:
Michael Slaghmuylder

ANNUAL OUTPUT:
6,500 hectoliters

BREW STYLES: Dubbel, spiced ale, pale ale, pils

CONNOISSEUR'S RATING

WITKAP-PATER SINGEL
6% ABV

BROUWERIJ
ST. BERNARDUS

TRAPPISTENWEG 23, B-8978 WATOU-POPERINGE, BELGIUM
(32-57) 38-80-21

Nestled in the heart of the West Flanders "Le Plat Pays" hop growing region, the St. Bernardus brewery is named for the patron saint of Watou. Brouwerij St. Bernardus brewed licensed imitations of the Westvleteren Trappist beers for the nearby St. Sixtus Abbey until 1992, and, since that time, versions without the "St." attached to the name in Belgium and France. The brewery is most proud of the water it uses in brewing, which is pumped from a depth of nearly 500 feet. The well water is estimated to be rainwater that fell during Joan of Arc's time and has seeped down through the permeable sand strata.

The St. Bernardus beers are produced in the traditional Belgian top fermentation tradition, with three months of maturation before being bottled unfiltered with a fresh dose of yeast and sugar. The brewery recommends serving their beers at 54–59°F. The number designations in the names overleaf refer to the old Belgian brewing degrees and appear on the bottle cap.

BREW FACTS
FOUNDED: 1946
HEAD BREWER: Euy Clous
ANNUAL OUTPUT: 13,000 hectoliters
BREW STYLES: Strong ale, dubbel, tripel

TASTING NOTES

ST. SIXTUS ABT 12: *10% ABV. A dark Belgian strong ale with a hefty sweet nose of malt and fruit and a dominating sweetness from end to end. Finishes long, with a lingering syrupy aftertaste. Best served as a slowly-sipped nightcap.*

ST. SIXTUS PATER 6: *6% ABV. Deep brown to black in color with a heavy roasted malt and fruit aroma. Arguably this brewery's best offering. Well balanced, smooth, deeply complex, and satisfying. If you like your dubbels on the sweet side, this ripe fruit, chocolate, and coffee-flavored ale is for you. A classic dubbel.*

ST. SIXTUS PRIOR 8: *8% ABV. Sometimes classified as a dark tripel, this ruddy, idiosyncratic beer has some of the sharp, sour notes of a Flanders brown amidst a deep layering of malty sweetness, gently spicy hops, and fruit.*

ST. BERNARDUS TRIPEL: *7% ABV. A great example of the Belgian tripel style, softly melding sweet, dry, and bitter flavors. Golden amber in color, with a powerful fruity aroma. Well hopped, smooth, full, ripe, and complex.*

CONNOISSEUR'S RATING

ST. SIXTUS ABT 12

ST. SIXTUS PATER 6

ST. SIXTUS PRIOR 8

ST. BERNARDUS TRIPEL

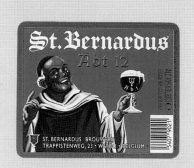

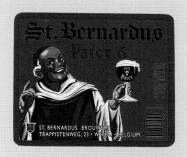

BIERBROUWERIJ ST. CHRISTOFFEL

14 BREDE WEG, 6042 GG ROERMOND, THE NETHERLANDS
(31–475) 341447

Named after the patron saint of Roermond, this tiny (15 hectoliter) brewery was founded by Leo Brand, a descendant of Edmond Brand, founder of the Netherlands' oldest and most important brewery. Because of the Brand Brewery's regional significance, Leo Brand decided to brew his own version of Dutch lager. His range of superior quality pilsners are regarded as some of the world's best, particularly his unfiltered Christoffel Blond.

BREW FACTS

FOUNDED: 1986

HEAD BREWER:
Leo Brand

ANNUAL OUTPUT:
4,000 hectoliters

BREW STYLES: Pilsner, Münchner lager

CONNOISSEUR'S RATING

CHRISTOFFEL BLOND
12 °P/1.048 o.g., 45 BU, 5% ABV

ST. STAN'S BREWERY

821 L STREET, MODESTO, CALIFORNIA 95354
(1-209) 524-2337

St. Stan's Brewing Company truly began in 1973, when Garith Helm and his wife, Romy, became interested in brewing German-style beers as a hobby after returning from a trip to Germany. After many experimental brews and several subsequent visits to Germany, they successfully produced an alt like those made in Düsseldorf. Encouraged by the reception given to their beers by friends, Romy and Garith built a modest brewery adjacent to their Modesto home.

BREW FACTS
FOUNDED: 1981
HEAD BREWER: Garith Helm
ANNUAL OUTPUT: 16,416 hectoliters
BREW STYLES: Düsseldorfer alt, wheat beer, pale ale, specialty beers

Construction of the 1,368-hectoliter brewery began in 1981 and was completed in 1984. The rapidly growing popularity of St. Stan's required the building of a new brewery in downtown Modesto in 1990. It now includes a gift shop, a 175-seat restaurant, and California's largest brewpub. What started as a tiny mom-and-pop operation with beer available only in kegs now produces beers in a variety of packages that are shipped throughout the U.S. and around the world.

St. Stan's alts are all produced in the Düsseldorfer altbier style; that is, with top-fermenting yeast and a warm primary fermentation followed by a cold maturation period to produce the smooth, rounded, character of a lager. St. Stan's alts are unpasteurized and, therefore, should be stored cold for maximum shelf life and flavor retention.

TASTING NOTES

AMBER ALT: *12 °P/1.048 o.g., 5.8% ABV. A nice Düsseldorf-style amber ale with a creamy, smooth malt flavor and just enough bitterness to balance. Bittered with Cascade and Fuggles hops; aroma hops are Cascade and Tettnang. Not as interesting as the dark version, this is still a solid beer to match with hearty foods. Silver medal winner in the 1995 World Beer Championships.*

DARK ALT: *13 °P/1.052 o.g., 6.2% ABV. Also in the Düsseldorfer style but with a higher ratio of caramel and chocolate malts in the grist. Fuggles and Bullion are used for bittering; Cascade hops for aroma. A dark, rich beer with full roast coffee and chocolate flavors and a smooth, malty finish. Perhaps America's best German-style alt. Gold medal winner in the 1995 World Beer Championships. A superlative example of the altbier style.*

RED SKY ALE: *12 °P/1.048 o.g., 5.6% ABV. Brewed from 98% barley malt/2% wheat malt. Fuggles and Tettnang hops are used for bitterness; Fuggles and Cascade hops for aroma. A red pale ale with a subtle sweetish flavor and crisp hop bitterness. The wheat aids head retention and adds a subtle, smooth dryness.*

CONNOISSEUR'S RATING

AMBER ALT	🍺🍺🍺
DARK ALT	🍺🍺🍺🍺🍺
RED SKY ALE	🍺🍺🍺

BRASSERIE ST. SYLVESTRE

1 RUE DE LA CHAPELLE, F-59114 ST. SYLVESTRE-CAPPEL, FRANCE
(33) 28-40-15-49

I n the heart of French Flanders hop growing country, three hills—Mont des Cats, Mont des Recollets, and Mont Cassel—surround the village of St. Sylvestre, where this artisanal farmhouse brewery is located. The products of Serge and Françoise Ricour are based on the beers brewed in a Trappist monastery outside the village many years ago and on the artistic methods taught to Remy Ricour when he took over operation of the brewery in 1918. All of their beers are of similar gravity to the flagship 3 Monts, with variations of hops, malt, and yeast. These beers might be pigeonholed into the bière de garde style category, but they are as individualistic as the products of their neighbors in Belgian Flanders to the north. All of these handcrafted beers are best served at cellar temperatures of 45–55°F.

St. Sylvestre also produces a seasonal bière de mars which, unlike the Mars "small beer" of Belgium that is brewed from the low gravity runoff of the mash, St. Sylvestre's is quite strong at 7.5% ABV and is available only in late winter, rather than in summer.

BREW FACTS

FOUNDED: 1918

HEAD BREWERS:
Serge Ricour and
François Ricour

ANNUAL OUTPUT:
22,000 hectoliters

BREW STYLES: Christmas beer, strong ale

TASTING NOTES

BIERE DE NOEL: *18.75 °P/ 1.075 o.g., 8.5% ABV. Labeled Flander's Winter Ale for the English-speaking market, this seasonal ale is top fermented and lagered for six weeks at 32°F. Ingredients include locally grown Munich malt and hops. Deep, coppery red in color with a lacy, tan head. Deeply aromatic with a mixture of fruit and hops over an earthy base. Feels sharply carbonated in the mouth, but develops to a smooth, fruity-malty palate with hints of cellar flavors and the dryness of hops. Finishes dryly with a lingering earthy aftertaste. Rounded, mature, and exquisitely balanced.*

3 MONTS: *18.75 °P/ 1.075 o.g., 8.5% ABV. Subtitled "Flanders Golden Ale," 3 Monts is top fermented and lagered for one month at 32°F. Ingredients include French spring malt, 51% French Flanders hops, and 49% German hops. A blond, aromatic beer of impressive, earthy character. Enjoy with full-flavored cheeses.*

3 MONTS GRAND RESERVE: *18.75 °P/ 1.075 o.g., 8.5% ABV. Top-fermented and lagered for one month at 32°F. Ingredients include French spring malt and German aromatic malts. Features a discreet earthiness, with estery notes of honey, apple, and cloves reminiscent of a Bavarian weissbier. The flavor is equally complex and earthy, with layers of hops, spice, and fruit. Brewed once in spring and once in fall, this cork-finished, bottle-conditioned classic is refermented in the bottle for three weeks. Suitable for laying down for months or even years.*

CONNOISSEUR'S RATING

BIERE DE NOEL

3 MONTS

3 MONTS GRAND RESERVE

STAROPRAMEN
BREWERY

NADRAZNI 84, 150 54 PRAGUE 5, CZECH REPUBLIC
(42-2) 245-91456

Acclaimed by the brewery as "Prague's favorite beer," Staropramen is at last gaining worldwide popularity after surviving Nazi occupation, two world wars, and forty years of communism. Bass Plc became a strategic partner of Staropramen's parent, Prague Breweries, in 1994 and is largely responsible for the current wide distribution of this Bohemian beer. Staropramen also produces a variety of other products, primarily for Czech and German markets.

BREW FACTS

FOUNDED: 1869

HEAD BREWER:
Information not available

ANNUAL OUTPUT:
1.1 million hectoliters

BREW STYLES: Pilsner, dark pilsner, alcohol-free, low-calorie, diät pils

CONNOISSEUR'S RATING

STAROPRAMEN
12 °P/1.048 o.g., 5.2% ABV

STOUDT'S
REAL BEER

P.O. BOX 880, ADAMSTOWN, PENNSYLVANIA 19501
(1–717) 484–4387

Carol Stoudt holds the distinct honor of being the first woman to oversee the design and development of an American microbrewery from start to finish. Her mission—"to provide fresh and authentic European style beers of the highest quality"—may seem like a promotional slogan dreamed up by a marketing department, until you look at her record. Carol Stoudt's beers have been awarded an amazing eighteen medals at the Great American Beer Festival since 1988.

BREW FACTS

FOUNDED: 1987

HEAD BREWER:
Carol Stoudt

ANNUAL OUTPUT:
10,260 hectoliters

BREW STYLES: Bock, mai bock, doppelbock, weizen, dubbel, tripel, fest, pils, export

Stoudt's beers are made in accordance with the Bavarian Reinheitsgebot and employ both infusion and decoction mashing. Ingredients of choice include pale, Munich, wheat, black, and chocolate malts; and Cluster, Hallertau, Tettnang, Cascade, and Saaz hops. Stoudt's beers are currently available only in a few eastern states. Hopefully, one day they will be available nationwide, because they are certainly among America's best.

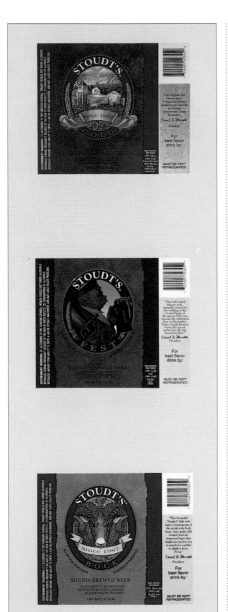

TASTING NOTES

FEST: *13 °P/1.052 o.g., 5% ABV. Deep copper gold in color with a rich head of foam meant to be coaxed with a vigorous pour. Its overall personality is of freshness, from the lush, caramel aroma to the long, malty palate and gently dry finish. Smooth, almost buttery in the mouth with the rich, satisfying maltiness and secondary hop bitterness intended for this style.*

GOLD: *13 °P/1.052 o.g., 5% ABV. Deep amber gold in color with an ample rocky head of foam that is equally full of hop and malt aromas. Smooth, full, and satisfying in palate, with a delicately sweet taste of malt on a nice foundation of hops that emerge quickly toward the finish. Dry and hop accented, but not bitter in the aftertaste. Wonderfully easy to quaff.*

HONEY DOUBLE MAI BOCK: *17 °P/ 1.068 o.g., 7% ABV. Deep, ruddy amber in color with an aroma of honeyish fruit, caramel, and flowery hops. Weighty and malty sweet in the mouth with a sharp attack of bitter hops. Slightly rough in the middle but a more rounded, mellow character appears toward the finish.*

CONNOISSEUR'S RATING

FEST

GOLD

HONEY DOUBLE MAI BOCK

STRAFFE HENDRIK

WALPEIN 26, B-8000 BRUGES, BELGIUM
(32-50) 33-26-97

This small home brewery in the heart of the historic town of Bruges produces but one beer in bottles and on draft. The brewery, whose name translates to "Strong Henry," has achieved a hoppy masterpiece through its concentration on a single product, and is destined to be regarded as a classic Belgian pale ale. Straffe Hendrik was taken over by the Riva Group in the late 1980s, instituting more uniform brewing practices and, recently, marketing this uncommonly characterful ale in the U.S.

BREW FACTS

FOUNDED: 1856

HEAD BREWER:

Lorenz Lambrecht

ANNUAL OUTPUT:

7,500 hectoliters

BREW STYLES:

Belgian pale ale

CONNOISSEUR'S RATING

BRUGSE STRAFFE HENDRIK
6% ABV

The manual bottle filler as used at the turn of the century.

FURSTLICHE BRAUEREI THURN UND TAXIS

15-17 HAUPTSTRASSE, 8306 SCHIERLING, BAVARIA, GERMANY
(49-941) 78460

The aristocratic Bavarian family Von Thurn und Taxis has a long and successful history in the brewing industry dating back to the end of the Napoleonic period. Thurn und Taxis lager brewing is centered in their home city of Regensburg, while their Roggenbier, which was introduced in 1988, is brewed in Schierling, in a brewery that traces its origins to a thirteenth-century convent. The colorful Thurn und Taxis family now controls a large brewing empire that has nonetheless managed to keep many small Bavarian brewery traditions intact.

BREW FACTS

FOUNDED: 1834

HEAD BREWER:

Werner Meyer

ANNUAL OUTPUT:

Figures not available

BREW STYLES: Rye beer, export, doppelbock, helles, märzen, weizen, dunkel, pilsner, alcohol-free

CONNOISSEUR'S RATING

SCHIERLINGER ROGGEN *12 °P/ 1.048 o.g., 15 IBU, 40–45 EBC, 5.2% ABV*

FÜRSTLICHE BRAUEREI

Thurn und Taxis

UNERTL
WEISSBIER

LERCHENBERGER STRASSE 6, 83527 HAAG I. O.B., GERMANY
(49–8072) 82 97

The origins of this small, family-run brewery east of Munich sprang from a brewpub founded by Franz Schissl in 1898. Today the brewery is owned by Alois Unertl. Although still tiny, with only twelve employees, the reputation of this wheat beer brewery is gargantuan. In August 1995, it was voted "The Best of the Best" among Bavarian wheat beer breweries by *Der Feinschmecker* magazine and has a loyal following across Germany.

BREW FACTS
FOUNDED: 1898
HEAD BREWER: Alois Unertl
ANNUAL OUTPUT: 20,000 hectoliters
BREW STYLES: Hefe-weizen, weizenbock, light weizen

The original brewpub (located next door) is now a popular restaurant and *gasthaus* serving Unertl's much-beloved beers. The popularity of these beers may be due to their individuality. They are less carbonated and maltier than the mass-market weissbiers of Munich. They are also darker in color, reflecting the traditional character of the weissbiers of the past. Unertl uses only organic Bavarian Hallertauer hops and Bavarian wheat and barley malts. They employ a single decoction mash and open fermentation.

LEICHTES WEISSE: *7.1 °P/1.028 o.g., 2.6% ABV. Paler and more like some of the major breweries' standard gravity wheats. Less characterful, obviously than Unertl's other superb beers, but above average among other low-calorie weissbiers.*

WEISSBIER: *11.2 °P/1.045 o.g., 4.9% ABV. Hazy, amber brown in color with a creamy head of off-white foam. Deep, richly sweet aromas of pear preserves, ripe bananas, and peppery spice carry through into the flavor profile. Tart, spritzy, and dry in the mouth with a smooth, fruity finish. Very full-bodied, individualistic, and fresh tasting. Dark and rich enough to straddle the line between dunkles and helles weissbiers in pairings with light summer meals and heartier German-style fare.*

WEISSER BOCK: *16.2 °P/1.065 o.g., 6.7% ABV. Auburn gold in color with an impressive head of foam that explodes with rich esters of cinnamon, cloves, apples, and nutmeg. The flavor is equally praiseworthy for its cornucopia of fruity, spicy, and malty depth. Develops slowly with a long, lingering finish of fruit and spice and eventual wheat dryness.*

CONNOISSEUR'S RATING

LEICHTES WEISSE

WEISSBIER

WEISSER BOCK

WARSTEINER
BRAUEREI

59564 WARSTEIN, GERMANY
(49–29) 02–88–0

W arsteiner has become widely available in the U.S. in recent years, due largely to an aggressive campaign by the brewery to distribute its products. Although Warsteiner strictly adheres to the Reinheitsgebot, even for beers exported to the U.S., it also heavily stresses modern technology and production volume, which probably accounts for the somewhat "industrial" image of its lagers. Nevertheless, theirs is an extremely well crafted version of a modern German "Premium Pilsner."

BREW FACTS

FOUNDED: 1753

HEAD BREWER:
Albert Cramer

ANNUAL OUTPUT:
7 million hectoliters

BREW STYLES: Pils, low-calorie, alcohol-free

CONNOISSEUR'S RATING

PREMIUM VERUM
11.25 °P / 1.045 o.g., 4.8% ABV

CHARLES WELLS LTD.

THE BREWERY, HAVELOCK ST., BEDFORD MK40 4LU, ENGLAND
(44-1234) 272766

The father of Charles Wells' childhood sweetheart can be thanked for the existence of this independent craft brewery. As the story goes, when the young sea captain Wells asked for the hand of Josephine Grimwade in the late 1860s, her father said that he would never let his daughter marry a man who would be away from home so much. It was then that Charles embarked on a long and successful career as a brewer, and the people of Bedford have been eternally grateful.

The brewery is still family owned four generations later, brewing from secret recipes dating back to 1876 and using water from the original well sunk by Charles Wells. Brewery output is restricted by the limited amount of water that can be drawn from that well in a given year, because it is believed that the exceptional purity of the water greatly affects the taste of their beers.

BREW FACTS

FOUNDED: 1876

HEAD BREWER:
Robert Knox

ANNUAL OUTPUT:
821,500 hectoliters

BREW STYLES: Bitter, IPA, strong ale

TASTING NOTES

BOMBARDIER PREMIUM BITTER: *10.5 °P/ 1.042 o.g., 4.3% ABV. Deep chestnut brown with golden highlights. Fruity, malty, nutty, and dry, this medium-bodied beer has a big, robust character that remains tightly organized from start to finish with a clean, fruity dryness and just a whiff of roasted malt.*

FARGO FULLY MATURED STRONG ALE: *12.5 °P/1.050 o.g., 5% ABV. A mouthful to say and to drink, this hearty brew seems bigger than it should be at 12.5 °P. It is richly aromatic with a pronounced fruity, woody-hoppy nose and a broad, earthy palate that is indeed fully mature in flavor. Develops with a lingering dryness rising to the surface toward the finish. Its only fault is that, like the Bombardier, it seems to lose its condition toward the end of the glass, becoming slightly thin in body.*

CONNOISSEUR'S RATING

BOMBARDIER PREMIUM BITTER

FARGO FULLY MATURED STRONG ALE

YAKIMA
BREWING & MALTING
COMPANY

1803 PRESSON PLACE, YAKIMA, WASHINGTON 98902
(1–509) 575–1900

I n 1981, at a wine tasting in Yakima, Washington, the homebrewed beers that Bert Grant offered to his friends won such raves that several of the tasters offered to finance a small microbrewery to brew his beers commercially. Unlike many of his craft brewing peers, Bert Grant was no homebrewing college student at the time, but had a thirty-six year career in brewing that included positions as chemist with Canadian Breweries, research director with Stroh's, and technical director with the major hop producer, S.S. Steiner. Grant has always placed a strong emphasis on overseeing the entire brewing process and on brewing beers that reflect his Scottish heritage, with a decidedly American twist reflected in a generous use of Cascade hops.

BREW FACTS

FOUNDED: 1981

HEAD BREWER:

Bert Grant

ANNUAL OUTPUT:

68,400 hectoliters

BREW STYLES: Mild, Scottish ale, spiced ale, American wheat beer, IPA, imperial stout, porter, fruit ale

TASTING NOTES

CELTIC ALE: *8.5 °P/1.034 o.g., 2.9% ABV. Not an "Irish Red" as the label might suggest, but a ninety-nine-calorie beer brewed to approximate more of a session mild than the watery light beers of the megabreweries. Medium-brown in color with a light malty profile and the fresh dryness of a solid hopping. Great as an all-round thirst quencher or as a cool-weather session beer, this beer doesn't impress at first in comparison to more assertive beers, but quickly grows on you.*

IMPERIAL STOUT: *16.8 °P/1.067 o.g., 6.3% ABV. Deep, almost opaque reddish brown. Immensely thick, creamy, and rich, this is deservedly one of Grant's most popular brews. Powerful, but restrained, and hopped well enough to make this incredibly drinkable—I once attended a beer festival in ninety-degree weather where this was the most popular entry.*

INDIA PALE ALE: *11.5 °P/1.046 o.g., 4.3% ABV. Bert Grant is largely credited with renewing interest in authentic versions of this style and his version has long been one of the best. Bright golden colored with a blast of Cascade hops in the aroma. A style tailor-made to Grant's regard for hops, this version is wonderfully refreshing, dry, and bitter, with hops dominating end to end.*

SCOTTISH ALE: *12.5 °P/1.050 o.g., 4.6% ABV. The flagship brew of this pioneering brewery has the creamy, caramel malt character of the Scottish versions, and is equally hearty and full bodied with a touch of fruity sweetness.*

CONNOISSEUR'S RATING

CELTIC ALE

IMPERIAL STOUT

INDIA PALE ALE

SCOTTISH ALE

RISING STARS

Abita Brewing Co., Inc. ● Brasal Brasserie Allemande ● Brasserie La Binchoise ● Brick Brewing Company ● Brooklyn Brewery ● Carlton & United Breweries ● Deschutes Brewery, Inc. ● Dixie Brewing Company ● Dock Street Brewing Company ● Full Sail Brewing Company ● Granville Island Brewing Company ● Great Lakes Brewing Company ● Braurei Heller-Trum, Schlenkerla ● Brasserie Jeanne d'Arc ● Schlossbrauerei Kaltenberg ● Lakefront Brewery ● Matilda Bay Brewing Co. ● La Brasserie McAuslan ● North Coast Brewing Company ● Otter Creek Brewing ● Pavichevich Brewing Company ● Summit Brewing Company ● Tooheys Pty. Limited ● Unibroue ● Upper Canada Brewing Company ● Weeping Radish ● Wellington County Brewery Ltd. ● Wild Goose Brewery ● Würzburger Hofbräu

ABITA
BREWING CO., INC.

P.O. BOX 762, ABITA SPRINGS, LOUISIANA 70420
(1-504) 893-3143

Situated across Lake Pontchartrain from New Orleans and the more famous Dixie Brewing, Louisiana's first microbrewery has quietly produced exceptional brews for more than a decade, progressing from the days of delivering fifty barrels a week in a pickup truck to their current distribution in more than a dozen states. Abita's range of European-influenced beers is only now gaining much-deserved acclaim.

Abita's beers are brewed in small, thirty-barrel batches from imported Munton and Fison malts, German yeasts, and primarily American hop varietals.

BREW FACTS

FOUNDED: 1986

HEAD BREWER: Jim Patton

ANNUAL OUTPUT: 41,040 hectoliters

BREW STYLES: Amber lager, Oktoberfest, porter, strong lager, American wheat, pale bock, fruit beer, pilsner, Christmas beer

TASTING NOTES

AMBER: *11 °P/1.044 o.g., 15 BU, 3.8% ABV. Fruity and nutty (pecans?) in aroma with a definite British character of crystal malt sweetness and balancing hop bitterness. Finishes rounded, smooth, and tangy with a sweetish, fruity finish. An excellent session lager or accompaniment to deep-fried seafood dishes and pecan pie.*

FALLFEST: *14 °P/1.056 o.g., 23 BU, 4.9% ABV. Features rich caramel malt and gentle hop aromas; a smooth, rounded malty flavor; and an equally smooth finish with a cleansing hop bitterness. Serve with traditional Oktoberfest cuisine and Louisiana Creole cooking.*

TURBODOG: *00 °P/1.054 o.g., 28 BU, 4.9% ABV. Brewed from an eclectic mix of British malts, American hops, and German alt yeast, the dry-hopped Turbodog is dark reddish brown in color with hints of chocolate malt and Willamette hops among an understated malty sweetness that develops toward a clean, dry finish. A nice blend of traditions suitable with Westphalian ham as well as steak and kidney pie or fish and chips.*

CONNOISSEUR'S RATING

AMBER

FALLFEST

TURBODOG

BRASAL BRASSERIE ALLEMANDE

8477 RUE CORDNER, VILLE LASALLE, MONTREAL, QUEBEC H8N 2N2, CANADA (1-514) 365-5050

Quebec's largest microbrewery was founded by the Jagermann family in 1989 in the city of LaSalle, Montreal. Brasal's four brews are decidedly German in flavor and are brewed under the Reinheitsgebot. This brewery has gained a host of accolades in the past two years after winning a string of major awards. Brasal also imports the highly regarded Clausthaler alcohol-free beer from Germany.

BREW FACTS

FOUNDED: 1989

HEAD BREWER:
Harald D. Sowade

ANNUAL OUTPUT:
10,000 hectoliters

BREW STYLES: Strong lager, bock, low-calorie, amber lager

TASTING NOTES

BOCK: *7.8% ABV. Contains three types of European two-row malt, three types of imported hops, and a Swiss yeast strain. Lagered for three months in oak barrels. Gold medal winner: 1994 Brewmaster's Best Awards, 1994 World Beer Championships, and 1995 California Beer Festival. Recommended pairings include roast duck, pizza and spicy foods, as well as desserts. Seasonal.*

HOPPS BRAU: *4.5% ABV. Serve between 45–50°F. The flagship brand of Brasal, Hopps Bräu is a medium golden lager with a malty-hoppy aroma with hints of vanilla and fruit. Mellow malt features strongly in the mouth, with a soft hop bitterness beneath that gives this the rounded feeling of a Bavarian helles. Finishes clean and dry with a faint bite of malt in the aftertaste and some resiny hops.*

LEGERE: *3.1% ABV. Burnished gold colored featuring a very full, malty-fruity aroma for a light beer, and a softly sweet, malty palate that is fairly thin. Becomes bittersweet toward the end,* with a faintly bitter aftertaste. It is hard to bring the same rich, fresh flavor of a standard-gravity microbrew to a low-calorie lager, but this does surprisingly well; better than most. One of the most flavorful light beers on the market.

SPECIAL AMBER: *6.1% ABV. Brewed from three types of two-row barley malt, four types of European hops, and Swiss lager yeast. Lagered six weeks. Smooth, rich, and malty, with a clean European flavor. Gold medal winner, 1994 Brewmaster's Best Awards and the 1995 World Beer Championships.*

CONNOISSEUR'S RATING

BOCK	🍺🍺🍺
HOPPS BRAU	🍺🍺🍺
LEGERE	🍺🍺🍺🍺
SPECIAL AMBER	🍺🍺🍺

BRASSERIE LA BINCHOISE

FAUBORG ST. PAUL 38, 7130 BINCHE, BELGIUM
(32-64) 33-61-86

This excellent brewery was established by an ardent homebrewer, André Graux, and his wife, Francoise, in 1988 in the village of Binche. Mr. Graux is the brewmaster and president of the brewery, his wife takes care of the administrative functions. A malting house from the eighteenth century was chosen as the site for the brewery, which sits atop the ramparts that once protected Binche during medieval times.

Binchoise employs just five people and is truly an artisanal brewery. It quickly became highly regarded in Belgium for its unique range of ales, and now that they are newly available in the U.S., will no doubt enjoy a loyal following here.

BREW FACTS

FOUNDED: 1988

HEAD BREWER: André Graux

ANNUAL OUTPUT: 700 hectoliters

BREW STYLES: Blond ale, brown ale, honey ale, Christmas ale

TASTING NOTES

BIERE DES OURS: *18 °P/1.072 o.g., 21 BU, 14 EBC, 8.5% ABV. The name translates to "Beer of Bears," in reference to that animal's favorite food, honey, which flavors this strong ale. Top-fermented, unfiltered, and unpasteurized; using pale malts, Kentish and Slovenian hops, and more than a pound of honey per case of twelve 750 ml/27 fl. oz champagne bottles. Hazy gold and incredibly light-bodied considering its strength, this intricate, bottle-conditioned ale is a style unto itself. Fruity, spicy, and pleasingly sweet in aroma and palate with an earthy and mature character that carries through to the dryish finish. Won a gold medal in the 1995 World Beer Championships. Serve in a Burgundy-style glass at 45–55°F with hearty game or lamb chops and with rich sauces and desserts.*

SPECIALE NOEL: *20 °P/1.080 o.g., 18 BU, 36 EBC, 9% ABV. A top-fermented, spiced Christmas ale produced in July for holiday enjoyment. Brewed from pale, Munich, and caramel malts; Kentish and Slovenian hops; and a selection of spices. This seasonal masterpiece features a reddish brown color; an explosion of spicy vanilla, apple, and nutmeg aromas and a very complex tapestry of every holiday spice imaginable, fruit, and caramel malt sweetness. Won a platinum medal in the 1995 World Beer Championships. Serve in a Burgundy-style glass at 50–55°F; with hearty yuletide feasts and highly spiced, seasonal desserts, or contemplatively by the fire on a snowy evening.*

CONNOISSEUR'S RATING

BIERE DES OURS

SPECIALE NOEL

BRICK
BREWING COMPANY

181 KING STREET SOUTH, WATERLOO, ONTARIO, CANADA
(1-519) 576-9100

Although Jim Brickman's dream of creating a small craft brewery was not realized until 1984, the odyssey began six years earlier with visits to sixty-eight breweries in twenty-nine countries around the world. The "little brewery that could" overcame innumerable obstacles to become Ontario's first micro, but now can enjoy the fruits of its perseverance. Brick has expanded six times since 1984, garnered twelve prestigious medals, and won a legion of loyal fans in eastern Canada.

BREW FACTS

FOUNDED: 1984

HEAD BREWER:
Perry Witt

ANNUAL OUTPUT:
60,000 hectoliters

BREW STYLES: Lager, bock, dunkel, light ale, pils, dry, American golden ale

CONNOISSEUR'S RATING

RED CAP ALE
5% ABV

PREMIUM LAGER
5% ABV

RED BARON
5% ABV

BROOKLYN BREWERY

79 NORTH 11TH STREET, BROOKLYN, NEW YORK 11211
(1-718) 486-7422

Brooklyn Brewery was founded in 1988 by Stephen Hindy and Tom Potter with its beers being brewed under contract by F.X. Matt in Utica, New York. After quickly garnering several medals at the Great American Beer Festival, it seemed only a matter of time before they would have their own brewhouse. Brooklyn Brewery's growth and development has been greatly assisted by the hiring in 1994 of Garrett Oliver as brewmaster. His Black Chocolate Stout causes scores of otherwise blasé New York beer lovers to feverishly horde cases of the seasonal holiday brew whenever it is released. The brewery seems poised to return Brooklyn, once one of America's most prolific brewing centers, to its rightful place of prominence.

BREW FACTS
FOUNDED: 1988
HEAD BREWER: Garrett Oliver
ANNUAL OUTPUT: Figures not available
BREW STYLES: Lager, brown ale, weizen, IPA, imperial stout

CONNOISSEUR'S RATING

BLACK CHOCOLATE STOUT
21.7 °P/ 1.087 o.g., 8.3% ABV

BROWN ALE
15.5 °P/ 1.062 o.g., 32 IBU, 5.5% ABV

EAST INDIA PALE ALE
17 °P/ 1.068 o.g., 40 IBU, 7.4% ABV

LAGER
12.5 °P/ 1.050 o.g., 4.5% ABV

CARLTON & UNITED
BREWERIES

77 SOUTHBANK BOULEVARD, SOUTHBANK, VICTORIA 3006, AUSTRALIA
(61-3) 9342 5511

Carlton & United Breweries (CUB) has its origins in Melbourne's old Carlton Brewery dating from the 19th century heyday of Australia's burgeoning brewing trade. When Carlton & United acquired Tooth's brewery, they obtained one of Australia's best. Tooth's is particularly famous for its dry Sheaf Stout, now gaining much deserved attention among craft beer connoisseurs. Today CUB is part of the Elders IXL group with Foster's as its main brand.

BREW FACTS

FOUNDED: 1907

HEAD BREWER:
Mel Miles

ANNUAL OUTPUT:
9 million hectoliters

BREW STYLES:
Lager, stout, bitter, pilsner

CONNOISSEUR'S RATING

SHEAF STOUT
14 °P/1.056 o.g., 5.7% ABV

DESCHUTES
BREWERY, INC.

1044 N.W. BOND STREET, BEND, OREGON 97701
(1-503) 382-9242

Originally founded by Gary Fish as a brewpub, Deschutes Brewery quickly caught the attention of a multitude of fans in America's microbrewery heartland. In the space of a year, public demand prompted Gary to begin distributing kegs of his handcrafted brew wholesale. Deschutes has grown steadily ever since, with a recently completed facility now in place to accommodate this microbrewery's meteoric rise and to allow bottling of some of Deschutes award-winning beers. Deschutes ales are unfiltered, cold-conditioned variations of classic English-style ales with a Pacific Northwest accent.

BREW FACTS

FOUNDED: 1988

HEAD BREWERS:

Mark Vickery and Bill Pengelly

ANNUAL OUTPUT:

27,360 hectoliters

BREW STYLES: Best bitter, porter, stout, holiday strong ale, golden ale

TASTING NOTES

BACHELOR BITTER: *12 °P/1.048 o.g., 5% ABV. A copper-colored, British-style best bitter. Dry hopped with Kent Goldings for an explosion of hop aroma. Features full-bodied maltiness with a classic, bitter hop foundation developing quickly and leading to a dry finish.*

CASCADE GOLDEN ALE: *10.5 °P/1.042 o.g., 4.1% ABV. Intended as a "transition beer" for those first venturing into the craft brew world. Golden, crisp, and light bodied. Not unlike a cream ale, a nice summer refresher or accompaniment to pub grub.*

JUBELALE: *(seasonal) 16.25 °P/1.065 o.g., 6.5% ABV. This Great American Beer Festival gold medal winner is brewed in the true English "winter warmer" style (unfortunately, most modern winter warmers are now standard strength in England). Big malt body proceeds to a powerful hop finish.*

MIRROR POND PALE ALE: *(seasonal) 12.5 °P/ 1.050 o.g., 5.3% ABV. Copper gold in color, with a pronounced Cascade aroma from dry hopping. Nicely balanced malt underpinning and crisp hop presence. The 1990 Great American Beer Festival bronze medal winner.*

OBSIDIAN STOUT: *(seasonal) 16.25 °P/ 1.065 o.g., 6.9% ABV. Named after the glassy, black volcanic rock, Obsidian bears the hallmarks of a rich, chewy, and rounded sweet stout. Deep, dark, and satisfying.*

CONNOISSEUR'S RATING

BACHELOR BITTER

CASCADE GOLDEN ALE

JUBELALE

MIRROR POND PALE ALE

OBSIDIAN STOUT

DIXIE
BREWING COMPANY

2537 TULANE AVENUE, NEW ORLEANS, LOUISIANA 70119
(1-504) 822-8711

When this icon of New Orleans culture and cuisine was founded, there were ten local breweries thriving in the Crescent City; today it is the only survivor. Dixie made it through Prohibition by producing ice cream, soft drinks, and a near-beer called "Dixo." It flourished during the depression years before toughing out World War II rationing. Dixie beers are similarly handcrafted today, and aged in the brewery's original Louisiana cypress wood tanks.

BREW FACTS

FOUNDED: 1907

HEAD BREWER:
Kevin Stuart

ANNUAL OUTPUT:
82,080 hectoliters

BREW STYLES: Dark lager, American premium lager, light, American amber ale

Considering that this Southern landmark was founded on October 31, 1907, it's hard to imagine why it took so long for them to produce a beer with such a decidedly Halloween image as their Blackened Voodoo. In any event, the groups in Texas who tried to ban this beer should know that this dark lager pays more tribute to the brewery's German immigrant founders than to that infamous night of mischief.

TASTING NOTES

BLACKENED VOODOO: *13 °P/1.052 o.g., 5% ABV. Brewed from five malts and Cascade and Mt. Hood hops. Ruby brown in color with a fast-fading head. Features a very light malt aroma, a medium-to-light body, and a slightly sour tang in flavor. A lively mouthfeel compensates for the thin head and brings out subtly sweet molasses and malt flavors and balances a smooth oiliness that develops toward the finish. Michael Jackson has compared it to a Bavarian Kulmbacher; it doesn't fit easily into either the Munchner dunkel or the schwarzbier category even though it has qualities of both. Despite its ominous packaging and dark color, it is understated enough to pair with the classic Cajun crawfish, chicken and fish dishes, especially spicier entrées such as blackened redfish. The 1995 Great American Beer Festival silver medal winner.*

DIXIE BEER: *11 °P/1.044 o.g., 4.5% ABV. Brewed from American barley malt, Louisiana rice, and Cascade and Cluster hops. Pale gold in color with an above-average presence of malt and hop aromas for an entry in the American Premium Lager category. The same can be said for the flavor, which is nicely balanced between hops and malt, with a subdued, dryish rice character. Serve as a warm-weather thirst quencher or with lighter pub grub and Creole/Cajun fare.*

JAZZ AMBER LIGHT: *7 °P/1.028 o.g., 3.25% ABV. Pale, bright amber in color with mellow rounded aromas of fruitiness and hops. Surprisingly full of "real beer" character for a light beer, with subtle caramel malt sweetness beneath a fresh hops presence. If for some reason you must drink light beer, this is one of the best. The 1987 Great American Beer Festival silver medal winner. Serve as a light thirst quencher and with appetizer courses and salads.*

CONNOISSEUR'S RATING

BLACKENED VOODOO

DIXIE BEER

JAZZ AMBER LIGHT

DOCK STREET
BREWING COMPANY

TWO LOGAN SQUARE, 18TH AND CHERRY STREETS, PHILADELPHIA, PENNSYLVANIA 19103 (1-215) 496-0413

Dock Street president Jeffrey D. Ware had always been different. In his youth, he sought out expensive bottles of imported English ales while his friends were buying cheap, megabrewery suds by the case. When Jeff learned of the British consumerist movement CAMRA, he decided that Philadelphians, too, would appreciate good beer if given the opportunity to experience it. Unlike a majority of his contemporaries, who had backgrounds in engineering before entering the brewing world, Jeff was an artist and a chef. That experience undoubtedly lead to the great success of the Dock Street Brewery and Restaurant in Philadelphia and the decision to open up a sister restaurant/brewery in Washington, D.C., in 1995.

BREW FACTS

FOUNDED: 1986

HEAD BREWER:
Bill Moeller

ANNUAL OUTPUT:
34,200 hectoliters

BREW STYLES: Amber ale, pilsner, doppelbock

TASTING NOTES

AMBER BEER: *12.75 °P/ 1.051 o.g., 27 BU, 5.3% ABV. Brewed from two-row pale and caramel malts and Cascade hops. Dry hopping gives this beer a great hoppy nose. Its flavor is full bodied, fruity, and complex with a subtle, smooth finish. Won "Monde Selection" gold medals in 1992, 1993, 1994, and 1995. Recommended with smoked fish, clams, steamed mussels, mushrooms, or sharp cheeses.*

BOHEMIAN PILSNER: *12.75 °P/ 1.051 o.g., 26 BU, 5.3% ABV. Expensive imported Hallertau, Saaz, and Zatec hops are largely responsible for this beer's resemblance to the authentic Bohemian Pilsners. Hazy gold in color, with the spicy, mellow aroma of European hops. Features a soft, layered palate of malt and hop bitterness. Finishes dryly with a lingering flavor of hops. "Monde Selection" gold medal winner, 1994; silver medal winner, 1995. Serve with such light, but flavorful dishes as lobster, paella, weisswurst, and chicken.*

ILLUMINATOR: *18.25 °P/ 1.073 o.g., 30 BU, 7.5% ABV. Deep ruby brown in color with a dense, rocky head, and aromas of malt and hops. Rounded maltiness with flavors of chocolate, caramel, and coffee that are balanced by Tettnang and Hallertau hops. Recommended with pâté, roast pork, sirloin, and rich desserts such as chocolate mousse.*

CONNOISSEUR'S RATING

DOCK STREET AMBER

DOCK STREET BOHEMIAN PILSNER

ILLUMINATOR

FULL SAIL
BREWING COMPANY

506 COLUMBIA STREET, HOOD RIVER, OREGON 97031
(1-503) 386-2281

Founded by Irene Firmat, Jerome Chicvara, and Margaret Roland in a renovated portion of the historic Diamond Fruit Cannery, this brewery and its products' names pay homage to the world-class windsurfing just beyond its main facility on the wild waters of the Columbia River. Brewing since 1987, Full Sail was Oregon's first modern craft brewery to bottle its products, and has since developed something of a cult following on the West Coast from Portland to San Diego for its fruity malt ales.

BREW FACTS

FOUNDED: 1987

HEAD BREWERS:

James L. Emmerson and John Harris

ANNUAL OUTPUT:

116,280 hectoliters

BREW STYLES: Golden ale, pilsner, stout, porter, winter ale, nut brown ale, IPA, ESB, barley wine, American amber ale, Oktoberfest

TASTING NOTES

AMBER ALE: *14 °P/1.056 o.g., 37 BU, 5.9% ABV. Solidly in the classic Pacific Northwest tradition of fruity, malty, and hoppy ales. This reddish brown beer's best feature is its immense perfumey nose that is itself intoxicating. Features a huge freshness of flavor with a clean, nutty sweetness gently surrendering to mellow hop bitterness and resiny flavor. A perfect example of American amber. The 1989 Great American Beer Festival gold medal winner.*

GOLDEN ALE: *12 °P/1.044 o.g., 31 BU, 4.4% ABV. Rich, bright gold in color, malty and lemony in aroma. Velvety-smooth in the mouth with a bright, hoppy flavor beneath a broad, grainy maltiness. Overall, a nicely woven personality of hops and malt with sweet, perfumey floral notes. Silver medal, 1995 World Beer Championships.*

WASSAIL WINTER ALE: *12 °P/1.044 o.g., 40 BU, 6.5% ABV. Reddish brown in color with a lacy, tan head. Subdued, but very well balanced; characterful and rounded in flavor, featuring interlaced flavors of hops, caramel, and coffeeish roasted malt. Ends with a touch of understated sweetness and a lingering dryness. Silver medal, 1995 World Beer Championships.*

CONNOISSEUR'S RATING

AMBER ALE	🍾🍾🍾
GOLDEN ALE	🍾🍾🍾
WASSAIL WINTER ALE	🍾🍾🍾🍾

GRANVILLE ISLAND
BREWING COMPANY

1285 WEST BROADWAY, #214, GRANVILLE ISLAND, VANCOUVER, BRITISH COLUMBIA V6H 3X8, CANADA (1–604) 738–9463

The brainchild of Vancouver businessman Mitch Taylor, Canada's first microbrewery was founded in the upscale shopping and artist community after a two-year fight to change Canadian microbrewery bottling laws. The premier brew, Island Lager, was an immediate success, leading the way to ten years of growth and expansion. This brewery's beers are brewed in accordance with the Reinheitsgebot, using step infusion mashing and a four-week maturation period for their lagers.

BREW FACTS

FOUNDED: 1984

HEAD BREWERS:

Joe Goetz and
Nick Bennet

ANNUAL OUTPUT:

50,000 hectoliters

BREW STYLES: Helles lager, pale ale, Irish-style ale, bock, low-calorie

CONNOISSEUR'S RATING

ANNIVERSARY AMBER ALE	🍺🍺🍺🍺
ISLAND BOCK	🍺🍺🍺
ISLAND LAGER	🍺🍺🍺
LORD GRANVILLE PALE ALE	🍺🍺🍺🍺

TASTING NOTES

ANNIVERSARY AMBER ALE: *13 °P/ 1.052 o.g., 5.5% ABV. Ingredients include Canadian two-row Harrington, English Carastan, and roasted black malts; Willamette, Spalt, and Tettnang hops. More assertive in flavor than the pale ale, the deep copper amber features the same perfectly balanced fresh malt sweetness and clean finish. Full of flavors of fruit, caramel candy, and nuts, this "Irish-style" ale has the reddish color and comforting maltiness of the originals, and with great depth of character. Bronze medal winner, 1995 World Beer Championships. Pair with Tex-Mex, Thai, Cajun, and Szechuan cuisines.*

ISLAND BOCK: *16.5 °P/1.066 o.g., 6.5% ABV. Ingredients include Canadian two-row Harrington, English Carastan, and roasted black malts; Willamette, Spalt, and Tettnang hops. Dark, reddish brown in color with a voluminous, creamy head of persistent foam. Surprisingly light in body and easily drinkable, with a pronounced sweetness held in check by a good backdrop of hops. Soft, smooth, and well produced. Serve with grilled or roasted beef and stir-fried chicken or pork dishes.*

ISLAND LAGER: *11.5 °P/1.046 o.g., 5% ABV. Ingredients include Canadian two-row Harrington malts; Willamette, Spalt, Hallertau, and Tettnang hops. Pale gold in color with a rocky dense head. Subdued, mellow aroma of a helles-style lager. A good smack of hop bitterness leads to a rounded maltiness and a clean finish with a lingering malt aftertaste. Silver medal winner, 1995 World Beer Championships. Recommended with chicken, tomato-based pasta dishes, and fish.*

LORD GRANVILLE PALE ALE: *12 °P/ 1.048 o.g., 5% ABV. Ingredients include Canadian two-row Harrington, English Carastan, and roasted black malts; and Willamette and German Tettnang hops. Deep copper gold with a fresh, herbal, fruity aroma of hops and roasted malt. An extremely smooth, distinguished, and mellow pale ale with the sweet caramel notes of the Scottish style, but with a much cleaner, drier finish. Very well done. Recommended with Asian fare, venison, lamb, and salads.*

GREAT LAKES
BREWING COMPANY

2516 MARKET STREET, CLEVELAND, OHIO 44113
(1-216) 771-2490

Acclaimed as the Best Microbrewery of the Year in 1994 by the Beverage Testing Institute, Great Lakes Brewing Company typifies the new spirit of pride that exists in Cleveland. Great Lakes' beers are beyond doubt some of America's best, simultaneously conquering beer styles as diverse as dortmunder, porter, Vienna, IPA, Belgian white, and Scotch ale, and winning major awards with each.

In a story that is repeated in successful craft breweries worldwide, Cleveland's first microbrewery was the product of two well-traveled homebrewers, Dan and Pat Conway, who left secure career paths to leap over the edge into professional brewing. Their skill and courage have now been amply rewarded in the critical acclaim they've received.

BREW FACTS

FOUNDED: 1988

HEAD BREWERS:
Thaine Johnson,
Andy Tveekrem, and
Mark Richmond

ANNUAL OUTPUT:
16,416 hectoliters

BREW STYLES: Bitter, pilsner, dortmunder, porter, winter warmer, Irish ale, strong ale, Belgian ale, Scotch ale, brown ale, spiced ale, IPA, Vienna

TASTING NOTES

THE COMMODORE PERRY INDIA PALE ALE: *16 °P/1.064 o.g., 80 BU, 6.9% ABV. Pale gold, with a malty complexity balanced by a massive hop bitterness and overall dryness provided by Galena hops. Medium- to full-bodied and assertive, this beer best complements robust flavors associated with red meat and strong cheeses. The 1991 Great American Beer Festival bronze medal winner.*

DORTMUNDER GOLD: *14 °P/1.056 o.g., 25 BU, 5.4% ABV. True to style, this golden amber lager is drier than a helles, but maltier than a pils. Finely balanced malt sweetness and drying hop bitterness develop to a cleansing, dry finish with subtle aftertastes of mellow malt. Serve as a quaffing beer and with pasta salads, broiled fish, or barbequed chicken. Gold medal, 1990 Great American Beer Festival. Gold medal, 1995 World Beer Championships.*

EDMUND FITZGERALD PORTER: *15 °P/1.060 o.g., 60 BU, 5.9% ABV. Dark reddish brown in color and full of robust chocolate, roasted malt, and coffee aromas. Medium-bodied and dry with a well organized development of complex malt, roast, and bitter flavors that carry over into the dry finish. Serve at 52°F with barbequed ribs, oysters, smoked meats and cheeses, or with rich chocolate desserts. Gold medal, 1993/1991 Great American Beer Festival. Platinum medal, 1995 World Beer Championships.*

THE ELIOT NESS: *14 °P/1.056 o.g., 35 BU, 5.4% ABV. Brewed from two-row, Munich, and caramel malts; and Hallertau and Tettnang hops. Reddish amber in color with a pronounced malt aroma and flavor above a firm base of German hop bitterness. Rich, smooth, and full of specialty-malt roundness in body. Goes well with spicy foods, pork, and chicken, as well as traditional German fare. Silver medal, 1995 World Beer Championships.*

THE MOON DOG ALE: *12.5 °P/1.050 o.g., 55 BU, 5% ABV. Pale copper colored, dry, and well hopped in the classic English bitter style, with generous additions of Northern Brewer and Kent Goldings hops. Serve as an aperitif or warm-weather refresher. The 1994 and 1995 gold medal winner in the World Beer Championships; 1991 Great American Beer Festival gold medal winner.*

CONNOISSEUR'S RATING

THE COMMODORE PERRY IPA	🍺🍺🍺
DORTMUNDER GOLD	🍺🍺🍺🍺
EDMUND FITZGERALD PORTER	🍺🍺🍺🍺
THE ELIOT NESS	🍺🍺🍺
THE MOON DOG ALE	🍺🍺🍺🍺

BRAUEREI HELLER-TRUM, SCHLENKERLA

6 DOMINIKANER STRASSE, 8600 BAMBERG, GERMANY
(49–951) 56060

Before the development of modern malt kilns, many beers—such as the brown beers of the Bavarian monasteries and the brown ales of England—had distinct smoky notes because their malts were dried over oak or beechwood fires. Today, beers with a smoky flavor and aroma have found a renewed following in the craft beer renaissance.

A world-class smoked beer has its origins in the Schlenkerla Tavern in Bamberg. The Heller family were early tenants; the current owners, the Trums, have been there five generations. From the early days, the beer was taken to nearby caves for lagering. The classic brewhouse at Schlenkerla is gleaming and pristine copper with brass rails, white-tiled walls, and a quarried tile floor. The beer is now lagered in cellars beneath the brewery. Despite its recent entry into the U.S. market in April 1995, Schlenkerla Rauchbier has gained a wide acceptance among craft beer connoisseurs and was a silver medal winner in the 1995 World Beer Championships.

BREW FACTS

FOUNDED: 1678

HEAD BREWER:
German Trum

ANNUAL OUTPUT:
Figures not available

BREW STYLES: Märzen rauchbier, bock, helles

CONNOISSEUR'S RATING

AECHT SCHLENKERLA RAUCHBIER *13.5 °P/1.054 o.g., 29–32 BU, 52 EBC, 4.9% ABV*

BRASSERIE
JEANNE D'ARC

38 RUE ANATOLE FRANCE, 59790 RONCHIN/LILLE, FRANCE
(33) 20-53-62-85

In 1898, a Monsieur Van Damme created the Brasserie Jeanne d'Arc in a small town famous for the purity of its well water, which was well suited to brewing beer. This small town, Ronchin, is located near Lille, capital city of French Flanders. The well VanDamme sank in 1898 is still being used for today's beers.

After the 1930s, the Brasserie Jeanne d'Arc became more regional in scope, recently expanding into foreign markets. It is now the fourth-largest brewery in northern France, but still remains strongly traditional, with family ownership and only eight employees. Its current owner, Dominique LeClercq, grew up in this family brewery, working his way up through a variety of technical positions to become chairman in 1991.

Because the two beers described here have been filtered, they are not intended for laying down and should be consumed by the date noted on the label. Serve both at 46–50°F.

BREW FACTS
FOUNDED: 1898
HEAD BREWER: René LeBec
ANNUAL OUTPUT: 102,000 hectoliters
BREW STYLES: Bière de mars, bière de garde, Scotch ale, Christmas ale, lager

TASTING NOTES

AMBRE DES FLANDRES: *16 °P/1.064 o.g., 22 BU, 40 EBC, 6.4% ABV. Brewed from Vienna malt, caramel malts, and French six-row winter barley from Gatinais and Flanders; Styrian, Saaz, and Brewers Gold hops; spring water; and lager yeast. Deep red in color with amber highlights and a spicy hop and nutty malt aroma reminiscent of a Bavarian märzen. Richly malty and earthy in flavor with a smooth, well-matured character and a clean, faintly sweet finish. Serve with hearty roasted fowl dishes, baked squash, wild rice, and freshly baked breads and soft cheeses.*

GRAIN D'ORGE: *21 °P/1.084 o.g., 20 BU, 13 EBC, 8% ABV. Brewed from three varieties of aroma hops and three malts, this beer calls itself a "Blond Beer of Flanders" but bears strong similarities to a Belgian Tripel. It is richly golden in color, with lush hop and soft fruity aromas. Features a full, clean maltiness backed by a rounded hop bitterness, developing to a sweet, lingering finish. Serve with any variety of fresh fish and seafood dishes, sharp cheeses, and fresh fruits, or light, but well seasoned chicken and pasta dishes.*

CONNOISSEUR'S RATING

AMBRE DES FLANDRES

GRAIN D'ORGE

SCHLOSSBRAUEREI KALTENBERG

AUGSBURGER STRASSE 41, 82256 FURSTENFELDBRUCK, GERMANY
(49–81 41) 2 43–0

The most unique aspect of this "Schlossbrauerei" is not the castle that forms the heart of the brewery, but rather its charismatic director, Prinz Luitpold, the great-grandson of Bavaria's last king. Prinz Luitpold's emphasis on quality and tradition, as well as his acute marketing savvy, have made Kaltenberg a major player in the craft beer renaissance in Germany and a tenacious competitor of the large, entrenched Munich breweries since he took over the brewery in 1976. The Kaltenberg Brewery is actually composed of two breweries: one at the fairy-tale Kaltenberg Castle, and a more modern one nearby in Fürstenfeldbruck. The brewery strictly supervises the production of the malt, hops, and yeast used in its beers. Kaltenberg has an extensive range of beers in three major brand categories, spearheaded by the selections detailed below.

BREW FACTS

FOUNDED: 1872

HEAD BREWER: Dieter Heiner

ANNUAL OUTPUT: Figures not available

BREW STYLES: Weissbiers, dunkel lager, pils, fest, seasonal lagers

KALTENBERG PILS: *11.7 °P/1.047 o.g., 5% ABV. The flagship brand of a range of pale lagers brewed by Kaltenberg that includes a Diät-Pils that is very popular in Britain. Along the lines of many mainstream pils found throughout southern Germany, although it is much fresher-tasting than most. Well constructed, with an initial maltiness giving way to a dominant hoppy dryness. Finishes clean and exceptionally dry.*

KONIG LUDWIG DUNKEL: *13.3 °P/ 1.053 o.g., 5.6% ABV. Brewed from Munich malt and triple decoction mashed. Darker and richer than the typical Munich dunkel, Kaltenberg's version is robust with firm bitterness and malty complexity. Impressively lively, fresh, and bold, this is justifiably one of the leaders in the reemergence of Bavaria's dark lagers.*

PRINZREGENT LUITPOLD WEISSBIER: *12.5 °P/1.050 o.g., 5.6% ABV. An incredibly aromatic, full-bodied wheat beer with volumes of fresh fruit and citrus aroma. Bittersweet in palate, with immense fruitiness and tart, balancing dryness that carries through to the dry, lemony finish. Like Kaltenberg's other products, this far exceeds many of its competitors with its lively, fresh taste.*

KALTENBERG PILS

KONIG LUDWIG DUNKEL

PRINZREGENT LUITPOLD WEISSBIER

LAKEFRONT BREWERY

818A EAST CHAMBERS STREET, MILWAUKEE, WISCONSIN 53212
(1-414) 372-8800

Milwaukee's only microbrewery is run by two brothers who once held homebrewing contests to determine who was the better brewer. This sibling rivalry eventually lead to today's successful commercial enterprise. Young and short of cash, the brothers patched together what they called the "Frankenstein operation" in an old bakery in the Riverwest neighborhood of Milwaukee in 1987, while enduring the drudgery of full-time, nine-to-five jobs.

BREW FACTS

FOUNDED: 1987

HEAD BREWERS:

Russell Klisch and Jim Klisch

ANNUAL OUTPUT:

2,736 hectoliters

BREW STYLES: Bock, Vienna, pilsner, pale ale

You've got to be on your toes with the Lakefront beer names, especially if you're a pedantic student of styles. Its Stein beer is classified by the brewery as a Vienna, but has the strength of a märzen; its Dark is actually a bock; and its Cream City may make you think of Genessee, not Young's, its closer relative. Lakefront's eye-catching labels are designed by noted homebrewing author Randy Mosher.

TASTING NOTES

CREAM CITY PALE ALE: *15 °P/1.060 o.g., 6% ABV.* Brewed from two-row, Munich, and carapils malts; Nugget and Cluster hops; and Wyeast Special London yeast. Dry hopped with Cascade hops. Lakefront's version is beautifully balanced, with a massive hop and fruit bouquet, firm, nutty maltiness, and assertive hop bitterness giving way to a very dry finish, and a gentle fruitiness in the aftertaste. Serve with hearty foods from the British Isles or with robust and spicy American-style pizzas, spaghetti, or grilled steaks.

EAST SIDE DARK: *15 °P/1.060 o.g., 6% ABV.* Brewed from two-row, Munich, black patent, and chocolate malts; Mt. Hood hops; and Schmitt 118 yeast. Dry in character with a rich, roast aroma and a chocolatey, coffeeish palate with a touch of sourness. The maltiness is very nicely balanced by a rounded hop bitterness and a dryish, roasty aftertaste. Winner of the 1992 First Place award, All-American Tasting of the Chicago Beer Society. A great match for German wursts or Polish kielbasa.

KLISCH PILSNER BEER: *15 °P/1.060 o.g., 6% ABV.* Brewed from two-row barley malts, Mt. Hood hops, and Schmitt 118 yeast. Hazy, lemony gold in color with the subtle hop and fruity malt aroma. An exceptionally clean, well balanced, and malt-accented lager with a fresh, satisfying malt sweetness and clean, light finish. Very good, but I'd call it a helles. A good, thirst-quenching quaffing beer to be served with hearty Bavarian or Polish foods or with spicy pepperoni pizza, pit-cooked barbeque, and buffalo wings.

RIVERWEST STEIN BEER: *15 °P/1.060 o.g., 6% ABV.* Brewed from roasted barley, two-row, Munich, and cara-pils malts; Mt. Hood and Cascade hops; and Schmitt 118 yeast. Auburn colored with a lush, rocky head of off-white foam that exudes a flowery, caramel-accented aroma. Malty and well organized with a clean dryness being the most noticeable quality. Ends with a dry fruitiness and a faint tinge of malt sweetness and sourness in the aftertaste. The 1991 Great American Beer Festival bronze medal winner.

CONNOISSEUR'S RATING

CREAM CITY PALE ALE	🍺🍺🍺🍺
EAST SIDE DARK	🍺🍺
KLISCH PILSNER BEER	🍺🍺🍺
RIVERWEST STEIN BEER	🍺🍺🍺

MATILDA BAY
BREWING CO.

130 STIRLING HIGHWAY, NORTH FREMANTLE, WESTERN AUSTRALIA
6159, AUSTRALIA
(61-9) 430-6222

Founded by a former brewer for the The Swan Brewery Company, Philip Sexton, Matilda Bay microbrewery was born out of the success of The Sail and Anchor Pub Brewery which were founded in 1984. Their aim was to elevate the image of, and interest in beer, and to brew traditional ales, stouts, and lagers which were styles that had been previously neglected in Australia. Matilda Bay's greatest success and world renown stems from its Red Back Original—a beer never before produced in Australia. Red Back is reminiscent of a South German weizenbier with a 50:50 ratio of wheat to barley malts. As a concession to the longstanding Australian brewing tradition, locally grown Pride of Ringwood hops are used, in addition to imported Saazer. The Sail and Anchor's brewpub in Fremantle was Australia's first and produces a variety of traditional English ales and a highly regarded sweet stout. Expansion and upgrading of their plant took place in 1994, and in July of that year, the brewery was selected in the Australian Best Practice Demonstration Program.

BREW FACTS

FOUNDED: 1984

HEAD BREWER: Information not available

ANNUAL OUTPUT: 450,000 hectoliters

BREW STYLES: Wheat beer, pils, dark lager

CONNOISSEUR'S RATING

RED BACK ORIGINAL
11.25 °P/1.045 o.g., 4.7% ABV

LA BRASSSERIE McAUSLAN

4850 ST. AMBROISE, #100, MONTREAL, QUEBEC H4C 3N8, CANADA
(1-514) 939-3060

After two years of planning and building, Peter McAuslan's brewery began operating in January 1989, and released its first beer a month later. With famed British brewmaster Alan Pugsley formulating the recipe, St. Ambroise Pale Ale was an immediate success. In four short years, Peter McAuslan released three new beers and saw his brewery mirror the phenomenal success of North American microbrewing as a whole.

McAuslan's St. Ambroise line is named for Frère Ambroise of the Sulpician Order, a religious order that was granted the territory of Montreal by King Louis XIII of France. Brother Ambroise is reputed to have been the first brewer on the island of Montreal.

BREW FACTS

FOUNDED: 1988

HEAD BREWER:
Ellen Bounsall

ANNUAL OUTPUT:
14,000 hectoliters

BREW STYLES: Pale ale, oatmeal stout, brown ale, Canadian golden ale

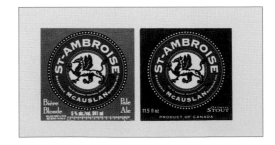

GRIFFON BROWN ALE: *12 °P/1.048 o.g., 25 BU, 4.5% ABV. Brewed from two-row Canadian barley malt, torrefied wheat, and imported Carastan malt and roasted barley. Hops include Tettnang, Willamette, and Kent Goldings. Mahogany brown in color with a rich roasted barley and hops aroma. Complex, full-bodied, and moderately sweet in the mouth with a clean wheat and hops dryness and a long hoppy finish. Serve at 52–60°F with roast beef, lamb, and sharp English cheeses.*

GRIFFON EXTRA PALE ALE: *12.5 °P/ 1.050 o.g., 24 BU, 5% ABV. Bright gold color with a large, creamy white head of mixed bubbles that leaves a nice lace. Flowery citrus aroma of fresh hops. Features a dry, tart, and hoppy start that develops to a fruity, rounded, and sweet maltiness that could be more assertive, and a dryish finish with a quick hop aftertaste. Serve at 42–47°F with fish and lightly spiced meals.*

ST. AMBROISE PALE ALE: *12.25 °P/ 1.049 o.g., 32 BU, 5% ABV. Reddish gold in color, with a citrusy hop bouquet. Robustly malty and gently sweet in front, but with the fresh and clean character that is the trademark of Cascade hopping. Full-bodied and flavorful enough to serve at 50°F with the heartiest of meals.*

ST AMBROISE OATMEAL STOUT: *16.25 °P/1.065 o.g., 37 BU, 5.5% ABV. Rich black in color with a nose of roasted malt, perfumey fruitiness, and roasted malt. Features an idiosyncratic roasted, almost burnt black malt taste and a smooth, oily mouthfeel. The underlying malt sweetness and the softness contributed by the oats offset the dry, espresso-like malt character, making this "Biere Noire" complex and extremely drinkable. This beer confounds at first, but soon wins you over. I give this beer the highest rating simply for its uniqueness. Serve at 55–65°F with dark chocolate desserts.*

GRIFFON BROWN ALE	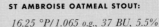
GRIFFON EXTRA PALE ALE	
ST AMBROISE PALE ALE	
ST. AMBROISE OATMEAL STOUT	

NORTH COAST
BREWING COMPANY

444 NORTH MAIN STREET, FORT BRAGG, CALIFORNIA 95437
(1-707) 964-2739

Mark Ruedrich, president and brewmaster, became interested in "real beer" while living in England and quickly began homebrewing. Like so many of his counterparts, his success made him believe that he could brew commercially in a country lacking in high quality beer. North Coast Brewing Company opened its doors for business in August of 1988. The building, which had formerly housed a church, a college, and a mortuary, was refurbished by founding partners Mark Ruedrich, Tom Allen, and Joe Rosenthal. Red Seal Ale, Scrimshaw Pilsner, and Old No. 38 Stout were the three original brews on tap, soon followed by distinguished seasonal beers. Incorporated since 1994, Mendocino County's North Coast has expanded its capacity from 1,642 to 20,520 hectoliters per year. North Coast Brewing Company beers are now available in twenty-two states and are perennial winners at the Great American Beer Festival.

BREW FACTS

FOUNDED: 1988

HEAD BREWER: Mark Ruedrich

ANNUAL OUTPUT: 20,520 hectoliters

BREW STYLES: American wheat beer, stout, American amber ale, pilsner

TASTING NOTES

BLUE STAR GREAT AMERICAN WHEAT BEER:
14.5 °P/1.058 o.g., 4.8% ABV. A good version of the American wheat style beer. Pale, clean, and dry with a soft, bready aroma, a light refreshing palate, and dry finish. A perfect "lawnmower" beer or a match for light summer picnic foods. Silver medal, 1995 World Beer Championships.

OLD NO. 38 STOUT: *14.5 °P/1.058 o.g., 5.6% ABV. One of America's most popular stouts, this exceptionally fresh tasting version is silky smooth with a nicely organized palate of roasted malt, chocolate, coffee, and malty sweetness. Finishes well hopped and dryish with a subtle roasty flavor. Silver medal, 1994 World Beer Championships. Silver medal, 1993 Great American Beer Festival. Bronze medal, 1992 Great American Beer Festival.*

RUEDRICH'S RED SEAL ALE: *14.25 °P/ 1.057 o.g., 5.5% ABV. Richly amber colored with a gentle hoppy, fruity aroma. The epitome of a good American ale, full of fresh hops and malty flavors balanced by a good hop dryness, with the clean fruity notes of a warm ferment. Finishes with a mellow malt flavor and a refreshing taste of hops. Gold medals, 1995 and 1994 World Beer Championships. Silver Medal, 1992 Great American Beer Festival.*

SCRIMSHAW PILSNER: *1.045 o.g., 4.5% ABV. The nose is full and fresh with hops, malt, and a hint of caramel. Mingled flavors of hop bitterness and malt sweetness attack from the outset and develop throughout, with a finish reminiscent of a classic pilsner. Smooth, soft, and well organized with a lingering fresh hops aftertaste. Try with lemon and garlic flavored seafood dishes, particularly shrimp scampi. Gold medal, 1992 Great American Beer Festival. Silver medals, 1995 and 1994 World Beer Championships.*

CONNOISSEUR'S RATING

BLUE STAR GREAT AMERICAN WHEAT BEER	🍺🍺🍺
OLD NO. 38 STOUT	🍺🍺🍺
RUEDRICH'S RED SEAL ALE	🍺🍺🍺🍺
SCRIMSHAW PILSNER	🍺🍺🍺🍺

OTTER CREEK BREWING

85 EXCHANGE STREET, MIDDLEBURY, VERMONT 05753
(1-802) 388-0727

At the ripe old age of twenty-eight, Lawrence Miller has seen his five-year-old Otter Creek Brewing Company become the bestselling craft brewery in Vermont, and with draft beer sales in the state second only to Anheuser-Busch. This wunderkind of New England brewing began in much the same way as many of his peers, as an enthusiastic homebrewing college student who traveled to Europe in search of greater brewing knowledge. Miller was aided by the friendship he had formed with the owners of Widmer Brewing in Portland while studying at Reed College. Widmer sold the twenty-three-year-old Lawrence some used brewing equipment in the summer of 1990, and, by Thanksgiving, test batches of Otter Creek's flagship Copper Ale were being formulated. Seasonal ales were introduced in 1991, and bottled beers appeared in March 1993. The rise of Otter Creek has been nothing short of meteoric ever since, with production rising nearly 300 percent per year. A custom-designed, state-of-the-art brewhouse was completed in September 1995 to accommodate the growing popularity of this brewery, which has shyly stayed away from major competitions and high-profile advertising.

BREW FACTS

FOUNDED: 1990

HEAD BREWER: Lawrence Miller

ANNUAL OUTPUT: 13,680 hectoliters

BREW STYLES: Altbier, smoked beer, bock, wheat beer, porter, Oktoberfest, winter ale, helles

COPPER ALE: *12 °P/1.048 o.g., 21 BU, 5.2% ABV. Copper gold in color with an herbally, malty aroma and a subtle woodiness. Nutty, malty, and earthy in flavor with a balancing hop dryness. Finishes with a malt-inspired dryness and a unique complexity of malt flavors. Based on the German altbier style, this ale has enough personality to match with an assortment of flavorful, well-seasoned dishes, particularly pizza, barbequed chicken, and grilled Italian sausage.*

HELLES ALT BEER: *10.75 °P/1.043 o.g., 18 BU, 4.5% ABV. Burnished gold in color with a gently hoppy aroma. Features an appropriately subdued hoppiness and rich malt character. Nicely balanced with an emphasis on malt character, this top-fermented version of the Bavarian beer hall favorite is exceptionally clean and rounded in malt flavor with a long malty finish. A solid session beer and a good match for German cuisine, robust deli meats, and lighter summer fare.*

HICKORY SWITCH SMOKED AMBER ALE: *12.5 °P/1.050 o.g., 18 BU, 4.9% ABV. Brewed using a malt that is cold-smoked at the brewery, this ties with the Mud Bock as my favorite Otter Creek brew. Deep reddish amber in color, medium bodied, and dry, Hickory Switch has a rich, yet balanced, smokiness on par with the famous smoked beers of Bamberg. Nicely complemented by a faintly sweet malt presence and*

a backdrop of fresh hop dryness. Finishes clean and well organized. A perfect match for smoked fish and cheese, of course, and blackened Cajun cuisine or southern barbeque.

MUD BOCK SPRING ALE: *14.75 °P/1.059 o.g., 31 BU, 5.8% ABV. Deep, reddish brown in color with a rich creamy head that persistently maintains a fruity, malty aroma to the end of the glass. Smooth, clean, and very lager-like in character, despite the fact that it is an ale. Medium- to full-bodied, with a rich, orderly layering of malt, hops, and fruit flavors mingled with subtle notes of chocolate and roasted malt.*

COPPER ALE	🍾🍾🍾
HELLES ALT BEER	🍾🍾🍾
HICKORY SWITCH SMOKED AMBER ALE	🍾🍾🍾🍾
MUD BOCK SPRING ALE	🍾🍾🍾🍾

PAVICHEVICH
BREWING COMPANY

383 ROMANS ROAD, ELMHURST, ILLINOIS 60126
(1-708) 617-5252

Ken Pavichevich, the charismatic and energetic chairman and CEO of the publicly-held brewing company that bears his name, spent five years as a Chicago police officer before joining the business world. His stint with an oil company took him overseas, where he first became obsessed with the notion of brewing lagers as good as those found in Europe. Pavichevich built the brewery in a very organized and businesslike manner, with years of planning and months spent dragging his head brewer around Germany, Austria, and the Czech Republic before the first beer was released in 1989. Pavichevich Brewing's beers, dubbed Baderbräu after a friend of the founder, are fire-brewed in a copper kettle and in compliance with the Reinheitsgebot. Baderbräu beers are brewed from both six-row and two-row pale malts, with Saaz comprising ninety-five percent of the hops used.

BREW FACTS

FOUNDED: 1986

HEAD BREWER:
Douglas R. Babcook

ANNUAL OUTPUT:
27,360 hectoliters

BREW STYLES: Bock, pilsner, winter lager

CONNOISSEUR'S RATING

BADERBRAU BOCK BEER
5.4% ABV

BADERBRAU PILSNER BEER
4.8% ABV

SUMMIT
BREWING COMPANY

2264 UNIVERSITY AVENUE, ST. PAUL, MINNESOTA 55114
(1-612) 645-5029

The Midwest has often been ignored in discussions of successful American microbreweries, but St. Paul's pioneering Summit Brewing Company has labored quietly since 1986 and, despite lacking the press that is often given to East and West Coast breweries, has grown steadily and profitably. Founded by forty-something antiwar protestor turned capitalist Mark Stutrud, Summit's founder typifies the microbrewers who are successful, fiercely independent, stubborn, and determined to do things the traditional way.

Seasonal brews in addition to the Winter Ale include: India Pale Ale (14 °P), Heimertingen Maibock (16 °P), Hefe Weizen (10.8 °P), and Düsseldorfer-Style Alt Bier (12.5 °P).

BREW FACTS

FOUNDED: 1986

MASTER BREWER:
Mark Stutrud

ANNUAL OUTPUT:
19,152 hectoliters

BREW STYLES: Pale ale, porter, winter warmer, maibock, weizen, altbier

CONNOISSEUR'S RATING

SUMMIT EXTRA PALE ALE

GREAT NORTHERN PORTER

WINTER ALE

TASTING NOTES

EXTRA PALE ALE: *12.1 °P/1.048 o.g., 4.9% ABV. The subtle, fruity aroma of hops, malt, and caramel belies the intense hop bitterness to follow, in the style of the classic West Coast pale ales. Clean, fresh, and well balanced despite the definite hop presence. After the palate acclimates itself to the hoppy assault, Summit Extra becomes a dangerously easy-drinking pale ale to accompany sweet and sour foods that need a palate-cleansing tonic.*

GREAT NORTHERN PORTER: *13.3 °P/ 1.053 o.g., 5.4% ABV. Ingredients include pale, caramel, and black malts; Fuggles, Eroica, and Cascade hops. Features a sweet toffee over roasted barley aroma. A deep, opaque black color with the slightest hints of ruby and a small but long-lasting head. Light bodied, bitter, but well balanced, without too much dry roast. Incredibly easy to drink, with a faintly sweet and dry finish and just a touch of roasted barley in the aftertaste. An excellent session porter to accompany lengthy winter meals. Gold medal winner at the 1987 Great American Beer Festival.*

WINTER ALE: *(seasonal) 14.5 °P/1.058 o.g., 6.1% ABV. Brewed from pale, caramel, and black malts; and Fuggles, Willamette, and Tettnanger hops. Summit's Winter Ale is lightly carbonated; features a deep, ruby red color; lingering, sweet, candied fruit nose; and medium-bodied, malty, and warm flavor. One of America's best winter ales.*

TOOHEYS PTY LTD.

29 NYRANG STREET, LIDCOMBE NSW 2141, AUSTRALIA
(61-2) 648 8611

The Tooheys brewery was founded by John and James Toohey, two sons of Irish immigrants who had come to Melbourne in 1841. In 1981, Tooheys merged with Castlemaine Perkins. In 1992, along with Castlemaine and Swan in Western Australia, Tooheys was acquired by the Lion Nathan brewing group. Toohey's makes a large assortment of mass-market oriented beers, but its most famous is its Old Black, which was reputedly first brewed in 1869. Old Black is often thought of as an English style ale, but the brewery insists that it bears a greater resemblance in name and brewing technique to the altbiers of Germany. The Hahn Brewing Company founded as a microbrewery in the Sydney suburb of Camperdown in 1988, was acquired in 1992.

BREW FACTS

FOUNDED: 1869

HEAD BREWER: Patrick Goddard

ANNUAL OUTPUT: 3 million hectoliters

BREW STYLES: Wheat beer, pils, dark lager

CONNOISSEUR'S RATING

OLD BLACK ALE
10.2 °P/1.041 o.g., 4.4% ABV

HAHN PREMIUM LAGER
11.25 °P/1.045 o.g., 4.5% ABV

UNIBROUE

80 DES CARRIERES, CHAMBLY, QUEBEC J3L 2H6, CANADA
(1-514) 658-7658

Founded in 1990 by Belgian-style ale enthusiasts André Dion and Canadian rock star Robert Charlebois, Unibroue produces a wide range of idiosyncratic, award-winning beers "On Lees" (bottle conditioned). Their progressive combination of Old World brewing tradition and unique beer styles has quickly gained them international recognition. Having a talented Belgian brewmaster at the kettle doesn't hurt either. In addition to Unibroue's divergence from the product lines normally associated with Canadian brewing, Unibroue has some of the most stunning, suitable-for-framing artwork drawn from Canadian legend and cultural heritage.

BREW FACTS

FOUNDED: 1990

HEAD BREWER:
Gino Vantieghem

ANNUAL OUTPUT:
40,000 hectoliters

BREW STYLES: Witbier, strong ale, spiced ale, smoked beer

TASTING NOTES

BLANCHE DE CHAMBLY: *5% ABV. Bottle-conditioned, spiced wheat beer with the citrusy, earthy aroma of a Belgian wit. Tart, dry, and refreshing. Silver medal winner in the 1995 World Beer Championships Wheat Beer category. Serve with salads, raw vegetables, grilled poultry, pasta, fish, and crustaceans. Suitable for laying down for up to two years at cellar temperatures. Serve at 41°F.*

MAUDITE: *8% ABV. Deep, hazy reddish brown. Features a sweet aroma and sweet, spicy homebrew taste with hints of ripe fruit. Fairly light bodied for an 8% alcohol beer. Won a gold medal in the Belgian-Style Red Ale category of the 1995 World Beer Championships and a silver medal in 1994. Serve with pasta, red meat, and spicy dishes. Suitable for laying down for up to five years at cellar temperatures. Serve at 45–50°F.*

LA FIN DU MONDE: *9% ABV. Deep yellowish gold in color with a voluminous creamy head and many similarities to a Belgian wit. Sweet, tangy, and fruity, with alcohol warmth. Intense, fruity orange and spicy liqueur aroma. The name means "End of the World," implying that you'd have to go to the ends of the earth to find such a powerful, but dangerously alluring beer. Platinum medal winner in the Belgian-Style Golden Ale category of the 1995 World Beer Championships and silver medal winner in 1994. To complement fine dining, cheeses, and desserts. Suitable for*

laying down for up to ten years at cellar temperatures. Serve at 45–50°F.

RAFTMAN: *5.5% ABV. Gold medal winner in the 1995 World Beer Championships Whiskey Malt category. A hazy, honey-colored brew with an aroma of dried fruit and a dense, creamy head. Fruity-spicy Belgian ale flavors with a distinct smokiness intertwined. Finishes with a tangy sweet aftertaste vaguely reminiscent of orange juice. Serve with smoked fish and meats and mildly spiced foods. Suitable for laying down for up to two years at cellar temperatures. Serve at 41–45°F in a Belgian-style tulip glass.*

LA GAILLARDE: *5% ABV. Reportedly brewed according to a medieval recipe, with herbs and spices used in place of hops; unpasteurized and unfiltered. Serve with fruits, sorbets, fowl, rabbit, and terrines. Suitable for laying down for up to two years at cellar temperatures. Serve at 45°F.*

CONNOISSEUR'S RATING

BLANCHE DE CHAMBLY	🍾🍾🍾
MAUDITE	🍾🍾🍾
LA FIN DU MONDE	🍾🍾🍾🍾
RAFTMAN	🍾🍾🍾🍾
LA GAILLARDE	🍾🍾🍾

UPPER CANADA
BREWING COMPANY

2 ATLANTIC AVENUE, TORONTO, ONTARIO, CANADA
(1-416) 534-9281

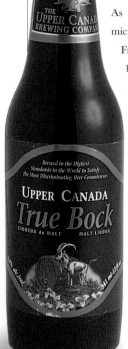

The Upper Canada Brewing Company was founded in 1985 by Frank Heaps to fill a gap in the Ontario beer market left by large Canadian breweries, who were turning their attention toward increasingly bland products. As an early investor in Canada's first microbrewery, Granville Island of Vancouver, Frank had been exposed to the joys of good beer and wanted to do the same for his hometown.

Situated in a c.1900 warehouse in central Toronto, Upper Canada brews a wide variety of German, British, and North American styles in strict conformance with the Reinheitsgebot. It trucks in water from the Caledon Hills, thirty miles away, in order to ensure that it is chemical-free. As a result, Upper Canada's beers are available in more European markets than any other brewery in North America, with exports to Germany, the Netherlands, Belgium, Luxembourg, Sweden, and Switzerland.

BREW FACTS

FOUNDED: 1985

HEAD BREWER:
Dr. Richard Rench

ANNUAL OUTPUT:
72,000 hectoliters

BREW STYLES: Bock, lager, light lager, low-alcohol, stout, wheat, pale ale, brown ale, strong lager

TASTING NOTES

PALE ALE: *11.5 °P/1.046 o.g., 4.8% ABV. Brewed from Canadian two-row, Carastan, and black malts; Cluster and Cascade hops. Amber gold in color with a classic English aroma of estery malt and floral/herbal hops. Pleasantly bitter with a background of malty sweetness and an appropriate dry and bitter hop finish. Recommended with garlic or herb dishes and spicy Chinese fare.*

COLONIAL STOUT: *11.75 °P/1.047 o.g., 4.8% ABV. Brewed from Canadian two-row, Carastan, and black malts; Challenger and Cascade hops. I would describe this more as a porter than a stout because of its medium-bodied, easy-drinking character. Nonetheless, a very well-balanced, complex black brew with a deft combination of English hop bitterness, roast malt dryness, and sweetness. Its dry and bitter finish makes this a wonderful accompaniment to robust breads and strong cheeses.*

LIGHT LAGER: *9.25 °P/1.037 o.g., 4% ABV. Brewed from two-row Canadian barley, Hallertau Northern Brewer and Hersbrucker hops. Pale golden in color, with delicate aromas of hops and faint esters. Slightly sweet on the palate with a subtle bitter aftertaste. Pair with fresh summer salads, curry, or Szechuan seafood.*

PUBLICAN'S SPECIAL BITTER ALE: *11.5 °P/ 1.046 o.g., 4.8% ABV. Brewed from Canadian two-row pale, Carastan, and black malts; Challenger and Hallertau Hersbrucker hops. Copper colored with aromas of roasted malt, fruit, and hops. Full-bodied with the classic British balance of sweet malt and bitter hops.*

WHEAT: *(Seasonal) 10.25 °P/1.041 o.g., 4.3% ABV. Brewed from two-row Canadian barley and wheat malts, and Hallertau Northern Brewer hops. Pale golden color with delicate aromas of malted wheat and understated flavors of fruit. Add a lemon slice to enhance the light-bodied, dry, Bavarian kristall-weizen character. Pair with salads, fish, cold pasta, and white meats.*

TRUE BOCK: *15.5 °P/1.062 o.g., 6.5% ABV. Brewed from Canadian two-row pale, Carastan, and black malts; Hallertau Northern Brewer and Hersbrucker hops. Ruby amber in color, with an aroma of roasted malt, hops, and black cherries. Fruity malt flavors dominate with a generous amount of bitterness to balance. Finishes fairly dry with a fruity aftertaste of malt sweetness. Try with a robust cheese, as an aperitif, or as a nightcap.*

CONNOISSEUR'S RATING

PALE ALE	🍺🍺🍺🍺
COLONIAL STOUT	🍺🍺🍺
LIGHT LAGER	🍺🍺
PUBLICAN'S SPECIAL BITTER ALE	🍺🍺🍺
WHEAT	🍺🍺🍺🍺
TRUE BOCK	🍺🍺🍺

WEEPING RADISH

HIGHWAY 64 EAST, MANTEO, NORTH CAROLINA 27954
(1–919) 473–1157

Bavarian immigrant, Uli Bennewitz and his wife, Eileen, opened the Weeping Radish Restaurant and Brewery back in 1986, when few people on the East Coast—especially on the wild and windswept Outer Banks—had ever heard of a thing called a "brewpub." This pioneering brewery has only recently begun to expand beyond Manteo, where most of the beer is consumed in its family-oriented restaurant/pub/biergarten, to open a sister brewery in Durham. Weeping Radish has also just now ventured cautiously into wider mid-Atlantic distribution of its products, an area often fraught with danger for an unfiltered, unpasteurized lager that must constantly be kept refrigerated. The name of this exceptional microbrewery is taken from the classic Bavarian beer snack, a sliced radish that appears to weep after being sprinkled liberally with salt.

BREW FACTS

FOUNDED: 1986

HEAD BREWERS:
Paul Hummer

ANNUAL OUTPUT:
2,736 hectoliters

BREW STYLES: Helles, fest, dunkel, pilsner

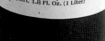

CONNOISSEUR'S RATING

BLACK RADISH BEER
13 °P/1.052 o.g., 5% ABV

COROLLA GOLD PILSNER
11.25 °P/1.045 o.g., 4.5% ABV

FEST BIER
13 °P/1.052 o.g., 5.3% ABV

WELLINGTON COUNTY BREWERY, LTD.

950 WOODLAWN ROAD WEST, GUELP, ONTARIO N1K 1B8, CANADA
(1-519) 837-2337

Brewed from ingredients such as English pale and specialty malts, Styrian, Goldings, Fuggles, and East Kent Goldings hops, these Canadian brewed beers have the necessary foundation of the traditional English ales to which they successfully aspire. True to their British heritage, Wellington has the distinction of being the first commercial brewery to offer cask-conditioned ales in North America.

BREW FACTS

FOUNDED: 1985

HEAD BREWER: Mike Stirrup

ANNUAL OUTPUT: 8,000 hectoliters

BREW STYLES: Bitter, lager, strong ale, stout

CONNOISSEUR'S RATING

COUNTY ALE
13 °P/1.052 o.g., 5% ABV

IMPERIAL STOUT
5.5% ABV

IRON DUKE
16.25 °P/1.065 o.g., 6.5% ABV

WILD GOOSE
BREWERY

20 WASHINGTON STREET, CAMBRIDGE, MARYLAND 21613
(1-410) 221-1121

Wild Goose Brewery was one of the first microbreweries in the mid-Atlantic states, leading the way in what is becoming one of America's fastest-growing centers of great brewing. Founded by Rich Klein, Ted Garrish, John Byington, and brew master Alan Pugsley, Wild Goose is located on Maryland's historic Eastern Shore in the old Phillip's Packing Company. Their first offering was Wild Goose Amber, which was based on a traditional English bitter. Since 1989, Wild Goose has expanded from a 34-hectoliter brewhouse to a 103-hectoliter system. After Jim Lutz joined the company as president in 1991, Wild Goose greatly expanded and improved its range of year-round and seasonal beers, and is now one of the most successful microbreweries on the East Coast.

BREW FACTS

FOUNDED: 1989

HEAD BREWER: Mark Scease

ANNUAL OUTPUT: 19,152 hectoliters

BREW STYLES: American amber ale, IPA, golden ale, porter, oatmeal stout, American wheat

TASTING NOTES

AMBER BEER: *12.75 °P/1.051 o.g., 5% ABV. Brewed from British two-row pale and specialty malts, this ale is rich in fruity maltiness with a mellow, rounded sweetness counterbalanced by a refreshingly hoppy blend of German, American, and British varieties. Finishes dry and fruity with a fresh, citrusy hop aftertaste. Bronze medal, 1995 World Beer Championships. Serve with softshell crab, crabcakes, and other Chesapeake Bay classics.*

IPA: *14 °P/1.056 o.g., 5.3% ABV. Richly aromatic of ripe fruit, caramel malt, and resiny hops. Softly sweet in front, developing to a mature hoppy flavor that is reminiscent of hearty Scottish IPAs. Very British in its full, but not overdone, use of hops. Finishes with a long, hoppy dryness and a gentle fruitiness. Bronze medal, 1995 World Beer Championships.*

SNOW GOOSE: *1.064 o.g., 6.4% ABV. Deep mahogany in color. Roasty, silky, and malty with a fairly dry, hoppy finish and a bittersweet aftertaste. Flavors of herbs and almost minty spice with faint hints of smoke and charred wood. Lingering roasted malt aftertaste. Elusive, multilayered flavors puts this English old ale-inspired seasonal on my list of top five American Christmas beers.*

CONNOISSEUR'S RATING

AMBER BEER	🍺🍺🍺
IPA	🍺🍺🍺
SNOW GOOSE	🍺🍺🍺🍺

WÜRZBURGER
HOFBRÄU

HOCHBERGER STRASSE 28, 8700 WÜRZBURG 1, GERMANY
(49-93) 14 109 105

At the northern end of the "Romantic Road" in the heart of Franconian wine country is the city of Würzburg. Würzburg was Christianized in the seventh century by the Irish missionary Saint Killian. By the eleventh century, the missionary monks had become the prince-bishops of the city and, therefore, the right of brewing was their prerogative. The first official brewery was established in 1643 by Prince-bishop Johann Philip von Schonborn. By 1867, Würzburger Hofbräu beer was being served on tap in New York City. Its availability was eventually interrupted by Prohibition and two world wars, but returned in April 1983 and has in recent years offered a broad range of Bavarian styles not widely available in the U.S.

BREW FACTS

FOUNDED: 1643

HEAD BREWER:
Richard Schuller

ANNUAL OUTPUT:
Figures not available

BREW STYLES: Weissbier, fest bier, dunkel, maibock, doppelbock, helles

TASTING NOTES

BAVARIAN DARK: *13.5 °P/ 1.054 o.g., 40 EBC, 4.5% ABV. Medium brownish gold in color with an aroma of roasted malt and piney hops. Full, smooth, and fuzzy in the mouth with a hoppy sourness developing after an initial malty sweetness. Finishes with a lingering caramel nuttiness and hop bitterness. One of a few Bavarian dunkels being imported into the U.S.*

BAVARIAN HOLIDAY: *18.5 °P/ 1.074 o.g., 90 EBC, 6.5% ABV. Deep reddish gold with a sweet, fruity aroma. A big, malty, bock-strength fest bier with a spicy, fruity sweetness that dominates from start to finish. A dramatic break from the hoppy dryness of the other Würzburger brews, this seasonal specialty shows its cleansing bitterness only at the end, and this is best sipped slowly on a cold holiday evening.*

FALLFEST: *13.5 °P/ 1.054 o.g., 36 EBC, 4.5% ABV. Brownish amber in color with a slightly skunky aroma, probably the result of the green bottle. Well balanced between specialty malt sweetness and rounded hop bitterness, but predominantly dry—a hallmark of this brewery. Not as big and malty as a traditional Oktoberfest should be, but richer than many of the progressively pale fest biers of late. Very similar to the Bavarian Dark.*

JULIUS ECHTER HEFE-WEISSBIER: *12.5 °P/ 1.050 o.g., 11 EBC, 4.4% ABV. Brewed from a nineteenth-century recipe of 70 percent wheat, 30 percent barley, and Hallertau hops. Ruddy*

gold in color with a fluffy head that emits soft aromas of apples, bananas, and bread. Lively, tart, and fruity in the mouth and full of wheaty dryness, but very full bodied and firm, making it better suited to year-round enjoyment than many of its lighter peers. Serve at 40–45°F with meaty deli sandwiches and sharp cheeses or with spicy, hot cuisine.

MAY BOK: *16.5 °P/ 1.066 o.g., 18 EBC, 5.6% ABV. Rosy golden color with an aroma of sweet, fruity malt and alcohol. Predominantly malty and creamy up front, becoming hoppy, resiny, and dry toward the finish with a lingering fruity aftertaste of caramel and pears.*

CONNOISSEUR'S RATING

BAVARIAN DARK	🍺🍺
BAVARIAN HOLIDAY	🍺🍺🍺
FALLFEST	🍺🍺
JULIUS ECHTER HEFE-WEISSBIER	🍺🍺🍺🍺
MAY BOK	🍺🍺

ASSOCIATIONS

American Homebrewers
Association
736 Pearl Street
P.O. Box 1679
Boulder, CO 80306–1679
(1–303) 447–0816
Fax (1–303) 447–2825

CAMRA Ltd.
(Campaign for Real Ale)
230 Hatfield Road, St. Albans,
Hertfordshire AL1 4LW,
England
(44–1727) 867201
Fax (44–1727) 867670

De Objectieve Bierproevers
(Belgian Beer Consumer's
Organization)
Postbus 32
2600 Berchem 5
Belgium

Home Wine and Beer Trade
Association
604 N. Miller Road
Valrico, FL 33594
(1–813) 685–4261

Association of Bottled Beer
Collectors
4 Woodhall Road, Penn,
Wolverhampton WV4 4DJ
England
(44–1902) 342 672

British Beermat Collectors'
Society
10 Coombe Hill Crescent
Thame
Oxfordshire OX9 2EH

Brewers and Licensed
Retailers Association
42 Portman Square
London W1H 0BB
(44–171) 486–4831

The Inn Sign Society
2 Mill House, Mill Lane,
Countess Wear, Exeter
Devonshire EX2 6LL
(44–1392) 70728

Institute of Brewing
33 Clarges Street
London W14 8EE
England
(44–171) 4998144

Promotie Informatie
Traditioneel Bier (PINT)
(Dutch Beer Consumer's
Organization)
Postbus 3757
1001 AN Amsterdam
Netherlands

Siebel Institute of Technology
4055 W. Peterson
Chicago, IL 60646
(1–312) 463–3400
Fax (1–312) 463–4962

Society for the Preservation of
Beers from the Wood
61 De Frene Road
London SE26 4AF

Svenska Ölfrämjandet
(Swedish Beer Consumer's
Organization)
Box 16244
S-10325 Stockholm
Sweden

MAGAZINES FOR THE BEER LOVER

Zymurgy/New Brewer
736 Pearl Street
P.O. Box 1679
Boulder, CO 80306–1679
(1–303) 447–0816
Fax (1–303) 447–2825

Brewing Techniques
P.O. Box 3222
Eugene, OR 97403
(1–503) 687–2993
(1–800) 427–2993
Fax (1–503) 687–8534

Suds 'n Stuff
Bosak Publishing Co.
4764 Galicia Way
Oceanside, CA 92056
(1–619) 724–4447
Fax (1–619) 940–0549

American Brewer/Beer: The Magazine
P.O. Box 717
Hayward, CA 94543–0717
(1–510) 538–9500

All About Beer
Chautauqua, Inc.
1627 Marion Ave.
Durham, NC 27705
(1–919) 490–0589
Fax (1–919) 490–0865

American Breweriana Journal
American Breweriana
Association
P.O. Box 11157
Pueblo, CO 81001

The Malt Advocate
3416 Oak Hill Road
Emmaus, PA 18049
(1–610) 967–1083
E-Mail: maltman999k aol.com

Beer Magazine
102 Burlington Cr.
Ottawa, Ontario K1T 3K5
Canada
(1–613) 737–3715

BEER NEWSPAPERS

Ale Street News
P.O. Box 1125
Maywood, NJ 07607
(1–201) 368–9100
Fax (1–201) 368–9101

BarleyCorn
P.O. Box 2328
Falls Church, VA 22042
(1–703) 573–8970

Beer & Tavern Chronicle
277 Madison Ave.
New York, NY 10016
Fax (1–914) 227–5520

Brew Hawaii
P.O. Box 852
Hauula, HI 96717–9998
(1–808) 259–6884

Celebrator Beer News
P.O. Box 375
Hayward, CA 94543
(1–510) 670–0121
Fax (1–510) 670–0639

Midwest Beer Notes
339 6th Avenue
Clayton, WI 54004
(1–715) 948–2990

Rocky Mountain Brews
251 Jefferson
Fort Collins, CO 80524
(1–303) 224–2524

Southern Draft Brew News
702 Sailfish Rd.
Winter Springs, FL 32708
(1–407) 327–9451

Southwest Brewing News
11405 Evening Star Drive
Austin, TX 78739
(1–512) 467–2225

What's Brewing
(CAMRA Newspaper)
230 Hatfield Road, St. Albans
Hertfordshire AL1 4LW,
England
(44–1727) 867201
Fax (44–1727) 867670

What's Brewing
(CAMRA Canada Newspaper)
P.O. Box 30101
Saanich Centre Postal Outlet
Victoria, B.C. V8X 5E1
Canada
(1–604) 386–2818

The Yankee Brew News
Brasseur Publications
P.O. Box 8053
J.F.K. Station
Boston, MA 02114
(1–617) 846–5521

NEWSLETTERS

Northwest Brew News
22833 Bothell-Everett Hwy,
Suite 1139
Bothell, WA 98021–9365
(1–206) 742–5327

On Tap: The Newsletter
P.O. Box 71
Clemson, SC 29633
(1–803) 654–3360

The Pint Post
12345 Lake City Way N.E.
#159
Seattle, WA 98125
(1–206) 365–5812

What's On Tap
P.O. Box 7779
Berkeley, CA 94709
(1–800) 434–7779

BEST HOLIDAY BEERS

Bière de Noël—*St. Sylvestre*
Celebration Ale—*Sierra Nevada*
Festive Ale—*Felinfoel*
Noël Christmas Ale—*Affligem*
Our Special Ale—*Anchor*
Scaldis Nöel—*Dubuisson*
Snow Cap Ale—*Hart Brewing*
Snow Goose—*Wild Goose*
Spéciale Noël—*La Binchoise*
Stille Nacht—*De Dolle Brouwers*

AUTHOR'S FAVORITE BEERS

Anchor Porter
Celis White
Frank Boon Kriek
Fuller's ESB
Lord Granville Pale Ale
Maisel's Hefe-Weisse Bier
Orval Trappist Ale
Paulaner Salvator
Pike Place Pale Ale
Sierra Nevada Pale Ale
Spaten Export Dunkel
Traquair House Ale
Unertl Weisser Bock
Weeping Radish Fest

BEST SUMMER BEERS

Anderson Valley High Roller's Wheat Beer
Aylinger Bräu Weisse
De Kluis Hoegaarden White Ale
Frank Boon Kriek
Liefmans Frambozen
Lindemans Peche
Portland Wheat Berry Brew
Saison Dupont
Silly Titje Blanche
Spaten Franziskaner Club-Weissbier

BEST LOW-CALORIE BEERS

Brasal Légère
Dixie Jazz Amber Light
Grant's Celtic Ale
Granville Island Light
Unertl Leichtes Weisse
Upper Canada Light Lager

AUTHOR'S FAVORITE NORTH AMERICAN MICROBREWERIES

Abita Brewing Co., Inc.
Alaskan Brewing & Bottling Company
Anchor Brewing Company
Anderson Valley Brewing Company
Catamount Brewing Company
Celis Brewery
Granville Island Brewing Company
Great Lakes Brewing Company
Lakefront Brewery
Mendocino Brewing Company
North Coast Brewing Company
Pennsylvania Brewing Company
Pike Place Brewery
Redhook Brewery
Riverside Brewing Company
Rogue Ales
Sierra Nevada
Stoudt's
Sudwerk Privatbrauerei Hübsch
Unibroue

THE BEER DIRECTORY'S STRONGEST BEERS

Brugse Tripel: *9% ABV*
Eldridge Pope Thomas Hardy's Ale: *11.7% ABV*
Hürliman Samichlaus: *14.7% ABV*
Imperial Russian Stout: *10% ABV*
Saint-Rémy-Rochefort 10: *11.3% ABV*
Scaldis: *12% ABV*
Sierra Nevada Bigfoot Barleywine: *10.6% ABV*
St. Bernardus Abt 12: *10% ABV*
La Trappe Quadrupel: *10% ABV*

BEST CRAFT BEERS TO PAIR WITH FOOD

Anchor Liberty Ale
Anderson Valley Boont Amber Ale
August Schell Weizen
Baderbräu Pilsner
Brasal Bock
Brick Brewing Red Cap Ale
Catamount Bock
Celis Grand Cru
Dock Street Bohemian Pilsner
Frankenmuth Dark
Grant's India Pale Ale
Heckler Fest Märzen
Hickory Switch Smoked Amber Ale
Hübsch Hefe Weizen
Lakefront Klisch Pilsner Beer
McAuslan St. Ambroise Pale Ale
North Coast Scrimshaw Pilsner
Pennsylvania Brewing Helles Gold
Riverside Brewing Victoria Avenue Amber Ale
Wild Goose India Pale Ale

BEST BEERS TO CELLAR*

Chimay Grand Réserve: *three to ten years*
Corsendonk Noster Pater: *one to five years*
Courage Imperial Russian Stout: *two- to ten years*
Eldridge Pope Thomas Hardy's Ale: *three to twenty years*
Gouden Boom Brugse Tripel: *one to three years*
Het Anker Gouden Carolus: *one to ten years*
Hürlimann Samichlaus: *five to ten years*
Liefman's Goudenband: *five to seven years*
Orval Trappist Ale: *one to five years*
Rochefort 10: *five to twenty years*

Corked bottles should be stored on their side in the cellar. Crown-capped bottles should be kept upright.

Style	Prime Commercial Examples
Altbier	Diebels Alt • St Stan's Dark Alt • August Schell Schmaltz's Alt
American Wheat Beer	Catamount Wheat • Upper Canada Wheat • Anchor Wheat
Barley Wine	Anchor Old Foghorn Barleywine • Sierra Nevada Bigfoot Barleywine • Rogue Old Crustacean Barley Wine
Belgian Red Ale	Rodenbach Grand Cru
Belgian Strong Ale	Dubuisson Scaldis • Het Anker Gouden Carolus
Bière de Garde	Castelain Blonde • St. Sylvestre 3 Monts • Jeanne d'Arc Ambre Des Flandres
Bière de Paris	Lutèce Bière de Paris
Bière de Mars	Castelain Bière de Mars
Bitter	Fuller's ESB • Marston's Pedigree Bitter • Courage Director's Bitter
Bock	Einbecker Ur-Bock Dunkel • Frankenmuth Bock • Catamount Bock
Bock, Doppel	Paulaner Salvator • Ayinger Celebrator • Heckler Doppel Bock
Bock, Eis	Kulmbacher Reichelbräu Eisbock
Bock, Mai	Sierra Nevada Pale Bock • Stoudt's Honey Double Mai Bock
Brown Ale	Brooklyn Brown Ale • Samuel Smith Nut Brown Ale • Pyramid Best Brown Ale
California Common	Anchor Steam Beer
Cream Ale	Riverside Raincross Cream Ale
Czech Pilsner	Pilsner Urquell • Budweiser Budvar • Baderbräu Pilsner Beer • Penn Pilsner
Dortmunder-Export	Stoudt's Export Gold • Ayinger Jahrhundert-Bier
Dubbel	Westmalle Dubbel • Rochefort 6 • St. Bernardus Pater 6 • Corsendonk Monk's Brown Ale
Faro	Frank Boon Pertotale
Fest Bier	Würzeburger Hofbräu Bavarian Holiday
Framboise	Lindemans Framboise • Frank Boon Framboise
German Pils	Jever Pilsener • Bitburger Premium Pils • Warsteiner Premium Verum
Grand Cru	Celis Grand Cru
Gueuze	Frank Boon Gueuze • Lindemans Gueuze • Cantillon Super Gueuze
India Pale Ale (IPA)	Brooklyn Brewery East India Pale Ale • Marston's India Export Pale Ale • Anchor Libery
Irish Red Ale	Kilkenny Irish Beer

Kellerbier	St. Georgen Bräu Kellerbier
Kölsch	Pyramid Kälsch
Kriek	Lindemans Kriek • Frank Boon Kriek
Kulmbacher	Dixie Blackened Voodoo
Lambic	Frank Boon Lambic/Lindemans Lambic • Cantillon Lambic
Light Beer	Upper Canada Light Lager • Dixie Jazz Amber Light
Märzen/Octoberfest	Stoudt's Fest • Weeping Radish Fest • Hübsch Märzen
Mild Ale	Adnams Southwold Mild • Grant's Celtic ale
Münchner Dunkel	Frankenmuth Dark • Spaten Export Dunkel • Penn Dark
Münchner Helles	Heckler Hell Lager • Paulaner Premium Lager • Hübsch Lager
Old Ale	Gale's Prize Old Ale
Oud Bruin	Liefmans Goudenband • Liefmans Frambozenbier
Pale Ale	Royal Oak Pale Ale • Ind Coope Double Diamond • Pike Place Pale Ale • Granville Island Lord Granville Pale Ale • Lakefront Cream City Pale Ale
Porter	Samuel Smith's Taddy Porter • Anchor Porter • Catamount Porter
Rauchbier	Aecht Schlenkerla Rauchbier • Otter Creek Hickory Switch Smoked Amber • Alaskan Smoked Porter
Saison	Saison Dupont
Schwarzbier	Köstritzer Schwarzbier
Scotch Ale	Traquair House Ale
Scottish Ale	Caledonian Golden Promise • Grant's Scottish Ale
Steinbier	Rauchenfels Steinbier
Stout, Dry	Guinness Extra Stout • North Coast Old No. 38 Stout
Stout, Imperial	Courage Imperial Russian Stout • Samuel Smith Imperial Stout • Wellington County Imperial Stout
Stout, Sweet	Young's Oatmeal Stout • Anderson Valley Barney Flats Oatmeal Stout • Samuel Smith Oatmeal Stout
Trappiste Ale	Chimay Première • Orval Trappist Ale • La Trappe Quadrupel
Tripel	Rochefort 8 • Gouden Boom Brugse Tripel
Vienna	Lakefront Riverwest Stein Beer • Abita Amber Lager
Weisse, Berliner	Berliner Kindl Weisse
Weizen, Dunkel	Pschorr Weisse Dunkel • Franziskaner Hefe-Weissbier Dunkel
Weizen, Helles	Franziskaner Weissbier • Hübsch Hefe-weizen
Weizen, Kristall	Franziskaner Club-Weissbier
Weizenbock	Schneider Aventinus • Unertl Weisser Bock • Erdinger Pikantus
Witbier	Celis White • De Kluis Hoegaarden • Gouden Boom Blanche de Bruges